All
the
Rage

HARPER

An Imprint of HarperCollins*Publishers*

All the Rage

Mothers, Fathers, and the Myth of Equal Partnership

DARCY LOCKMAN

ALL THE RAGE. Copyright © 2019 by Darcy Lockman. All rights reserved. Printed in the United States of America. No part of this book may be used or reproduced in any manner whatsoever without written permission except in the case of brief quotations embodied in critical articles and reviews. For information, address HarperCollins Publishers, 195 Broadway, New York, NY 10007.

HarperCollins books may be purchased for educational, business, or sales promotional use. For information, please email the Special Markets Department at SPsales@harpercollins.com.

FIRST EDITION

Designed by Bonni Leon-Berman

Library of Congress Cataloging-in-Publication Data has been applied for.

ISBN 978-0-06-286144-3

19 20 21 22 23   LSC   10 9 8 7 6 5 4 3 2 1

For Liv and Tess

CONTENTS

All
the
Rage

The Problem That Has No Name

Married with Children

Am I being unfair to my husband?

It is a gray spring Saturday in 2016, the day before Mother's Day. There've been ten days of rain preceding this one, and I've spent half of those in Michigan with my kids, without their father, visiting my parents. I love taking my daughters to Detroit, but solo-parenting Liv and Tess is draining, not least because I am the only person available to issue and enforce the dreary commands of early childhood, the ones that begin upon waking and do not cease until it is night and the weight of their petal-soft eyelids has finally become too heavy to resist. Use the potty. Brush your teeth. Put on your socks. Put on your shoes. Don't hit your sister. Clean up the basement. Take off your shoes. Put on your shoes. Don't hit your sister. Take off your shoes.

When we return to New York, I decide that what I'd like most on the occasion of this Mother's Day is time to myself. I ask George to take our girls, then six and three, to visit his mother at her nursing home in Pennsylvania overnight. Ruth will be elated. George will feel good about spending the holiday with his mom. The kids will eat ice cream and play at Chuck E. Cheese and swim in the hotel's indoor pool. Everybody wins.

As George is leaving for the gym that morning before the trip, he stops, choosing his words with the care of the married, and says to me: "I'm going to pack for the kids, but if you can think of anything that I might forget, could you lay it on the bed?"

If you are a mother or a father, or have kept close company with a person who is a mother or a father, it probably will not surprise you to learn that George has never packed for our children. In the six and a half years since we became parents, I have done all the packing and all the other things like packing, and my husband knows—both because I have insistently brought it to his attention for the past few years and because I have deemed its occurrence nothing less than the starting point for a book— that I am no longer happy to take care of it for him. The social science research underscores that we are well within the norm in two regards. Our transition to parenting has not been easy on our relationship, and our division of labor has been front and center in that unease, a dusting of gunpowder ever ready to blow.

I am as careful as my husband when I respond. I want to be kind without losing my commitment to refusing responsibility for every detail and reinforcing this maddening system we have constructed in which I am the handler of all things. I ask him, "What is it that you think you are likely to forget?"

He thinks. "Their bathing suits," he says.

"Well, see, now you've remembered," I say, sounding to my ear like the equanimous badger mother in the Frances children's books. I love her. He nods and heads out the door.

A part of me feels good about the exchange. I've stood up

for myself, I've been good-humored about it, and George will remember the bathing suits (which the girls will gleefully sleep in when he ultimately forgets their pajamas). But the devil on my shoulder—the one internalized over decades of white noise about women and their responsibilities and their relative place—eggs me on: You're not being fair to him. He's taking them away, after all. Just throw some stuff together. It's only a one-night trip. It'll take you thirty seconds. What's the god-damn big deal? I gather the iPad and some toys and put them in a bag, an offering to the devil, and to my husband, to whom I wish above all else to be fair.

I Didn't See It Coming

In 2003, when I was thirty, my friend Tanya gave birth to her first child. She was a few years older than I was and—because this was New York, the city of advanced maternal age—the first of my local peers to have a baby. Some months later, she became the first of my group to become a full-time working mother, and then the first to fall out of touch because of the new demands on her time. We'd try, about every six weeks, to get together, but it never seemed to happen. Finally, one afternoon on the phone, Tanya explained to me, as if it all made perfect sense, that she just was not ever going to be able to meet for dinner because her husband couldn't be alone with the baby all evening long. John's job entailed entertaining clients, so I knew Tanya was often by herself after work with their son. If she could manage that, why couldn't he? I wondered. She hemmed before offering, "He wouldn't." I asked why not. We went back and forth like that for some time. I hung up feeling puzzled by and disdainful of what she seemed to be letting her husband get away with, the renunciation of so much responsibility. Both of them worked. Why would they be less than equal partners at home? It defied all reasonable explanation.

The punch lines to this story are neither few nor far between. Suffice it to say that six years later, I found myself co-parenting with a husband as well. This was a fortunate situation, all nicely planned and smoothly realized. But it wasn't long after our first daughter was born that I remembered Tanya's plight because now it was mine, and if it was mine, it was also that of most of the working mothers I came to know in my dual-breadwinner neighborhood in a leafy stretch of Queens. Like me, the women I met through the comings and goings at preschool and playground worked full-time, and like me, postpartum, they'd found themselves shouldering the bulk of all the theretofore unimagined burdens at home. I saw this not only among my neighborhood friends but also, because I'm a therapist, among my patients. In my office on the border between Chelsea and Midtown, I watched it begin as early as pregnancy. Twenty-eight weeks along and in her maternity work clothes, a woman would observe with some surprise and a nascent exasperation: "Jason seems really invested in what kind of stroller we get, but he's also completely taking for granted that I'm going to do all the research." I'd hold my tongue because my first reaction seemed unkind and overly cynical. But what I couldn't help thinking was: And so it begins.

Here is where it began for me. The first fight I had with my husband about the shared responsibilities of parenthood occurred when our daughter Liv was not yet a month old. I was on what passes for maternity leave, taking eight unpaid weeks off from the clinic where I was finishing my post-doc hours. George, whom I'd met in grad school, was working as a psychologist for the NYPD, a city job with good benefits and a nine-to-five schedule. I was enjoying my time at home with the baby as much as anyone on an infant's sleep schedule with engorged breasts can. Unable to rest during the day, I took computerized practice tests for my licensing exam while Liv napped, and on a few beautiful fall afternoons, she and I met friends taking their lunch hours on the lawn in Bryant Park. It all looked downright hedonistic to my husband, also tired, and stuck in a small, windowless office in Lefrak City Plaza, interviewing police officer candidates seven and a half hours a day.

George had been accustomed to going to the gym most nights after work, and a couple of weeks following our daughter's birth, he wanted to resume. It was a benign enough request from his perspective—which was then and, really, to this day remains much different from mine. He had long days at the office and wanted to work out. I had long days at home with our newborn and wanted some relief. Though I can no longer remember with great clarity what was so hard about being alone with one baby (ask any mother of two or more children, she is likely to say the same thing), I do recall the frayed nerves stoked by Liv's uninterrupted wailing each evening between four and seven o'clock in those first months. It's called "the witching hour." Google it along with the word "baby," and you'll be directed to a series of websites that advise mothers how to manage this daily period of extreme fussiness. The sites direct their reassurances to women: "Remember, you haven't done anything wrong, you're not a terrible mother, and this is normal." If George came directly home after work, he arrived at five-forty-five; the gym meant seven at best.

When I explained this to my husband, he did not immediately come around to my position. George believed me unsympathetic to his need to blow off steam. He was wrong—my consideration of him simply didn't extend so far as to obliterate my own needs in unrelenting service to his. There were a few days of mutual hostility before we managed to agree that he would go to the gym before work. His concession solved the material problem but presented with some umbrage. Despite having arrived at a solution that took both of us into account, George seemed to hold on to the idea that I was in the wrong— and also feeble (clearly) and capriciously imposing. In my mind, our very mutual and well-considered decision to start a family was now putting limits on his freedom, as it was on mine. In his mind, or so his attitude implied, those limits were not meant to be borne by him. We'd been together six years, and I'd learned to read his glances—before Liv, rife with love or good humor or the desire to be left to himself. When our daughter was born, a new category of glance: What (the fuck) was my problem? Why had I become so demanding? At great cost, I took this to heart. Maybe I should just accept my role as primary parent with grace. It wasn't like he didn't help at all.

I continued to struggle against this glance—both internally and with him—as the years passed and we had a second child. My requests for more help were sporadically heeded, but only after some fighting and a fraught reminder or two, each one serving to reinforce the same implicit bottom line: Our children's needs were my responsibility. "My resentment" became a topic of conversation in our eventual couples therapy, George oblivious to the punch he delivered to my gut each time he referred to my anger in that way, as if it were a rash on my back that had broken out spontaneously, nothing to do with him. Speaking from experience, our avuncular therapist offered this: "The way we actually live seems to have not caught up with our relatively new ideals." Why had no one told me this before?

Of course, Tanya had, six years earlier, but I'd imagined her as one woman and not every. Gender dynamics had changed so much since my own childhood—at least that was the impression I had before becoming a parent. And yet here were George and I, adhering to these domestic scripts long past their sell-by dates. By the time Liv turned one, I'd gleaned that any story I might have told about my husband's striking ability to abdicate domestic burdens—to fail to even know of their existence—might have been relayed by any mother I knew. There were small children dressed in the wrong season's clothes, permission slips that remained in folders unsigned, the consistent failure to pack any sort of supply. ("Did you remember diapers?" George would ask me in a slightly accusatory tone each time we got into the car.) A message was delivered, unspoken but clear. Not my job.

The husbands I knew, my own included, were engaged in myriad ways with their children—nothing like the retro stereotype of the guy who rarely left the office and refused to wipe a tiny dirty ass. But once they'd outpaced Don Draper in the annals of fatherhood, these men seemed content to retreat to their beds with their phones. We each, male and female, lived with an awareness of a recent past in which nothing much was expected of fathers at home. So who were all us mothers to be angry, to fail to greet every participation by our partners with less than a dozen roses and applause?

As for these otherwise decent men, their awareness that they were more involved than the fathers of yesteryear also led to much confusion, to their inability to absorb and respond to their wives' levelheaded rejoinders that this *more* was not enough. I became my own worst enemy, conflicted about my right to ask, self-conscious about my rising anger, and too often stuck with the choice between fighting or just taking care of it, whatever it was, on my own. It was disheartening. All around me, women articulated their frustrations to each other before minimizing them into oblivion. "At least he helps," I heard these women say, abashed by their own fury and protective of their partners' best intentions. That no man in history had ever been in the position to utter that phrase—"At least she helps"—was a thought we weren't eager to entertain. A mother, by writ of her sex, was partnered in the joys of parenthood but not likewise in its recalcitrant burdens: the packing of diapers, the buying of presents, the planning of meals, the searching for child care, the sorting and storage of hand-me-downs. We could question the moral rightness of this truth but not ever hope to one day see it change.

It takes time, in those early years of parenthood, for some difficulties to become self-evident, and I cannot recall when annoyance turned to deep disharmony for me, at what juncture watching my husband start to eat while I once again cut up our toddler's food became enough to leave me aggrieved for hours. It was the constant thrum of little things.

Together we adored Liv. Alone I made lists in my head of the particulars necessary to sustain her. Did my eagerness to gestate and nurse our child lead to a tacit agreement that her maintenance was my responsibility? I took it on as if this were so. If I hadn't looked for a babysitter and then day care, would George have?

Once I found a preschool, I became responsible each Sunday night for packing Liv's bag for the week and making sure it arrived Monday morning (my day for drop-off), clean sheet for naptime inside. Only on the rare week with a Monday holiday was I confronted by the fact that George, responsible for Tuesday drop-off, didn't even know about the Sunday-night bag, with its fresh linens and extra clothes. Those weeks, if her teacher failed to mention it, Liv would nap on a bare cot because her father had failed to bring in her things, and then the same held true for our second daughter three years later. Hardly the end of the world for the kids. But then for me it was. Because, you see, I was living like a second-class citizen in my own home. I tried to communicate my unhappiness to George, but he could only hear it as criticism, and then I never got through. Bag? What damn bag?

None of Us Saw It Coming

In light of social progress, when much has changed for women in the public realm, one might be forgiven for not intuiting the limitations of those changes in the private one. Among that morass, George and I became parents—with the vague assumption that we were in it together, and no concomitant sense of all we were working against or the effort it might take to achieve that. I took to reading about the problem.

At a friend's recommendation, I picked up *The Second Shift*,

sociologist Arlie Hochschild's thirty-year-old detailed account
of the ways in which heterosexual couples of the 1970s and '80s
organized their work and home lives. I identified so strongly
with the thin-stretched mothers in her study that it became the
first academic book to ever make me cry (this was after the
birth of our second daughter, Tess, at which point all the managing had really worn me down). Hochschild follows a handful
of families over the course of some years, observing each of the
men and women involved as they work to make cognitive peace
with the always uneven distribution of labor in their homes—
that many of those couples wound up divorcing illuminates at
what cost the chimera of harmony.

What stood out most to me, though, was Professor Hochschild's revelation in her preface that her female undergraduates
at Berkeley in the '80s didn't "feel optimistic that they [would]
find a man who plans to share the work at home." By the 1990s,
my classmates and I at the University of Michigan would have
predicted just the opposite: Of course our husbands would
share. Clearly, our expectations for our lives near the turn of
the century were more optimistic than Hochschild's sample. It
is only in retrospect that we can know they have gone largely
unrealized.

Once I started reading, there was no shortage of material.
At the end of 2015, *Newsweek* reported on a study of two
hundred couples out of Ohio State, "Men Share Housework
Equally, Until the First Baby." The study found that members
of working couples each performed fifteen hours per week
of housework before having kids. Once they had children,
though, women added twenty-two hours of child care while
men added only fourteen, the latter also compensating by

eliminating five hours of house care (women maintained their fifteen).

Younger dads, who came of age in more theoretically egalitarian times, were no better. "Millennial Men Aren't the Dads They Thought They'd Be," wrote *The New York Times* in July 2015, citing social science research out of the University of California, Santa Barbara, that found that men eighteen to thirty have more contemporary attitudes about gender roles in marriage than their predecessors, but "struggle to achieve their goals once they start families."

A Pew Research Center survey in the same year found that men believe they are carrying equal weight at home, but their wives see it differently. Sixty-four percent of mothers reported they did more to manage their children's needs than their husbands. Forty-one percent of fathers versus 31 percent of mothers told Pew that their responsibilities were shared equally. A 2017 *Economist* survey of parents in eight Western countries bore approximately the same result (46 percent of fathers versus 32 percent of mothers reported that tasks were shared). Multiple observations of the problem in social science publications read something like this one from the *Journal of Marriage and Family*: "Because of the potential benefit of sharing family work, the rapid increase in women's labor force participation, and increasing popular endorsement of equity ideals in marriage, many . . . predicted that the division of household labor would become more gender-neutral. Nevertheless, studies . . . seem to offer little support for this notion. This left researchers with a major unanswered question: 'Why don't men do more?'"

This was the question, too, in the background of the lives of the mothers I knew, even the ones who'd married self-identified feminists and assumed their shared ideology would translate into lived experience. Most often it did not. And so my friend Lisa, at the apex of her rage about her husband's general absence and failure to participate, sliced her hand open while chopping vegetables, a too literal Freudian slip that left her heavily bandaged and unable to complete a slew of necessary tasks with their toddler for weeks. My friend Beth refused to have a second child when her husband wouldn't promise greater involvement the next time around (they eventually had another anyway; at least this time she knew what she was getting into, she told me with a sigh and a shrug). My friend Sara, to ensure her husband's equal sharing upon the birth of their second son, devised a plan in which neither would ever be alone with their boys, necessitating shifts in both their work schedules and a relinquishing of all adult-exclusive social activities. In need of help in the mornings before work, my patient Andrea created a Google calendar that went as far as to schedule wake-up times for her husband during the week; on the many days he still chose to sleep in, she made the family's lunches with a half-dressed toddler tugging at her skirt. Other women I knew managed as well as they could until they couldn't any longer, and then fought with their children's fathers and watched as little changed. In the end, no effort ever seemed to take. This was just the way it was, and no one involved could say exactly why, or reconfigure the momentum in a more balanced and equitable way.

Why Don't Men Do More?

"I think it's biological," asserted my mother, in town for a visit, as we followed my daughters around the outdoor play space at the New York Hall of Science. "Women are naturally more in tune with their children's needs." I cringed at the suggestion. It irritated my intellectual sensibilities. My mother—a social worker who'd once marched for the Equal Rights Amendment and had spent my adolescence telling me how much happier she would've been had she worked outside the home when my sister and I were young—had recently begun calling herself a conservative and saying things like "I wish I had just realized that my children were the most important thing." But I balked, too, because I'd had the same thought about nature and its inescapable proclivities. My hypervigilant orientation to my daughters' requirements often felt outside of my control, no easier to resist than a rubber tomahawk to the knee. George could arrive home late from an evening out with two tired kids and immediately disappear into the bathroom to brush his own teeth. I wanted the girls changed and in front of the sink themselves before I might begin to consider my own needs. "I'd have taken care of it if you had just waited," my husband would chide me once they were in bed. But really, I could not.

"It's a personality thing," said Ellen Seidman, a writer, editor, and mother of three in New Jersey whose blog post about her "seeing superpower"—the motherhood equivalent of leaping tall buildings in a single bound—had attracted my attention on Facebook. "It's my experience, between me and my friends, that women tend to be more detail-oriented about household tasks and child care." With this, Seidman was offering a less deterministic version of my mother's paean to biology. She went on, "I happen to be especially detail-oriented. I notice things. I have my systems in place. I know that I need to call the doctor next week to book my kids' physicals for the fall, and that I need to hire the photographer we see once a year to take our family photos. I have material and mental lists. My husband doesn't. It's not his MO." Clearly, women are no more likely than men to be inherently organized, and Seidman also acknowledged that this tendency to be more attentive to the needs of others is one that she's chosen to cultivate in her home life, sparing her husband the trouble.

Calling herself powerful underscores her pride in her capability and in the good care she takes of her family. I can relate. It also tempers her frustration with the lower-status position she occupies in her home, the one left to do all the seeing. "We watched our mothers running our households and our fathers passively letting that happen," she said, adding that she hopes for something different for her own daughter. "Those are the gender stereotypes we learn. They don't just go away because more and more couples are dual income. It's a cycle. I'm not sure how one breaks it."

"Male privilege," said my then-childless best friend from college when I asked her what she made of it. Patriarchy, the relic I once thought I'd dodged by being born in the right place at the right time. (Ha.) It is a truism that motherhood makes many women feminist. As Jane O'Reilly wrote in the cover story of the inaugural edition of *Ms.* magazine back in 1971, "In the end we are all housewives, the natural people to turn to when there is something unpleasant, inconvenient or inconclusive to be done." Nothing in modern life so much as parenthood creates more tasks befitting that description—all those endless loads of laundry, all those breakfasts to prepare. And maybe the question of why men don't do more was best answered by a male guest at a dinner party thrown by O'Reilly in the time preceding her article's publication. "I'll go along with some of it, equal pay for equal work, that seems fair enough. . . . [But] you can't tell me Women's Lib means I have to wash dishes, does it?"

"It's structural," State University of New York sociologist Veronica Tichenor, who specializes in division of labor in families, told me over the phone. "Work hasn't changed. Workplaces still act like everyone has a wife at home. Everyone should be the ideal worker and not have to leave to take care of a sick kid. If one family struggles to balance it all, it's a personal problem. All these families with the same problem? That's a social issue." Certainly Tichenor has a point, as do the authors of the articles and books that explicate the problems in our system that make twenty-first-century family well-being difficult to sustain: from the near-twenty-four-hour demands of many occupations, to the implicit disapproval (or downright job-threatening consequences) faced by workers who put family obligations first, to the stultifying dearth of institutional supports for caretakers in the United States (and some other Western nations plagued with the problem). Men don't do more because the world has made it difficult for them to do so. "The structure of work needs to change," Tichenor emphasized. But if better arrangements in women's personal lives can be achieved only through sweeping shifts in our political and economic ones, I am not, at the time of this book's writing, optimistic for my daughters, nor for theirs.

Unfulfilled, Rising Expectations

The most recent time-use diary information collected by Pew Research and the Bureau of Labor Statistics in the U.S. consistently finds that women who work outside of the home shoulder 65 percent of child care responsibilities, and their male partners 35 percent. Those percentages have held steady since the year 2000. In the last twenty years, that figure has not budged. Some academics and parents alike detail anecdotes of more egalitarian setups, and of course there are exceptions to the rule. But the plural of anecdote is not data, and no one disputes the empirical work demonstrating that women, despite their ever-increasing economic power, are still living somewhat disempowered lives at home.

Ohio State sociologist Claire Kamp Dush even suggested to me that the household time-use studies—which look at men and women overall rather than husbands compared with their own wives—actually present an overly sunny take on progress. "I question what we know from time-use diaries. Our pattern of results, looking at couples on the same day, is different. It shows that men do even less." That's a grim reality for the generations of women who failed to anticipate such an impasse.

Expecting male partners who would share, we've been left with what political scientists call unfulfilled, rising expectations. Historically, these expectations lie at the heart of revolutions, insurgencies, and civil unrest. If so many couples are living this way, and so many women are angered or just exhausted by it, why do we remain so stuck? Where is our revolution, our insurgency, our civil unrest?

As I spoke with mothers and experts, they landed on three broad explanatory categories for the problem's tenacity: biology, cultural mandates around maternal devotion, and the ubiquitous prioritization of men's needs and desires relative to women's. I set out to look at each. Is there something inborn that keeps mothers, post-weaning, from lightening their load, or fathers from picking up slack? Are societal demands for hyperinvolved mothering so salient that even those of us who don't consciously subscribe to that ideal become destined to live it out, leaving our spouses behind in our wake? Are men so blindly entitled to the passive subordination of women that change is improbable at best?

I set out to interview a hundred mothers (I began with the friends and acquaintances of friends and acquaintances but ultimately relied primarily on mothers' groups on Facebook to recruit subjects). Once I got to about forty women, I began to see that the interviews were amazingly similar. No matter the age, race, region, or socioeconomic status of the woman (and my subjects ran the gamut), they largely had one story to recount. I wondered if this was an artifact of the limits of my journalistic skill.

I was relieved when the author Cheryl Strayed detailed a similar experience. For her *Dear Sugar* advice column, Strayed solicited letters from women about division of labor on her social media accounts. She noted an overwhelming response, and also that "Most of the letters could've been written by the same person—all of them women who described . . . a 'great guy' partner who doesn't do his equal share of the domestic and organization tasks required to run a household. . . ." I stopped at fifty mothers.

Sociologists Toni Calasanti and Carol Bailey have argued that "focusing on the persistence of the gender difference in the division of domestic labor rather than on factors accounting for the small amount of change may be more fruitful for understanding and eradicating inequality." The more we know about this trenchant norm, the better position we're in to combat it. As third-wave-feminist writer Amy Richards has acknowledged, "Feminism's crusade remains unfinished because examining the 'personal' is far more threatening than condemning the political." This book is ultimately a close inspection of the personal.

CHAPTER 1

On How Life Is

The Fallacy of the Modern, Involved Father

☑ Per every metric I've come across, men who live with their children today are more involved than the fathers of fifty years ago. Co-residential dads have tripled the amount of time they spend with their kids since 1965. Thirty-two percent of fathers in the most recent census reported being a regular source of care for their children, which is up from 26 percent a decade before. The National At-Home Dad Network estimates that there are 1.4 million stay-at-home fathers in the U.S., and that this is twice the number there were ten years ago. Roughly the same percentage of fathers as mothers report that parenting is extremely important to their identity. Mothers spent four times as many hours on child care as fathers in 1965, and only twice as many hours in 2010. Cross-nationally, between 1965 and 2003, men's portion of unpaid family work went from under 20 percent to almost 35 percent, where of course it has remained ever since.

Historians have documented significant changes in fatherhood in the last five hundred years. In colonial times (~1600–1800) work took place on family farms, and men

were responsible for their children's education and moral up-
bringing. During industrialization (~1800–1950), waged work
moved outside the home, bifurcating the lives of Western men
and women into separate spheres, the public and the private.
Women were tasked with unpaid domestic duty even when they
also brought in wages with home-based or other often marginalized efforts. Men went to work in factories and stores. Fathers
became distant and uninvolved. Finally, with urbanization in
the last half-century-plus, there was an increase in maternal employment and earnings, creating the conditions that spawned
the modern, involved father. He takes his kids to school. He
knows where they keep their socks. He's responsive to night-
mares and to vomit. He does not refer to being alone with his
children as babysitting. He attends parent-teacher conferences.
He makes dinner some of the time.

The arc of the moral universe is long, and it has bent toward
justice, and now women have it better than their mothers and
than theirs. You don't have to be a history major to have absorbed this merciful fact. It wasn't so long ago that married
women had no legal rights at all because they were their husband's property. (Single women belonged to their fathers: The
honorifics "Miss" and "Mrs." serve to clarify whether a woman
is beholden to a father or a spouse.) Until the passage of the
Civil Rights Act in 1964, it was legal for certain classes of em-
ployers to fire or refuse to employ a married woman because
she already had a job—as the physical and emotional laborer
of her family. Only in 1980 did the U.S. Census officially stop
calling every husband "the head of household." I came of age
in a time of equal opportunities in education and entry-level
employment for young women, and I assumed this trajectory to

have a boundless run. In podcasts, I'd hear women like Sheila Nevins, the longtime president of documentary films at HBO, born in 1939, explaining the difficulty of beginning a career in theater after finishing her MFA at the Yale School of Drama: "[My husband] wanted me home evenings. And he wanted me home weekends. So like theater is evenings and weekends so that nixed any chance of theater." (This was her first husband, whom she "long ago divorced.") But that was marriage in the 1960s. A man could assert his desires and expect his wife to cede to them, no matter the cost to her personhood. It sounded just so very long ago.

Or did it? When George and I moved into our first one-bedroom walk-up a few years before we got married, he soon after volunteered that he would do the vacuuming and the dusting. He liked those things, he told me, and he'd do them every week. What I didn't say in response, because I was a woman and he was a man, was that being left to clean the bathroom and the kitchen did not float my boat. He could have dusting, which I'd never bothered with anyway, but I wanted vacuuming. If I was going to scrub the bathtub, he needed to do the kitchen floor. I thought to say these things, but time froze, and instead, I didn't speak because wasn't I lucky that he wanted to do anything at all. We silently agreed upon the last part. This was in the year 2005.

It's easier to feel grateful for all that has changed than to acknowledge all that has yet to. Gratitude is the precursor to less conflict rather than more. For women raising children with the modern, involved father, there is some pressure—self-imposed and otherwise—to land on the side of appreciation, of sugar and spice and everything nice. ("When a dad comes, we clap," reports Jay Miranda, a mother and blogger from Los Angeles, describing her weekly mommy-and-me class.)

How lucky to share egalitarian ideals about marriage, even if they don't always manifest in behavior. After all, those ideals are still not universal. Molly, twenty-seven, a foster care worker and mother to a toddler in Tennessee, tells me, "It's unusual to see equal partnership around here. Even my friends without kids yet will say, 'I'm working late, so I have to make sure I have dinner prepared for my husband.' I would die if my husband ever threw a fit because I was working late and he had to feed himself. So when I say I'm grateful to be married to him, I mean it, even though I'm really spent from doing most all the work for our son."

Shannon, forty-two, an Oklahoma City mother who works as a court liaison, explains to me, "Where I live, it's still very backwards and old-school. My husband thinks he is supposed to bring home a check and do nothing else. He makes no bones about it. It's not that bad. He doesn't beat me. He doesn't drink excessively. I've learned how to manage things to where I can keep everything done. There's no point in fighting about it now, it's not going to change." Though she adds, "In all honesty, life would be easier if I were single. I wouldn't be expecting anyone to help me, and I wouldn't be upset if they didn't." Oklahoma, it's worth noting, is among the U.S. states with the highest divorce rates.

Given that there is always a nameless, faceless partner in the background whose laziness or inattentiveness is worse than your husband's, women who appreciate their lives and their relationships feel reluctant to acknowledge their displeasure. Sociology explains this with relative-deprivation theory: Only when one feels more deprived than other members of her reference group will she feel entitled to adamant protest. Michelle, forty-four, a Portland, Oregon, marketer and mother of a nine-year-old, says, "I don't know how equitable we are. But I do feel really lucky when I hear about other people's husbands. I have so many friends whose husbands have never put their child to bed because it's her job, because she's the mom."

Laura, thirty-eight, a New York City business owner and mother of a four-year-old, tells me she feels like a single parent but agrees with her husband that things could be a lot worse. Indeed, her partner's standard response whenever she tries to address their imbalance is "I do a lot more than other men," a sentence much easier to utter than "Yes, our arrangements are unfair to you, but that is the lot of women, so suck it up."

Erica, thirty-eight, a project manager in Portland, Oregon, and the mother of two kids under seven, expresses her mixed feelings like this: "He's great with the kids when he's here, and from friends I talk to, my husband does a lot more." She interrupts her thought to make sure I'll be changing her name (I am changing all parents' names). They've just started couples therapy, and she feels guilty talking about this. "He's on his phone or computer while I'm running around like a crazy person getting the kids' stuff, doing the laundry. He has his coffee in the morning, reading his phone, while I'm packing lunches, getting our daughter's clothes out, helping our son with his homework. He just sits there. He doesn't do it on purpose. He has no awareness of what's happening around him. I ask him about it, and he gets defensive. It's the same in the evening. He helps with dinner, but then I'm off to doing toothbrushing and bedtime, and he'll be sitting there on his phone."

Why do men act this way? Why do women tolerate it?

"Conventions embodying male dominance have changed much less in 'the personal' than in the job world," New York University sociologist Paula England, author of *The Gender Revolution, Uneven and Stalled*, tells me from behind the desk in her wide-windowed office overlooking Greenwich Village. "If you get down to it, we talk about equality, but the part people grasped on to was women changing. Women can have careers, be in the military, become clergy. But the fact is that all of that doesn't work if household stuff doesn't shift. And some things are more impervious to change than others. The implicit assumption that change is continuous is probably unrealistic."

Indeed, many of the women I spoke with—the partners of the modern, involved fathers—remain in what journalist Jill Filipovic, in her book *The H-Spot: The Feminist Pursuit of Happiness*, refers to as "a strange limbo where men's actions haven't totally caught up to women's expectations." Or, as Berkeley psychologists and pioneering family researchers Carolyn and Philip Cowan have put it, the ideology of the new egalitarian couple is way ahead of its time. Monique, thirty-two, the mother of a toddler in Queens, New York, explains how her husband sees the problem: "He notices the unfairness, but he just accepts it as something we have a disagreement about. I think he feels like there's nothing he can do. In fact, he's told me this before. There's nothing he can do, so it would be helpful if I wasn't so bothered by it."

I'll take the time to state here—and then, because it is obvious, I will not repeat it again in the course of this book—that the vast majority of modern, involved fathers are well-intentioned, reasonable human beings. Today fewer men are in touch with their children than at any time in history since the U.S. began keeping reliable statistics. While father involvement in two-parent families has increased in recent decades, there are also fewer father-present families. Clearly, the men who stick around to love and shepherd their offspring are not only to be maligned. Right now it is a Saturday, and George is spending the day with our daughters so that I can write. Earlier, he managed to find Liv's lost ballet slipper, saving her from missing her first class after summer break.

I'm at a neighborhood coffee shop, and sitting across from me are a father and son having hot chocolate, the dad's arm affectionately cast around his young son's shoulder. When they leave, they are replaced by another father-son pair, this boy a little older, these two arm-wrestling (really, they are). I get a text from the father of Liv's best friend who is sleeping over tonight for her birthday. Should he bring Maya's sleeping bag by this afternoon, or do we want to pick it up on our way home from dinner? Men are among the 3 to 5 percent of male mammals who contribute anything at all to their children post-insemination. Fathers in the U.S. work for pay three hours more per week than men without kids. A majority of U.S. men in relationships now report the belief that the egalitarian division of domestic labor is very important to a successful marriage. This is the glass half full. Amen.

But slow your roll. Reports of the modern, involved father have also been greatly exaggerated—or at least, as some researchers have argued, "this change is more in 'the culture of fatherhood' than in actual behavior." According to a 2018 Oxfam report, women around the world do between two and ten times as much unpaid care and domestic work as men (the global value of this work annually is estimated at $10 trillion). The ratio of women to men's free labor is smallest in the Scandinavian countries. In Norway—where, in 1993, the government earmarked a portion of paid parental leave exclusively for fathers—women spend three and a half hours a day in family work compared to men's three. This ratio is the largest for women in underdeveloped nations.

UN Women, a branch of the United Nations focused on gender equality, estimates that the unpaid labor gap is the largest in South Asia, where women carry out 90 percent of unpaid familial care work. In India, women perform six hours of free labor a day and men only one. These tasks can be particularly grueling in the third world. A woman with a family in Uganda is likely to spend six hours each day collecting water. Research from the international Organization for Economic Cooperation and Development (OECD) suggests that there is an important relationship between the gender gap in unpaid care work and prosperity—the smaller the gap, the wealthier the country.

MenCare, a global fatherhood campaign working toward child care parity in forty-five nations, estimates that at the current rate of change, it will be another seventy-five years before women worldwide achieve gender equity in their homes. The first world may be leading the way, but that does not mean we've arrived. This is easy to lose sight of in countries with modern infrastructure, in households without daughters or sons. Before kids, there just isn't all that much that needs to get done, and it seems harmless to let little things, like who spends more time scrubbing bathtubs and floors, pass by without remark. But as Mount Holyoke social psychologist Francine Deutsch puts it in *Halving It All*, her close study of the uneven distribution of unpaid labor between dual-earner American couples with kids: "Children . . . create an inequality of crisis proportions."

The Disillusionment of the Modern (Involved) Mother

Monique in Queens appreciates her circumstances. Hardworking and smart, she's built the life that middle-class girls like her, growing up in the last third of the twentieth century, knew was accessible to them. Interesting job in public service, loving marriage, one child and trying for another. "She's perfect," Monique tells me, referring to her daughter, "so I guess that means things are going well." She hesitates. She's ducked out of her office to meet me at a sleepy food court in Jamaica, Queens, in order to discuss her feelings about the inequity in her home life since the birth of her child—a wrench in her expectations, a thing that is not going quite very well at all.

She's adjusted to the demands of parenthood by making changes to her work life. She transferred to an office closer to home and has become less available to her clients in the evenings. She also enlisted both paid and unpaid child care—a part-time babysitter and her daughter's grandmothers. She loves her evenings with her toddler. That much she wouldn't change. But she's struck by how little her husband's priorities have shifted. She resents the liberties he continues to take with his time, his assumption that his involvement at home remains discretionary, and that all the many tasks invariably fall to her. "It's frustrating that I don't feel like we have the same responsibilities. He has a cushion that I don't have. If he has a big project at work, he's just like, 'Oh, I'm going to work late.' He doesn't have to worry about getting home so the nanny can leave in time to get back to her own kids. If something comes up for me at work, I've got to figure out, can my mom come, and if she can't, how is this going to go. For him, it's just, 'I've got to work, and someone else will take care of it.' It's a strain.

"When I was pregnant, we were talking about how it was going to go, and we ended up deciding on a babysitter for three days, and my mother would come from upstate to be with our daughter Thursdays and Fridays, and then my mother-in-law would leave work early on Fridays to watch the baby so that my mom could catch her bus back home. At some point I was like, 'This isn't going to work, this is just too many things,' and he was like, 'I don't understand why you can't make more of an effort here,' and I was like, 'You're the only one who's not ever coming home early or altering your schedule at all!' Eventually, this was the plan we settled on, and usually, it does work. All of the women have come together to make this work."

Monique and her female peers—like mine, like theirs—grew up with the heady rhetoric of gender equality. Girls can do anything boys can do. We got Title IX. We got grad school. But the rhetoric stopped with us, the obvious and necessary corollary never to be uttered. "Boys can do anything girls can do" doesn't exactly roll off the tongue. So now Monique is a lawyer, but her husband is not a primary parent.

The changes in their lives after the birth of their daughter more or less began and ended with her. "There's definitely resentment," she says. "It's not a deal-breaking kind of resentment, but it's there. So when the three of us are together, I'm edgy. If he suggests that our daughter needs something, I have an immediate visceral reaction, and it's hard not to start an argument because the implication is that I'm supposed to take care of it. I try to say something nicely. But I don't always say it nicely.

"Whenever we come up with ways we're going to change this or fix this, it doesn't stick for him, and I don't hold him to it. At one point we arrived at an agreement—he would be home and in charge Tuesday and Thursday evenings. And then it wasn't happening because he'd stay late at work or he'd schedule something. And then, like, 'Yes, yes, I'm sorry, it won't happen again.' But then it does. It's gone. I worry about the idea of us just arguing all the time about it. He knows how I feel, and it hasn't produced any meaningful, consistent change. How much convincing of the other person can you do?"

She continues, "I went to a liberal arts school, and I took a ton of women's studies courses. And there was all this conversation about the dynamics of marriage and how things just automatically tended to fall in a certain way, and I remember when I was in those classes being like, 'I don't know why they do that. That's not going to be me.' And then that's just the way it happened."

The Reality of the Modern, Involved Father

When researchers ask expectant fathers today how they anticipate dividing chores and child care, most say their wives will do a bit more, often because of nursing, but that they will not lag far behind. Six months into their children's lives, these same fathers report that mothers are doing more than expected, while they themselves are doing less.

What begins as a potentially time-limited necessity because of breastfeeding becomes precedent. Fathers have assumed a larger share of child care in recent decades, but the amount of change has been quite modest, even when compared to how much more housework men have taken on. Between 1980 and 2000, when women's labor force participation rose most dramatically, men's self-reported share of housework increased by ten percentage points, going from 29 to 39 percent.

That is in stark contrast with a self-reported increase in child care at the same two junctures: In 1980 fathers reported doing 38 percent of child care, and in 2000 they reported doing 42 percent. Mothers in 1980 estimated that their husbands did 31 percent of child care, while mothers in 2000 guessed they did about 32 percent. Today, per a range of studies, working women devote about twice as much time to family care as men. And in case you've considered moving to a more progressive nation to escape the problem, even in gender-egalitarian Sweden, fathers spend only about 56 percent as much time as their female partners do caring for their kids.

There is actually no known human society in which men are responsible for the bulk of all childrearing. Cross-cultural anthropologists report that in every part of the world, across a wide range of subsistence activities and social ideologies, mothers are more involved than fathers with the care of their young. In a 2018 report, the United Nations estimated that women average 2.6 times the amount of housework and child care that men do.

In the last seventy-five years, women with small kids throughout the developed world—in the collection of thirty-six countries that belong to the Organization for Economic Cooperation and Development—began working for wages in steadily increasing numbers. Across the OECD today, 71 percent of mothers with one child and 62 percent of women with two or more children are now employed for pay. Still, comparative-time-use studies suggest that fathers in these countries (which include the U.S., Canada, and most of Europe, as well as Mexico, New Zealand, and Japan, to name a few) spend less than a quarter of the time their female partners do in routine housework, and less than half as much time caring for children. A 2017 OECD report called the unequal distribution of unpaid work between men and women in the home one of the most important gender-equality issues of our time. In recent history, fathers all over the globe have made small changes in the face of greater demands from breadwinning mothers. But the story we tell ourselves—the one about great leaps toward the achievement of equally shared parenting—is a glass-half-full interpretation. Must we continue to be only grateful?

There is a raucous B-side to the gratitude. Research from cultures all over the globe consistently finds that new parents experience a qualitative change in their relationship that is, to quote one team, "abrupt, adverse in nature, relatively large in magnitude." Longitudinal studies find that marital satisfaction peaks around the time of the wedding and then declines, and at twice the rate for parents as for nonparents. Some work suggests that the steepest drops occur before a child's first birthday, others that they come later. Research out of the Gottman Institute in Seattle, Washington, where they've been studying families for twenty-plus years, has found that two-thirds of couples experience both a significant drop in relationship quality and a dramatic increase in conflict and hostility within three years of the birth of their first child. And as the number of children increases, so, too, does the discontent.

There are a number of reasons why this is so, including the buffeted pressures of time and money and sleep deprivation. As University of California, San Francisco, health psychologists have verified in the lab, "People who are sleep deprived tend to experience more negative emotions, are more reactive to negative events, and are worse at problem solving." But there is also the fact that the transition to parenthood is "a critical moment in the development of an unequal gap in time spent on routine household labor."

A 2008 study out of the University of Queensland, Australia, found that women increase their time spent on routine housework by about six hours a week following a first birth, "compared to the flat and static average housework hours for men." It doesn't get better from there. While a first child has no effect on men's time in housework, a second leads to its reduction. The Australian researchers "find evidence that men's time on routine housework declines as more children are born, suggesting that the gender gap in housework time widens as the demand for time on domestic work increases." Across the life cycle, only the transition from married to widowed, divorced, or separated significantly increases a man's time in unpaid domestic labor.

Child care is similarly skewed. Australian time-use data from a different study, also around 2008, showed that mothers compared to fathers spent more overall time with children, engaged in more multitasking, operated with a more rigid timetable, spent more time alone with kids, and had more overall responsibility for managing the care of their children. This is consistent with time-use data in the U.S. and elsewhere.

The persistent disparity between the shiny conception of the modern, involved father and his actual contributions has confounded scholars for years. Spend much time digging into the past decade's sociology journals, and you'll unearth a trove of phrases like these: "we are just beginning to understand why men do so little" and "we do not yet have a very good understanding of which men—or the conditions under which men—involve themselves in the care of others" and "increasing levels of maternal employment . . . have not resulted in more equitable gender distribution of housework and child care time" and "gender specialization is least pronounced when both spouses are employed full time, but even in these households, women generally do most of the housework and child care" and "fathers are changing . . . but change is gradual at best." One UCLA research team analyzed fifteen hundred hours of videotape from the homes of middle-class dual-earner couples with kids. They found that father-in-a-room-by-himself was the "person-space configuration observed the most frequently," a piece of data that now pops into my head whenever I'm in the living room with the kids while my husband camps out in our room playing *Game of War* on his phone.

The liberties fathers take with their time are meticulously chronicled by social scientists. They have found, for example, that fathers who work long hours have wives who do more child care, while mothers who work long hours have husbands who sleep more and watch lots of television; that working mothers with preschool-aged children are two and a half times likelier to get up in the middle of the night to tend to their kids; that fathers with babies spend twice as much weekend time engaged in leisure activity as mothers. Still fathers do not feel their privilege. Data from 335 employed, married parents suggests that women perceive the distribution of housework and child care activities to be significantly more unequal than men perceive it to be.

The stark reality is that it is only when husbands are unemployed and their wives earn all the income that ratios of mothers' to fathers' time in child care almost converge. The most egalitarian caregiving arrangement is between sole-breadwinner wives and unemployed husbands, though even that earnings arrangement fails to reach parity. In homes with stay-at-home fathers, mothers continue to take on more managerial care of their children—otherwise known as scheduling and keeping track of stuff.

Unlike housework, which goes down for women as paid work hours go up, mothers maintain their child care time almost regardless of their employment obligations. They accomplish this by cutting back on leisure time, personal care, and sleep. This hardly varies by race or ethnicity. Studies of African American and Hispanic American families replicate the pattern found for white Americans. Comparisons across ethnic groups reveal few differences in levels of co-residential father care, though African American men and women both tend to be more critical of gender inequality than whites, who tend to be more critical of gender inequality than Hispanics.

Way back in 1992, family psychologists the Cowans wrote that over the course of fifteen years of research, it became clear to them that behind the ideology of each egalitarian couple lies a much more traditional reality. All the talk about men and women sharing the responsibility, noted one mother in their study, "is just bullshit!" Two decades on, research from far and wide continues to support this observation. It is women's, rather than men's, daily lives that differ the most according to whether or not they're raising kids. Recent time-use studies by Pew Research and the Bureau of Labor Statistics in the U.S. consistently estimate that women employed outside the home shoulder 65 percent of child care responsibilities, and men 35 percent. To recap, those percentages have held steady since the year 2000. In the last twenty years, that figure has not budged.

Despite changing economic realities, we have one foot grounded in the past. The nuclear family with a breadwinning father and a homemaking mother was a historical anomaly steeped in race and class privilege. This cultural ideal has long been at odds with reality. Postwar, when women went back to the home—often after being forced out of their jobs in favor of the returning soldiers—their labor force participation figure hovered around 30 percent. That steadily rose between 1970 and 2000. In 1975, 39 percent of women with preschool-aged children worked; since 1994, that percentage has remained above 60 percent. In 1975, 54.9 percent of women with school-aged children were in the labor force; since the 1990s, that number has held around 75 percent.

Today, the Bureau of Labor Statistics reports that 70 percent of married women with children between six and seventeen work outside of the home (and 60.8 percent of married women with children under six do). According to the institutions that track such things, decade by decade, no group has ever seen labor force increases of such high magnitudes in such brief time increments. Living through it, you felt the cataclysm of those shifts.

Men's and women's home lives started to look more similar in two ways: First, over the last fifty years, there have been modest increases in men's housework and steep declines in women's.

Second, men and women both have increased their time in child care. Still, gender remains the most salient predictor of family work performance.

How It All Begins

We could chalk it up to biology, to gestation and lactation, in which men cannot partake. Once it is your job to nurse the baby in the middle of the night, it continues to be you who awakens with her in the darkness far past the point of midnight feedings. A body in motion stays in motion. An object at rest stays at rest. Data from countries with generous maternity-leave policies support this idea—by inadvertently reinforcing women's role as caregiver in the first year of a child's life, they've seen decreases in the recent gains made in fathers' unpaid work time. Women do less housework and men do more in countries with shorter maternal leaves. If it was more complicated for George and me early on, well, certainly, I couldn't remember.

To get the perspective of some new moms, I went to a meeting of a new-mothers' group in my neighborhood. The five women gathered that day had been getting together for a couple of months, led by a local doula who spearheaded discussions on topics from postpartum body image to returning to work. Their babies ranged from twelve weeks to ten months. I told them about my project and asked them to talk about their experiences.

Anne, forty-two, a vice president of operations for a small company whose firstborn had just turned seven months, said, "Sometimes I look at my husband after he's gotten up from a four-hour nap on a Saturday while I've been with the baby or taking care of things, and I really need a nap, too, but now it's too late in the day to take one, and I think, What is wrong with me, and us, that we're living like this?" She continued, "In our house, my husband pitches in financially, and I do everything else. We've been living together for eleven years, and for most of those he traveled a lot for work, so all the housework fell on me based on proximity. I never felt angry about it—that's a strong word. But when I would get frustrated, I'd let him know, and he would help out."

The others also described having been in charge of more of the housework before having children. "Before I was pregnant, I was doing everything," said Amber, thirty, who had worked as an administrative assistant before her son arrived. "I was a happy housewife with a job." She'd been less happy about this arrangement since giving birth. For the time being, she was at home because returning to work didn't make financial sense. Her husband was critical when the "everything" she'd always taken care of was no longer getting done. "If I don't do the laundry, he's like, 'Well, what did you do all day?'" The others laughed in recognition, but Amber, who said she was just pulling out of a period of postpartum depression, joined them only half-heartedly.

"My husband, he just hates to clean," said Kimberly, thirty-one, who'd recently returned to her work in educational publishing. "Not that I wake up in the morning going, 'I can't wait to dust today,' but I notice these things, and I want the house a certain way. It's the way we grew up. I take more pride in having a presentable home."

Tasha, thirty-two, a librarian, said that this resonated with her. "The ways we grew up influenced how we respond to getting things done. I'm one of four girls, both my parents worked, and in my family, my sisters and I were the housekeepers. My husband's mom stayed home, and she had help. There were different expectations of us. So now he does things when I ask, but he doesn't take initiative. We had discussions about that before the baby came. 'Discussions' is the polite word." The women laughed again.

Their husbands' lack of initiative seemed to be spilling over into child care now that the babies had arrived. These new mothers took care to speak of this gingerly, by which I mean without anger. Meredith—thirty-six, a psychologist—reported "surprise" about how much her spouse deferred to her around the care of their daughter. "He's a take-charge kind of person, but I'm home with her more, and certain things come more naturally to me. It's a new dynamic for our relationship." Meredith was back at work, but nothing had changed in terms of who was responding to her daughter's cries in the middle of the night. "When I wasn't working, I felt the responsibility to let him sleep. I still feel that way because he's working more, but I'm a little bit more resentful now that I'm back in the office. I'm sure if I said something, he'd get up."

Tasha was also the person in her family most likely to forgo sleep. "My husband is a night person. He'll stay up until whenever, so in the mornings, I get up with the baby. He says, 'You don't mind being up early.' And I'm like, 'Yes, but I like sleeping in once in a while, too.' If I said to him, 'Hey, tomorrow, when she gets up, can you take her?' he would a hundred percent do it, but I don't know if it's something that would ever just occur to him." At the time of our meeting, her daughter was ten months old, which meant that for ten months running, her husband had left it to her to get up with their daughter while he slept.

"Can you imagine," I asked her, "a world in which your husband got up early with the baby every morning for ten months running and you never once offered to relieve him?" She acknowledged that she could not. I could not, either. None of us could.

It went on in all of their homes. "I'm happy to do it if you ask," the modern, involved father's *cri de coeur*. His generally positive attitude toward being second in command has made it hard for his wife to feel frustrated without a generous amount of self-rebuke. "It's my fault for not speaking up," I heard these women conclude. Why they were left to speak up in the first place remained largely uninterrogated.

"It's just not part of his thinking," said Anne, as if in explanation. "I'm the one who's going to make whatever needs to happen happen."

Amber's husband reflexively hands her the baby when it's time for a new diaper. If Amber resists, "He's really happy to do it, and he goes with a smile."

Meredith's husband meets friends for dinner after work, but she can't fault him for that: "If I said I wanted to go out with a friend, he would be happy to come and watch Eliza for several hours."

Kimberly's husband had been pursuing professional development and also volunteer work more aggressively since the birth of their child. "We discussed that before kids," she said. "He wanted to make sure he could keep building himself in some way, never losing himself. I guess I thought once she came, he'd back off a little bit. Sometimes I'll be like, 'Do you really need to go to that happy hour for this nonprofit you're volunteering for?' But I don't ask him not to go. I mean, it is what it is right now, I guess."

I had heard these stories before. All of them. What struck me in the room that day was not the novelty of the women's accounts but, rather, that none of them seemed that much to mind. I realized that was the thing I had not quite recalled—the not minding. I had not minded once, too. Boys will be boys, the women acknowledged, in grand tradition, with their laughter. On that morning in that room, I felt upset about what these otherwise outspoken mothers were allowing, a feeling that they, at least so far, had managed to ward off.

Here Is What It Costs Us

An ever-growing body of research in family and clinical studies demonstrates that spousal equality promotes marital success and that inequality undermines it. Women who report that they do more child care than their husbands are 45 percent less likely to describe their marriages as "very happy" than women who say responsibilities are shared. Recent data published in the *Journal of Marriage and Family* suggests that couples in which men do more than a third of the household work have more sex than those who do less, and that these relatively egalitarian couples are the only ones to have experienced an increase in sexual frequency during three decades over which sex within marriage has declined worldwide.

Division of family labor is the primary source of conflict after couples have children. Mothers of kids under four report the

greatest sense of injustice. Female infidelity has risen 40 percent
over the last three decades, and Belgian psychotherapist and author Esther Perel has said that in her extensive work treating
couples in the wake of affairs, she has found that the most common reason women give for cheating on their husbands is the
desire to break free from their caregiving role. Perel has said,
"In truth we are not looking for another person. We are looking
for another self."

A male partner's contribution to child care is the most important factor predicting relationship conflict and mothers'
satisfaction. Not surprisingly, studies in the last decade in the
UK, Sweden, and the United States have all found that couples
with low levels of male partner participation in domestic chores
are more likely to separate than couples in which men do more.
As satisfaction with a male partner's help increases, so, too, do
positive marital interactions, closeness, affirmation, and positive affect. As it decreases, thoughts of divorce, negative affect,
and depression go up—for mothers. Although perceived unfairness predicts both unhappiness and distress for women, it
predicts neither for men, who often do not seem to fully register
the problem. It's worth noting that women initiate about 70 percent of all divorce. While domestic equality offers no guarantee
of marital bliss, as social psychologist Francine Deutsch found
in her family study: "In homes where both parents worked full
time and women did most of the work at home, free and easy
happiness never emerged."

If a mother believes that child care specifically is unfairly
portioned, this is more likely to affect her relationship happiness than a perceived imbalance in housework by one full standard deviation. The optimistic tale of the modern, involved

father means that women today believe they are signing up for something resembling 50/50. When it fails to manifest, there is trouble. .

Ultimately, if couples have parsed who will do what in advance, it doesn't matter if the labor is equally shared or not. This becomes especially clear in same-sex pairs. Gay couples also report labor imbalances. Still, they are less likely than their straight counterparts to feel angry about it, not because they are more even-tempered but, rather, because they have explicitly agreed to their respective roles. Without the double-edged sword of gendered assumptions, they are more likely to work to communicate their needs and preferences around parenting work. As obvious as it may seem, heterosexual couples often fail to do this.

In our marriage, it never occurred to us. In their book *When Partners Become Parents*, the Cowans expressed dismay that the couples they interviewed felt that inequality had just somehow happened upon them. They write, "It's not just that [they] are startled by how the division of labor falls along gender lines, but they describe the change as if it were a mysterious virus they picked up when they were in the hospital having their baby. They don't seem to view their arrangements as choices they have made."

Here is one additional consistent finding: Greater father involvement predicts smaller declines in both partners' marital satisfaction. Recent research has shown that a new father's active participation minimizes overall relationship dissatisfaction in the transition to parenthood. When fathers behave like equal partners, both members of a couple say they are more satisfied with their relationship. One longitudinal study found that dads who reported the largest contributions to child care six months postpartum manifested the new-parent equivalent of a unicorn, an increase in marital satisfaction at their child's eighteen-month mark. Their wives reported even greater increases in satisfaction during the same period. On the flip side, the less involved a father became with his baby's care over the first eighteen months, the more likely both members of a couple were to experience growing disenchantment with the relationship. A husband having more leisure time than his wife did not a happy marriage make.

It can even mean the end of a relationship. After writing an op-ed about couples and child care for *The Washington Post* in 2017, I received emails from women who'd ultimately left when their husbands refused to step up their game. "My husband's failure to be a partner around child care ended the marriage. He wouldn't watch our child to let me shower. He wouldn't get up to give me a few uninterrupted hours of sleep at night. He dumped all the responsibility for managing the kid and the house on me. I resented him so, so much," wrote one woman in New York.

"I'm a full-time, now single, career professional with two primary-school-age kids," wrote an American living abroad and working in international diplomacy. "While there were many factors that resulted in the end of my marriage two years ago, it was the gnawing grind of responsibility for every little thing, and the knowledge that my children were being shaped by seeing me put up with it, that eventually tipped me over the edge and saw my marriage conclude. Life is tough now. Certainly. But it's much clearer and calmer without the festering resentment that just added to my exhaustion at work, parenting, and everything else."

But even when relationship dissolution is not the end result, the cost of unequal partnership to women's well-being is high. Most working parents today report too little time for family life. Mothers, however, experience this time deficit differently than fathers. For a woman, having insufficient time to attend to her family is associated with a greater likelihood of depression, which epidemiologists say may explain why employed women are more likely than employed men to become depressed. A father's sense of well-being, in contrast, is more negatively impacted by not having enough time to himself.

A 2017 study published in the *Journal of the American Medical Association* found that female physicians were significantly more likely than their male colleagues to experience an increase in depressive symptoms during their demanding internship year, and that work-family conflict accounted for 36 percent of this disparity between the sexes. *The New York Times* noted, "Despite large increases in the number of women in medicine, female physicians continue to shoulder the bulk of household and child care duties." This sampling of one specific group of working women seems likely to be reflective of many.

Theorists propose that our culture's particular emphasis on feminine family devotion leaves women more vulnerable to guilt and then despair when they find themselves with outsize nonfamilial obligations. Employed women with young children also take a health hit. While advances in women's access to education and employment have brought about vast improvements in their health—once incorrectly presumed just innately more fragile than men's—those improvements are not borne out during the years when they're raising young kids.

Education and employment are among the most important

preventative factors in social epidemiology, for men of all family statuses, and for women with no children or with older ones. Being a family's primary caretaker in the early years leaves women more vulnerable to health problems, if only for a limited time. Carissa, a thirty-five-year-old public defender and mother to a seven-year-old and a three-year-old in Seattle, spoke to me while laid up in bed after foot surgery. "I developed a bone spur on the top of my foot. For months I was wearing shoes that hurt, but I didn't stop to buy other shoes because I have no time to go shopping. I kept wearing them and ignoring the problem. Finally, one of my friends said, 'What is wrong with your foot?' So here I am now, I had this surgery, and it's horrible, and recovery is painful, all largely because I did not stop last fall and do what I needed to do for myself. My foot is a casualty of this life where I go and go and go and go and go."

There's also a financial cost. Lack of parity in the home stalls movement toward greater gender equality in the labor market. Mothers' income trajectories fall when they move in and out of the workforce, cut back their hours, take less demanding jobs, and pass up or don't win promotions because of biases against mothers. In 2016, economists at the Center for American Progress calculated that a twenty-six-year-old woman earning the median U.S. income of $44,148 would lose not only her wages for taking one year off to be with her baby but also, and over time, $64,393 in wage growth and $52,945 in retirement and benefits. The overall economy then loses, too: A 2015 report from think tank McKinsey Global Institute estimated that the world economy would be $28.4 trillion (or 26 percent) richer by 2025 if the gender gaps in labor force participation and productivity were bridged.

Recent research indicates that the gender wage gap is really a motherhood gap. Women without children earn just barely less than men. It's not called "the motherhood wage penalty" for nothing. One reason for this is that commitment to one's job, in the last few decades, has become associated with the willingness or ability to work more than full-time. Since the 1970s, "overwork" (defined as fifty hours or more per week) is an ever more standard expectation, especially in managerial professions. By the mid-1990s, the years surrounding the apex of working moms, salaried workers who'd once faced a wage *penalty* for overwork began to see a wage *bump* for the same. The proportion of people who overworked increased, financial rewards for working long hours went up, and the attitude toward employees unable to make themselves perpetually available soared.

Attorney Joan Williams, the founding director of the Center for WorkLife Law and author of the 2014 book *What Works for Women at Work*, told me, "Not to be a conspiracy-theorist, but the wage penalty for overwork turned into a wage premium in exactly the same period that women started to enter professional life in a serious way. It's striking that when that happened, the ideal worker was redefined on the single vector in which women couldn't effectively compete, and that was time."

University of Indiana sociologist Youngjoo Cha studies the impact of overwork on labor outcomes. She's found that the increase in financial compensation for overwork plays a large role in maintaining the gender wage gap. She explains that if relative hourly wages for overwork had remained constant between 1979 and 2007, that gender wage gap would be about 10 percent smaller than it is today.

Legal scholars have argued that bias toward women as caretakers and men as breadwinners also manifests in workplace discrimination, further hurting women's career advancement and wages. Additionally, the so-called logic of gendered choices almost always trumps cold hard cash when it comes to decisions about who in the family will take leave or cut back. Even when mothers earn more, an increasingly common phenomenon, couples tend to decide that it should be she, rather than he, who becomes the secondary breadwinner. It is disproportionately women who forgo economic security and well-being when they become parents, costs that would be more easily borne were they only equitably distributed.

Though it's been illegal in the U.S. to fire a woman for becoming pregnant since 1978, in 2018 *The New York Times* reported, "Pregnancy Discrimination Is Rampant Inside America's Biggest Companies." The story detailed pregnant women's experiences being sidelined from work, refused accommodations, passed over for promotion, or fired for questioning all of the above. Hiring discrimination against mothers is also ubiquitous. "This commute would be too long for a woman with a young child," an older male psychologist at a Bronx hospital informed me toward the end of a job interview in 2010 (as I cursed my own judgment for mentioning I had a kid).

In 2007, sociologists spent eighteen months sending confederate résumés to entry- and mid-level business positions available in a large northeastern city. The gender and parental status of the made-up applicants varied, but their work history and education did not. Childless women were 2.1 times more likely to be offered interviews than mothers. In contrast, fathers were slightly more likely to be called than men without children.

A world in which both men and women are presumed to

shoulder outside obligations equally would necessarily render family commitments acceptable and expectable rather than inconvenient and deal-breaking. It might also shift public policy. For now, the male legislators who continue to make up the majority of Congress in the U.S. remain uninterested in proposing or passing policy changes that would support more livable family arrangements—paid parental leave and government-subsidized early child care come to mind. These men don't know parenthood's most grueling tribulations firsthand. Might their minds change if they did? (Never mind the problems inherent in having relatively few women in public office. As University of Wisconsin–La Crosse historian Jodi Vandenberg-Daves put it when we spoke, "One of the really unfortunate continuities in this country is that women have had so little say over the public allocation of resources.") The longer we all tolerate 65/35, the longer factors that support it will remain in place. If men had periods, tampons would be free in every public restroom. The same principle applies here. Until men bear the labor of family life as women do, other status quos seem unlikely to shift.

The women I spoke with described the personal toll of this status quo: intense disappointment in their partnerships, persistent underlying anger at their children's fathers, dampened sexual desire, and fantasies of escape. Tracy, forty-seven, a domestic violence advocate with two preteens in Washington State, ended our phone call in tears. "There's a huge amount of resentment. And the thought that, you know, If you're not going to help me more, I'll just check out," she said. "You hope that when the kids get older, things will get better. But I tell my friends, I'm one gas tank away from a small town and a new identity."

At a time when heady feminist battles are being fought boldly and publicly, parity in first-world homes might take its place among them. It is an essential piece of a bigger puzzle, one that undergirds the general struggle for the broad acceptance of women's basic humanity. We do not exist for the convenience and pleasure of men. We will not be equal anywhere until we are equal everywhere, until we stop colluding in the most widely accepted form of cultural misogyny. For now, we love our families as our partners do, but we remain more encumbered by the arrangements we accept in our private lives.

On Fairness

The following is an old finding, published in 1994, but as behavior hasn't changed much in the last twenty years, I think it bears mentioning. It's a breakdown calculated from the time diaries of couples, and their separate reports on their feelings about the distribution of labor in their homes. Time-diary studies require participants to record how they are spending their time at set intervals during the day for a limited number of days or weeks. Researchers can then take the time diary of each member of a couple and compute what percentage of the work he or she is doing in their home.

Once the researchers determined the relative percentages of the couples in the study (percentages that the couples were blind to), they compared the numbers to the participants' feelings about their arrangements. They found that men who performed 36 percent of their household's labor reported the strongest feelings of fairness. What might give us—and especially those of us who are female—a moment of pause is that women basically agreed with them. Women's "equity point" was actually even more generous to men. The women whose time diaries attested to the fact that they were doing 66 percent of their household's labor were the most likely to say that arrangements were fair.

The study's authors write, "These results show that fairness in housework does not mean sharing chores equally. Rather, both women and men appear to believe that women should do about two-thirds of household chores." The labor force participation of mothers with infants peaked in 1995, so this finding is not an artifact of the era of separate spheres. It makes some sense, then, that the division of child care labor has stalled here, 65/35, women/men. Our culture of sexism has reaped what it has sown.

More recently, Yale anthropologist Riché J. Daniel Barnes conducted a study of twenty-three professional African American women raising children with men. In 2016's *Raising the Race: Black Career Women Redefine Marriage, Motherhood and Community*, Barnes reports that 75 percent of them felt that their proportion of family work increased more dramatically than their husbands' after their first child was born. Still, Barnes writes, "Despite the mismatch, almost half of the women said they were pleased with the allocation of responsibilities. They all had complaints, but, for the most part, each of the women excused the imbalance as a function of the role as wife and mother."

We delude ourselves with ideology and the lip service we pay to female empowerment. Although sharing child care is associated with valuing gender equality, this value is neither a necessary nor sufficient condition for equally shared parenting.

Actually, there is limited support in the literature for gender attitudes determining family practices.

A 2001 study in Toronto looked at forty couples making the transition to parenthood. The subjects expressed "a stronger commitment to sharing the work . . . than is usual." Ultimately, the study found, most of them developed the gendered patterns typical in Canadian families, where women either cut back on paid work and take charge of the bulk of tasks at home, or don't cut back on paid work and take charge of the bulk of tasks at home.

Here's something more recent: While 65 percent of millennial men without children endorse combined breadwinner/caretaker roles for husbands and wives, only 47 percent of their peers with children continue to do so. Idealism is well and good before one has to accommodate its burdens. As British author Rebecca Asher writes in *Shattered*, her book about the state of her feminist ideals after children, "on becoming fathers, [men] find that patriarchy suits them rather well after all."

Less skeptical explanations for this difference between belief and practice have also been proposed. Arlie Hochschild wrote about "on top" versus "underneath" ideologies. Couples hold one set of beliefs about women's employment and men's domestic responsibilities on top but have a much different reality in lived experience underneath. Paula England attributes the gap to two competing cultural logics, that of individualism and the right to equal opportunity versus that of gender essentialism, the tacit belief that men and women have fundamentally different interests and skills.

Finally, exposure-based explanations argue that contact with other fathers who adopt primary caretaking roles will push more men toward doing the same, but also that immersion in a culture of female parenting just discourages men's shift. Social context can supersede gender ideology. Context influences whether attitudes will result in behavior, and when attitudes and behaviors conflict, we tend to reduce inconsistency by changing the former. Parents may ultimately become less egalitarian in order to minimize cognitive dissonance in relationships where egalitarianism is expected but inequality has forever been the norm.

Still, to say that gender ideology is totally and completely irrelevant to behavior is misleading. Rather, it is relevant only when the man's ideology is in consideration. Most studies have found that men with less traditional gender ideologies do a greater share of the household chores. These findings are confirmed in samples from Taiwan, Israel, China, Canada, Sweden, Great Britain, and the U.S. To quote the conclusion of the paper that examines this data, "Husbands' gender ideology may be a stronger determinant of housework divisions than the wives' gender ideology."

Along the same lines, a number of studies have found that fathers' (but not mothers') belief in equality is positively associated with paternal involvement with child care. Is it then any surprise that women who believe in sharing housework tend to have lower marital satisfaction than those who don't, and men who believe in sharing tend to have higher marital satisfaction than those who don't? Similarly, when men are more egalitarian than their wives, marital disagreements are fewer. When wives are more egalitarian than their husbands, marital disagreements abound.

What does this tell us about who wears the pants? Did you

know we were still asking that question? Wait, there's more. In terms of beliefs about marital roles, fathers' attitudes—but not mothers'—are significantly related to their children's attitudes regardless of the gender of those children. This seems to speak to kids' ability to identify power, to determine whose beliefs are more valuable and worthy of internalization. And while family of origin's effects on attitude formation recede during adolescence, we all know of the tenacious "underneath" quality of the ideas we acquire in our earliest years. Cultural messages about men and women maintain the rules of the gender system, and these rules have self-fulfilling effects on behavior. The rules give the system the ability to persist in the face of social shifts that might otherwise upend them.

Deanna, a teacher and mother of two in San Diego who was born in the Midwest in 1976, explained, "When my husband and I got together, we were totally equal partners in everything. Then we got married, and I wanted to do all the housework and take care of everything. It was part of my dream of meeting someone I adored. I thought I should assume the responsibility that being married, that being a woman, comes with. I know it sounds crazy now. At the time it really made sense." Her husband predicted she'd come to resent him (he was right). He went along with her anyway.

Deanna was rare among the women I spoke with in that she made a conscious and explicit decision to be her family's sole homemaker, if one with a full-time job. She and her husband agreed to live like a traditional couple. More common these days for dual earners is an arrangement that social scientists call the gender legacy couple. In these pairs, responsibility for children simply defaults to the woman, and if you are reading this book because of a personal connection to this problem, it is likely that you fall into this group. Mothers in the gender legacy pairs describe the most pronounced feelings of stress and burden associated with child care. Family researchers describe a "marriage between equals discourse" that bears little relationship to what actually goes on day-to-day. While couples report that their decisions are mutual, outcomes tend to favor the needs and goals of husbands much more than wives.

The language of equality—a belief in the modern, involved father—creates a myth central to the idea of these contemporary marriages. It conceals a sort of female subordination that would otherwise be intolerable in many twenty-first-century homes, the taken-for-granted notion that a mother is in charge of the tracking and the knowing and the thinking and the planning and the feeding and the caring and the checking and the doing unless she has worked to make other arrangements (which then entail more knowing and more thinking and more tracking and more doing). He's-happy-to-do-it-if-I-ask is yet another task; it's not a partnership.

Sometimes couples succinctly articulate the gap between their values and their behaviors. In other cases, they work hard to imagine that their arrangements live up to their ideals. In researching her 2003 book, *Unequal Childhoods: Class, Race and Family Life*, sociologist Annette Lareau noted how little organizing and managing fathers seemed to do, and she emphasized to me how blatantly this fact was denied. (This observation, not germane to her book's subject, grew into a separate paper she eventually titled "My Wife Can Tell Me Who I Know.")

Lareau told me that the dads "knew nothing about the kids' schedules and needs. But mothers and fathers swore otherwise.

For example, one couple insisted that the dad did all the soccer. I was there one day when there was a rainout, and there were seventeen phone calls, all fielded by the mom. They didn't even notice that she did all the snacks, the uniforms, the registration. They said, 'Oh, no, he does all the soccer.' It was hard to interview these people. They were so blinded by ideology. They didn't see all the invisible labor that went into moms structuring dads' time with the kids."

I heard similarly conflicting accounts from mothers I interviewed. Claudia, a forty-four-year-old bookkeeper in Atlanta with two children, said, "My husband is a hands-on dad," before adding that she has to harangue him to ask the kids how their days were, and "If he had to hire a babysitter, he wouldn't know where to start. I'm the one who knows what is due when, who reads emails from schools, goes through their folders. He takes my son to Boy Scouts, though sometimes he tries to get me to do it, and I'm like, 'Dude, you have to do one thing! I can't do every single thing. There are a bunch of guys there! Why don't you go encounter other male adults?' But then he will. He's not useless."

Couples that hang on to old gendered norms better suited to different social and economic times may be heading into choppy waters. The younger set of research subjects, not yet coupled or parenting, suggest as much. A large majority of undergraduates participating in New York University sociologist Kathleen Gerson's "Plan A/Plan B" research say they hope for egalitarian marriages. But when asked to predict how they'd decide to live if that didn't work out (their plan B), young men anticipate becoming breadwinners with primary caretaker wives, and young women anticipate divorce. Gerson wonders whether the differing fallback positions of self-reliant women and neotraditional men may point to a new gender divide. Of course, real life is stickier than theoretical situations posed to nineteen-year-olds in labs, and Occidental College sociologist Lisa Wade questions whether this finding speaks to anything that might ever come to pass. "You love the stupid guy, and he's the father of your children. Are you really going to table-flip your life because he won't pack a bag for your kids?"

But simply staying together is hardly a high bar for a marriage. Perceived unfairness in division of child care predicts marital unhappiness for women, but also, unhappy marital relationships predict decreasing involvement on the part of fathers. The two feed each other. Couples accept the myth of equality, fail to address their actual circumstances, and then enter into a despondent cycle. As long as they fail to recognize power dynamics in their relationship, it's hard for them to change. Studies of couples show that even when power issues are raised, they're generally not framed in terms of how husbands need to change but, rather, how wives do—you know, she needs to be more assertive. The women I spoke with demonstrated this, offering me earfuls about what they might have done differently (and to be clear, if someone had been interviewing me, I'd have sounded exactly the same). Tracy, the domestic violence advocate, said, "Why didn't he take on more? Because I did not force him to." She did, however, ask him to. He wasn't having it. "He'd say, 'You're doing just fine. You've got this under control. I'm going to play video games.'"

CHAPTER 2

The Naturalistic Fallacy

We Half Think It's Biology

In 2017, Pew Research found that 64 percent of Americans believe that men and women "approach parenting differently." Of that 64 percent, just under half attribute the difference to biology. Men are more likely than women to credit nature rather than nurture, 58 to 39 percent. There is no biological difference between the sexes that explains my husband's failure to download the classroom communications apps requested by our daughters' teachers, or to chop the quartered watermelons he regularly brings home and deposits in our refrigerator like an outdoor cat with bird kill on a porch. The frustrations expressed by the mothers I interviewed—full of similar themes—likewise preclude any reasonable organic explanation. However, when asked, "Why is it still this way?" most women list nature as they do their thinking aloud. It is such a comfortable place to land. It spares us some amount of anger or self-recrimination, and it has an intuitive feel.

Nicole, fifty-three, a college administrator in Portland,

Oregon, with two kids now finishing high school, remembers the years of arguing with her husband; finally, she laid down her sword. "The giving up happened when the kids were in elementary school," she says. "My husband just didn't quite get it. I made it a point to be around more. I thought, This is an important job, even if society doesn't hold it on a pedestal. I want to do it right. That was the conversation I kept having in my head. Maybe he's better at taking care of himself, and I was more willing to sacrifice. I think about how it would have worked had I pushed back more. But for a while, I was really pushing back.

"I think he saw it as more equal. I had to come to terms with it," she continues. "Compared to my father, who left, I have a husband who is giving his kids attention, he's good with their homework, he gives in the ways that he's good at doing. He would push back. 'Well, it's pretty equal,' he'd say, and he'd point out all the things he'd done.

"Some of my friends' marriages seemed more equitable, but you never know. Women, I don't know if they always talk about this, you just endure and you accept. There was grumbling. My marriage struggled. I went into it thinking we'd spend equal time tending to the kids' needs. I was doing accounting in my head for a while. It wasn't healthy."

This attitude toward accounting was something I got used to hearing from mothers, who considered it a scourge on a generous spirit. Accounting can also be a way of taking care. Jacqueline, a married lesbian in Colorado who reports feeling like a successful co-parent to her two elementary-school-aged kids, said, "We consider and then anticipate each other's needs. I know my wife took the kids to school and picked them up today, so I feel more responsibility to do the chores at the end of the night." As Jacqueline exemplifies, the problem with accounting comes not when both partners are doing it in recognition of the other's contributions but, rather, when it's left to a mother alone, stewing in the math of a father's apathy.

Not wanting to keep score, Nicole stopped instigating the "multiple spirited discussions" and accepted that women were just innately better at tuning in to the needs and concerns of others. "The multitasking and switching the brain, it's like switching to the needs of your baby and then jumping on the computer. We're good at that. There was a certain naturalness to it that was hard to fight. Intrinsically, women get the commitment at a deeper level. I almost think it's genetic or hormonal. Something is driving us that isn't driving them."

Here Is Why We Half Think It's Biology

Without naming it, Nicole nods toward gender essentialism, the idea that women share some innate essential property that differentiates them from men. It holds that intellectual, social, emotional, and psychological characteristics of human beings are related to the body, and then that biological sex directly results in gender expression.

In the twelfth century, gender essentialists were among the first Western feminist thinkers, contending that women weren't simply inferior versions of men—a bold assertion in its time, and maybe still. In the centuries since, gender essentialism has been used both to encourage women to bring their unique experiences to the table in the public sphere, and to justify discrimination against them. Men and women are essentially different. That is how many of us understand gender in contemporary society. But as philosopher Jennifer Hockenbery Dragseth explains in her book *Thinking Woman*, "Gender essentialists often claim that gender and sex is a natural division. But often times what seems 'natural,' 'innate,' or 'obvious' is actually a cultural habit."

Only women bear children. We know this much is true. What transpires postpartum might go any number of ways, but the logic of gender essentialism works to transform initial obligatory maternal investment into long-term exclusive maternal care. Conservative activist Phyllis Schlafly decried feminism as "doomed to failure because it is based on an attempt to repeal and restructure human nature," as feminist activist and Third Wave founder Amy Richards was experiencing "the stress of parenting much more than Peter does, and [beginning] to wonder if this is hardwired into me." Despite divergent goals, both women fell similarly prey to the naturalistic fallacy, the assumption that the current state of affairs, governed by laws of nature, is the only (and the best) possibility. "*What is*" comes to pass for "*what must be.*" Under scrutiny, though, most gendered differences attributed to hardwiring are rooted in social realities that, so far, are immovable but hardly biologically preordained.

Janet Shibley Hyde, a professor of psychology and women's studies at the University of Wisconsin, is a leading academic in the field of gender studies. Gender differences are not only the focus of broad public interest (exhibit A: John Gray's *Men Are from Mars, Women Are from Venus* has sold more than fifty million copies) but also a fertile area of psychological research. Name any presumed variation in emotion or cognition between men and women, and you are likely to find at least fifty studies on its validity. Hyde has counted.

In 2005, Hyde rounded up forty-six meta-analyses of gender difference studies whose domains included cognitive abilities, communication, social behavior, personality, and psychological well-being, to name a handful. Her goal was to determine the effect size, or statistical strength, of the variables in question. She found that the largest differences between men and women were in the domains of motor skills (like throwing velocity) and sexuality (like frequency of masturbation). But 48 percent of the variables had effect sizes in the statistically small range, and an additional 30 percent were hardly more than zero. That means that for 78 percent of the gender differences measured and remeasured and measured once again, there was actually as much of a difference within gender as between gender. Differences between two women or two men were at least as likely as differences between any female/male pair. She wrote, "This view is strikingly different from the prevailing assumptions of difference found among the general public and even among researchers."

Too often science, which is nuanced, is a poor match for conventional wisdom, which is not. This is why John Gray's *Men Are from Mars, Women Are from Venus* outsells neuroscientist Cordelia Fine's *Delusions of Gender: The Real Science Behind Sex Differences* twenty-five hundred to one. Gray reinforces popular myths about sex differences, exhorting his (millions of) readers that housework impacts oxytocin and testosterone production in ways that are salutary for women and downright dangerous for men: "to join in and share each day in her daily routines as a helper would eventually exhaust him." Fine rebukes Gray, writing, "Gender stereotypes are legitimated by these pseudo-scientific explanations. Suddenly, one is being modern and scientific, rather than old-fashioned and sexist."

Based on the findings of her meta-meta-analysis, Hyde proposed "the gender similarities hypothesis," which asserts that, distinctive reproductive systems aside, men and women are similar in more ways than not. Unless you are a gender scholar, however, you are likely less familiar with Hyde's work than you are with Gray's. In our current cultural climate, it is harder to absorb the less sensational, research-based propositions of Hyde or Fine or Michael Kimmel, director of the Center for the Study of Men and Masuclinities at Stony Brook University in New York, who succinctly states, "Gender difference is the product of gender inequality, not the other way around."

Here Is the Problem with Half Thinking It's Biology

If what drives the parenting gap is, as Nicole postulated, genetic or hormonal, how much effort should a reasonable parent exert toward fostering its reorganization? As Brown University professor emerita Anne Fausto-Sterling, a leading expert in biology and gender development, has written, "The belief in a biological explanation for a social phenomenon suggests that efforts to change the existing situation are futile."

How do we know this to be true? To test the impact of encountering a difference in a novel skill between a man and a woman, social psychologists at Princeton invited undergraduates to take part in an experiment on perceptual style. Subjects were administered a task either alone or in a mixed-sex pair. They were asked to scan a set of slides with dots on them, and to very quickly estimate how many dots were on each slide. Everyone who completed the task was then told (fallaciously, as no one was really scoring the task) that they had one of two perceptual styles, that of "underestimator" or "overestimator." The students who were tested alone learned their style one-on-one from the researcher. The mixed-sex pairs received their results alongside their co-participant and were told either 1) that they had different perceptual styles; or 2) that their perceptual styles were the same. Finally, the experimenter asked all participants to fill out a questionnaire to assess their beliefs about their (made-up) style: "What percentage of males do you think have your style? What percentage of females do you think have your style?"

Men and women in all three conditions guessed that members of their own biological sex category were more likely to share their perceptual style, but those tested in the mixed-sex pairs with differing outcomes reported the greatest likelihood that style was heavily influenced by sex. The presence of just one opposite-sex peer who exhibited a different style on a task not previously associated with a gender stereotype pushed them toward generalizing their own performance as being attributable to a sex-based essence.

Next, the researchers recruited additional students and told them they'd be participating in a task examining whether perceptual style was stable and consistent. In order to measure this, the students were told, they'd be administered a dot-estimation task two times. As in the first experiment, participants took the test either alone or in mixed-sex pairs. After completion of the initial dot-estimation task, students were given their (again fallacious) results alone or with their task partner. The mixed-sex pairs were told either 1) that they had different perceptual styles; or 2) that their perceptual styles were the same.

When the dot test was readministered—along with a reminder

to be accurate—both the solo participants and those in the pairs with the same (made-up) perceptual style attempted to improve based on the feedback. That is, they lowered or raised their estimates according to whether they were over- or underestimators. Participants from the mixed-sex pairs with purportedly differing styles, however, did not attempt to correct for their known errors. Their belief that their style represented their sex's tendency kept them from altering their performance even once they'd been told exactly how to improve. Their assumption that this trait was innate preempted any effort to change.

The researchers conclude, "When a woman and a man hold different opinions on an issue, a) they will be inclined to conclude that their difference of opinion is gendered, irrespective of whether or not this is true, and b) they will see the difference as entrenched, and therefore will be neither curious about one another's thinking nor optimistic that they can change each other's minds. When a woman describes a distinctive behavior of her male partner as a 'guy thing,' she is marking it as something she can accept, and perhaps even respect, but not something she can understand or hope to change."

What to do, then, about the dominant culture of parenthood that continues to reinforce the idea that men are just like that, just that way in their bones? Here is the way we talk—a 2017 exchange from an online mothers' group whose members live in the Midwest:

REBECCA: Mommas i just need to rant. I'm 30 weeks today and have a 20-month old. I'm finding it harder and harder to keep my cool since my husband just isn't understanding that I need help. He literally just sits there and barely interacts and even asking for help he does bare minimum. It's like he has blinders on and doesn't observe what's going around him.

ALISHA: I feel your pain. I have two kids and my husband works all the time and when he is home he sits on the sofa and tunes everyone and everything out! I'm like REALLY?!!

REBECCA: This is too true!! I also work 2 jobs but he is more important I guess.

CAROL: I have a voicemail saved of Bill calling me SCREAMING about the dishes while I was at work when it was his THIRD day off in a row.

SABRINA: Oh. Hell. No.

JACKIE: Whenever I feel like that I start asking my husband "which" he wants to do. As in "do you want to give the kid a bath in 10 minutes or unload and re-load the dishwasher now?" I let him choose but hold him responsible for whichever. It feels so silly sometimes, but I have found that's the only way I get the help I need.

LAUREN: Ha ha! That works really well with 3 year olds too!

BRIE: Ugh! My husband is horrible with timing. He's like a teenager that I have to yell at to get out of bed.

SABRINA: This is exactly why I'm thinking about stopping at 1 kid! My husband is the same. He does work really hard and late hours, but when he's home I still feel like I'm doing it all alone.

NICOLE: Ditto!!!!! Ughhhhh. It's extremely frustrating.

JANE: Do you ask him to get up and help (please come do the dishes, can you please help x kid with x)? Husbands need specific direction. Our job is to ask and it's the husband's job to do what we ask.

CAROL: I'm a believer of this as well, except then I get told I'm nagging. Like . . . do it the first time then! Men are more difficult than children!

LORI: OMG, this post is the STORY OF MY LIFE. I get so tired of asking my husband to help me that I eventually do most things myself.

CHARLOTTE: Ugh sounds like a lot of dads I know! Sorry Rebecca. You're an amazing mama!!!!

How many conversations like this do we have to absorb before we come to believe that men are impervious to change—unable to understand, in need of direction, more difficult than children? I, for one, have participated in more of such offline chats than I'd like to admit. While there's comfort in shared struggle, that comfort can be cold. The inferred inevitability of it all provides an (un)easy out. The familiar discourse minimizes our anger by allowing us to sink into those familiar tropes—boys will be boys and locker-room talk and guy things.

Tropes give us license to delicately petition our partners for more effort but not to confront them with our wrath. Even-keeled, we fail to communicate the stakes, and then again. Kristen, thirty-seven, a mother of two in Ann Arbor, Michigan, told me, "I read some article about training your husband like you train a dog. Reward good behavior and ignore bad behavior. So if he would do the dishes, I would be like, 'Thank you so much!'" The tropes calcify and reproduce until we are all the undergraduate dot estimators not bothering to recalibrate our efforts.

As Rosalind Franklin University of Medicine and Science neuroscientist Lise Eliot points out in her book *Pink Brain, Blue Brain: How Small Differences Grow into Troublesome Gaps—And What We Can Do About It*, a hundred years ago, women made up only 20 percent of college students and were rare in most professions. It was the general consensus that there was a fundamental, hardwired gap in both intelligence and ambition between women and men. Not until feminists began arguing the origins of this gap—asserting that it was social norms and not biology limiting women's potential—did things begin to change.

I'm not suggesting that women leave their online mothers' groups. I'm not suggesting any action at all. I am pointing out the way in which we breezily conflate men's prerogatives with their essential nature, prerogatives that are not actually innate but are learned, and which the luckiest among us are not forced to contend with so nakedly until men are living as our partners in our homes. Then, suddenly, the outgrowth of their privilege becomes breathtaking.

Compounding ideas about nature, parents with different experiences are less public about their lives. Danielle is a thirty-eight-year-old mother to a six-year-old girl in Boston. Her grad school requirements have meant that her daughter's father is the more involved parent. During her daughter's infancy, Danielle could not soothe her. The baby wanted her dad. They weren't falling back on traditional gender roles, and Danielle and her husband assumed their child's preference was learned as opposed to biological. They actively intervened to make sure their daughter would also be responsive to Danielle.

Danielle shared her guilt about her absence at home with her classmates at the time. "One of them was like, 'Danielle, if you were a man, you wouldn't even be worried about this. This would just be how it was.'" Danielle agreed. She also acknowledged shutting down when her mom friends begin complaining about their husbands. "Sometimes someone will ask me directly why I've gotten quiet, and I'll say, 'I'm listening and taking in.' Because Jeff and I are in the reverse situation. I'm the one that stacks the dishes on the sides of the sink." She told me that her reasons for holding back with other women were complicated. "There's this kind of narrative that is very true—I see it—of, like, gender roles in households, and on the one hand, I feel really lucky that I don't have to stick to that. On the other hand, I'm like, What's wrong with me that I'm not in that position?"

Derek, a twenty-nine-year-old stay-at-home father raising two young daughters in North Carolina, avoids friendships with other at-home men. "Even the dads who are at home full-time, when we hang out as families, the women are upstairs with the kids, and we're in the basement talking about fishing. I'm concerned about leaving the kids upstairs—the other dads aren't. I don't want to just leave both of them with Caitlin while

I'm doing something else by myself. That's not fair to her. I think even those dads still have nonprogressive views on family. They don't really acknowledge being at-home fathers. It's more like, 'I'm just in between jobs right now.'" (While this attitude frustrates Derek, there's likely some truth behind it. In 2016, only 24 percent of at-home fathers in the U.S. reported that they were there specifically to take care of their home or family.

Tiffany, a thirty-four-year-old social worker in Queens with a six-month-old son, has watched her friends raise their eyebrows in response to what goes on in her home. We drink tea on the couch in her railroad apartment while the baby naps nearby, and as her husband, Carlos, is in and out on errands. It's a Thursday afternoon, but Carlos, an office manager, requested and was granted permission to work from home one day a week after their baby was born. Tiffany herself has returned to work only part-time.

She explains that she's nursing, and that her husband gets up with her in the middle of the night whenever their son needs to eat. Carlos rubs her shoulders or gets her water or just keeps her company. They've been doing this together since night three, when she came home from the hospital after giving birth. Reflexively, I respond with a "wow." Tiffany replies, "I know. My friends are like, 'Why is he getting up?' Because he wants to, and he's helping me!" Tiffany feels like she has to defend their arrangements. I get that. My own reaction belied my belief that at least one of them should be sleeping, and of course, that would necessarily be Carlos. But my response—like Danielle's concern that there's something wrong with her, or Derek's experience of his fellow stay-at-home dads—was really just a symptom of the problem itself. It's one thing to believe that things should be different. It's another to see that belief through to its logical conclusion.

There's No Such Thing as a Maternal Instinct

Marisol, a twenty-nine-year-old ophthalmic assistant and military wife with a toddler and a baby in Las Vegas, tells me, "Before kids, we had an agreement that he paid all the bills while I took care of the house. The money I made, I got to keep to myself. Now that we have kids and I take care of them, mainly, I feel like the work should be divided evenly. He says he'll help, but it only lasts for a couple of days until he stops helping. Then I reiterate that I can't do everything on my own, and he starts to help again for another couple days. And it keeps going in a circle." I ask Marisol why it works this way, and it's clear that her assumptions about nature leave her capable of loving kindness but not outrage. "I think women generally take care because the maternal instincts come naturally to us, where for men, I feel like it is something that needs to be learned."

University of Oregon sociology professor emeritus and prominent family studies researcher Scott Coltrane believes it is the very idea that mothers are instinctively the most capable caregivers that underscores the pervasive inequality in the division of child care. The research backs him up. A 2008 study of young men and women in Iceland found the belief that women were naturally more adept at parenting was related to a more traditional division of labor. A 2007 study in the U.S. found that the rejection of essentialist beliefs about women's natural ability to parent was related to the opposite—a life in which both partners cut back at work and split child care in half.

Raj, a gay man raising a now-teenage son outside of Boston explained how he and his husband have divided their parenting responsibilities. "We've both always done what we're good at," he told me. Heterosexual couples divide responsibility the same way—but essentialist beliefs deem women the de facto presumptive better match for each and every kid-related task. And despite the enthusiasm for the idea of the modern, involved father, most Americans continue to believe that a mother knows best. In 2016, Pew Research found that breastfeeding aside, 53 percent of adults say that a mother is better equipped than a father to care for children (1 percent said a father is better; 45 percent that the two are equal).

Colloquially, we speak of maternal instinct, the presumably inborn, hardwired, and natural driver of the wisdom and devotion we ascribe to female parents alone. Biologists don't use the term because it's technically incorrect. By definition, an instinct is a behavior that does not have to be learned, shows almost no variation between members of its species, and manifests in a rigid sequence of behaviors performed in response to a stimulus. It's also called a fixed action pattern, or an FAP. In bears and pigeons, hibernation and homing are instincts. In some species, caring for newborns is instinctive. After a rat gives birth, she removes the pup from the sac, licks the newborn, and eats the placenta. Rich with prostaglandins, it stimulates lactation and helps the uterus to contract.

A pregnant rat does not go to birthing class. From animal to animal, this behavior shows no variation based on temperament or culture. It's programmed into her DNA. A rat has a maternal instinct. So, too, does a grayback goose, who immediately pushes any round object near her nest inside to incubate it, no matter if it is a billiard ball placed there by an impish ethologist or an actual egg. Round object (stimulus) produces rolling behavior (response). The less intelligent an animal, the more its survival depends on instinct.

In contrast, almost every aspect of primate behavior is mediated by a larger and more developed brain. Evolution has equipped us with a neocortex that requires us to learn in order to survive. With a neocortex, biology remains relevant but is no longer determinant. Natural selection ultimately favored flexibility. Animals that can rapidly adapt to shifting conditions have an advantage over those that can survive only a narrow range of circumstances.

The most defining characteristic of the primate brain is actually its plasticity. Plasticity allows us infinite potentials, at least in comparison to instincts, inflexible as glass. "The flip side of this escape from rigid, stereotypical responses is that *practice and learning become more important—even essential,*" University of California, Davis, anthropologist Sarah Hrdy writes in her seminal book *Mother Nature: Maternal Instincts and How They Shape the Human Species.* Humans no longer rely on reflexes or instincts, though we still have a handful, like raising our chin and eyebrows at the sight of an acquaintance. Instead we operate under the auspices of a sophisticated nervous system that interacts with the environment to alter the physical structures of the brain. This alteration is referred to as learning.

After she gives birth, a human mother is without a fixed action pattern. Her social world shapes her behavior. I gave birth in a hospital, guided by Western medicine. After each of my daughters was born, the doctor showed her to me, gave George scissors to cut the cord, wrapped her in white blankets with thin pink and blue stripes, and handed her to me to suckle before taking her away for her Apgar test. With my older daughter, the doctor asked for permission to send the placenta to a lab for study because it was heart-shaped, which she said was very rare.

In the hunter-gatherer society of the !Kung San in southern Africa, a woman gives birth alone, delivering the child into a small leaf-lined hole that she's dug in the sand about a mile from her village. She is instructed not to shout out in pain—crying during labor is thought to signal to the gods that she does not want the baby—but, rather, to grit her teeth or bite her own hand. She cuts the cord with sticks and places the placenta next to her baby to serve as its temporary guardian before return-ing to the village to fetch other women to join her in a ritual welcoming ceremony. In a Tanzanian tribe of hunter-gatherers called the Hadza, women give birth in huts, attended by their mothers and grandmothers. Men are intentionally excluded. The placenta is typically buried far outside of camp because it's considered dirty, unsuitable for male eyes. Culturally transmit-ted norms stand in for instincts.

The neocortex allows flexibility, but the loss of instinct also comes at a cost. Charles Snowdon, a professor emeritus at the University of Wisconsin, has spent his career studying marmosets and tamarins, cooperatively breeding New World monkeys. In most groups of tamarins, the young help to take care of babies, while in a minority of groups, they do not have this opportunity. In a field study of tamarins without prior infant-care experience, Snowdon and his team discovered that babies born to first-time parents never survived. They guessed that naive mothers and fathers didn't know enough either to parent on their own or to accept help from more experienced kin. Later, from comparative data, his team discovered that the survival rate was much better in the groups where young siblings had helped out with babies. Across primates, infants born to inexperienced parents are at higher risk of death. Snowdon explains, "When they don't have experience with infant-care skills, there's a very low breeding success rate. Parenting skills are learned. They're not innate, for males and females equally. Both are clumsy parents. You have to learn to tolerate a squirming infant on your back. You have to learn to share care of your baby. First-time mothers don't know how to position infants to nurse on the nipple. They hold them upside down."

The idea of maternal instinct doesn't apply just to birth and its immediate afterward but also to everything mothers do to care for their children over the course of a lifetime. It neutralizes thoughts of oppression, reflexively serving to undergird the notion that women make superior—and perhaps the only suitable—primary parents. It's meaningful that we fail to imagine a correspondent paternal endowment. Human culture has hardly allowed for the entertainment of such a notion.

In the 1800s, Victorian-era thinkers like Charles Darwin and Herbert Spencer fit emerging science into their lived experience and concluded that women alone had evolved an instinct that made them responsive to infantile helplessness. Spencer, an influential philosopher in his time, also believed that women's singular reproductive role had forestalled their mental development. Half the population, he wrote, had not developed higher intellectual and emotional faculties, the "latest products of human evolution." Darwin himself rejected the idea that social feelings grow out of experience and fell back on the concept of instinct. He wrote, "Maternal instincts lead women to show greater tenderness and less selfishness and to display these qualities toward her infants in an eminent degree."

It was an idea in search of a reality. A retrospective on human childrearing offers little support for so many Mother Teresas. In his *History of Childhood*, the psychohistorian Lloyd deMause describes recent centuries when abandonment, horrific abuse, and even infanticide were commonplace. As Darwin sat in his study in England dreaming of selfless women (and their correspondent unencumbered men), there was a long-standing epidemic of child abandonment under way in Europe.

Around that time in Paris, it was legal for poor women who gave birth at a state-run charity hospital to leave their newborns. The length of stay for these mothers varied, and in tracking the variations, the staff discovered a trend: Women who left the hospital on the day they gave birth had a fifty-to-one chance of departing without their babies, while women who remained just two days longer had only six-to-one odds of the same. When mothers were required to remain for a full week postpartum, abandonment dropped from 24 to 10 percent. Anthropologist Sarah Hrdy writes, "Neither their cultural concepts about babies nor their economic circumstances had changed. What changed was the degree to which they had become attached to their breast-feeding infants."

Anthropologists have found that across primates, whenever mothers leave babies, they almost invariably do it within the first seventy-two hours. Hrdy explains that while there's no critical period right after birth in which mothers and babies must bond, close proximity between mother and infant during this period produces feelings in the mother about her baby that make separation hard to bear. Hormones plus experience equals attachment. Nature and nurture work in concert. Mothering is biologically and socially determined.

To assert that there is no maternal instinct, then, is not to say that there is nothing innate about a mother's love. As Hrdy explains, every mother's response to her baby is influenced by a composite of biological responses of mammalian, primate, and human origin. "There is endocrinal priming during pregnancy, physical changes during and after birth, the feedback loop of lactation, and cognitive mechanisms that enhance preference for kin." But almost none of these biological responses is, as Darwin postulated, fixed (nor—mammary glands aside—are they exclusive to females). Instead, Hrdy explains, what women relative to other female mammals choose to invest in their children "is complicated by a range of utterly new considerations: cultural expectations, gender roles, sentiments like honor or shame, sex preferences, and the mother's awareness of the future. Such complexities do not erase more ancient predispositions to nurture.

"Our views of 'motherhood' . . . derive from . . . old ideas and even older tensions between males and females. The fact that most of us equate maternity with charity and self-sacrifice, rather than with the innumerable things a mother does to make sure some of her offspring grow up alive and well, tells us a great deal about how conflicting interests between mothers and fathers played out in our recent history." (You've got this under control; I'm going to play video games.)

Hrdy underscores that female primates have long been dual-career mothers, foragers with children to maintain, reliant on babysitters, and necessarily making compromises between their children's needs and their own—less giving trees than "flexible, manipulative opportunists." Continuous-contact mothering was always a last resort for primates, whose families thrived only with help from large support networks.

Male reproductive success, on the other hand, "has long depended upon viewing females as individuals to be coerced, defended and constrained." We derive our belief that primary maternal care is natural, inborn, and obvious from a long history of female subjugation. We call that history "nature" and continue to surmise that the sex bearing children must provide them with most of their care. Sciencey-sounding terms like "maternal instinct," which have no paternal equivalent, reinforce that thinking. The naturalistic fallacy shows up time and again in our ubiquitous commitment to the idea of mother as her baby's one and only, a convenient proposition that struggles to make actual sense.

The Modern, Involved Male Primate

At a glance, the mammal class and the behavior of half its members generally support the idea that males were not destined for meaningful parenthood. Pregnancy is invariably a female pursuit. The mother is the only parent guaranteed present at birth, the only one equipped to feed. The animal kingdom's most devoted fathers are not mammals but fish and birds, species that neither lactate nor gestate internally. The amphibian and the insect place second; still, you wouldn't want to marry one.

Only some fish parent at all, but when they do, exclusive male care is the norm, about nine times as frequent as female solo care. These males typically court passing females who love and leave. The males release milt over the eggs, defend their territory, and otherwise tend to offspring until a day or two after the hatch. In birds, while only females lay eggs, males are just as involved thereafter. Around 90 percent of birds exhibit a 50/50 division of parenting work. That's especially impressive when compared to the slight 3 to 5 percent of mammalian males who contribute anything whatsoever to childrearing. As anthropologists Kermyt Anderson and Peter Gray put it in their book *Fatherhood*, "Male investment in offspring can in principle (and in practice often does) end in ejaculation." Female investment, too, is less enduring in nonhuman mammals. It often ends at weaning. Many mammal mothers, on encountering their offspring years later, won't even recognize them.

According to Yale biological anthropologist Eduardo Fernandez-Duque, primate paternal behavior—action directed toward infants that has a positive effect on development, growth, well-being, and survival—remains poorly understood. Based on the fact that the primate species exhibiting paternal care are only distantly related, Fernandez-Duque and others in his field hypothesize that this care resulted from evolutionary trajectories that developed in varying circumstances. If parenting by male primates increased offspring survival under certain ecological or social conditions, then paternal care may have evolved. Still, fathering manifested only in some taxa. Even within the same genus, there can be huge variation in father involvement. Male macaques, a type of monkey, generally have little to do with infants. The closely related Barbary macaque males, though, love babies and, if you don't count nursing, provide as much care as the females. Males hold, carry, provision, nuzzle, and respond to cries of distress. Primatologists posit that Barbaries have lived in harsher environments, necessitating contact comfort, warmth, and protection by males for survival. There is also within-species variation. In the wild, rhesus macaques are absentee dads. In captivity, where the pressures of competition for food and mates are eliminated, they closely attend to their young. Caretaking behaviors are unisex potentials. They just don't emerge as freely in males.

"These days, those of us thinking about evolution of behavior, we run away from dialogue of learned versus instinct, nurture versus nature. If there's something we learn by the day, there tends to be some kind of underlying genetic component, but it's extremely flexible," says Fernandez-Duque.

There's also the issue of paternity certainty. Fernandez-Duque has spent his career studying owl monkeys and the titi monkeys of the Amazon. The two are among the taxa that show the most extreme paternal care. In studies of captive titi monkeys, the babies demonstrate a stronger bond with their fathers than their mothers. In the wild, when given a choice, the titi baby goes to its dad. Says Fernandez-Duque, "We've learned from them that paternal care happens more and in extreme forms when the risks of cheating—and then the likelihood of providing care to an infant you did not sire—tend to be reduced." Raising one's own offspring rather than some other guy's is so important in the animal kingdom that males in some polygynous species—a type of brown bird called the dunnock is one example—are able to calibrate their provisioning of a brood of chicks according to how often they mated with the mother. They determine the probability of being the biological father and then provide the correspondent percentage of necessary calories. Whether this capacity persists in humans is debatable, but one 2018 study of human fathers living apart from their babies found that those with children who resembled them spent more time with these infants in their first year of life.

Relative to mammals overall, a high percentage of primates mate monogamously (the exact numbers are "a huge topic of disagreement," according to Duque). Evolutionary biologists can agree that all primates evolved from polygynous ancestors. In some primate lines, polygyny eventually morphed into monogamy, and once monogamy developed in a given lineage, it never went back. Mating systems evolve when they increase reproductive fitness, or the reproductive success of the individual. The shift to monogamy must have involved upping the odds of catapulting one's genes into the next generation—and in ensuring that one's offspring survived to reproduce as well.

Today biological anthropologists surmise that in some primates, monogamy ultimately resulted in involved fatherhood. Researchers hypothesize that among early hominims, once adult pair bonds predominated, permanent relationships allowed for a greater sexual division of labor. Males could afford to spend their time looking for often-elusive prey while females gathered plant food, a more reliable calorie source than meat. Assuming couples slept next to each other at night, fathers would have found themselves in proximity to pregnant females and then offspring. More nuanced social relationships advantaged infants with more complicated brains. More complicated brains required more time to mature, and slow-growing offspring needed more care to reach independence than one adult could reasonably provide.

What seems to be true of both primates and humans dating back to hunter-gatherer tribes is that fathering behavior has long materialized when it was necessary for the well-being of all interested parties—fathers, mothers, and children. Hunting and gathering is how humans have subsisted for about 90 percent of evolutionary history. Today's remaining hunter-gatherers suggest how early humans may have lived.

Alyssa Crittenden, an anthropologist at the University of Nevada, Las Vegas, has studied and lived among the Hadza of Tanzania. She explained to me that today, Hadza men and women continue to divide labor according to sex, and openly acknowledge that women are the harder-working group in their camps. "The Hadza are egalitarian. Women are equal in terms of social status and position. That doesn't mean there's an equal distribution of labor. Women have equal decision-making power, but they also do way more work—the Hadza men talk about it.

"The men are in charge of meat, and the women are in charge of everything else. All the staple foods in the diet are foraged by women. Women are in charge of building houses, fetching water, collecting firewood, taking care of nursing infants. But Hadza women aren't mad. They don't think their husbands are louses. There are sisters and aunties around to help with children, and once the kids are toddling, they go off into the pack, where they do a lot of self-governing and self-care. There's a cooperative caregiving system in place that attenuates some of this cost and alleviates this burden for moms." (In contrast to what Crittenden has heard from the Hadza, many hunter-gatherer ethnographies do report that women routinely complain about men's failures to "meet sharing obligations.")

Crittenden also noted that, generally speaking, the level of paternal involvement among hunter-gatherers is dictated by the subsistence needs of the group. "Everything goes back to resources," she said, which helps to explain why humans show more variation in fathering activity than all other primate species combined. Male and female Aka Pygmies hunt together with nets, and fathers are intensely involved with their children. Among the Hadza, both men and women forage, though not usually together, and women do most but not all of the child care.

In tribes where men hunt big game alone and spend long periods away from camp, their interaction with young children is minimal. Male pastoralists relocate frequently in search of literal greener pastures, and have multiple wives and little involvement with their biological children. Historically and around the globe, participation varies according to how both parents earn a living. Adaptation to circumstance has forever been the rule.

Biology

In 2017 *The New York Times* published a short piece called "The Birth of a Mother." It explored something anthropologists have termed matrescence, or the process of becoming a female parent. The writer noted: "[T]his transition is also significant for fathers . . . , but women who go through the hormonal changes of pregnancy may have a specific neurobiological experience." The nod to fathers is cursory. The "but" that follows makes the sentence's main point: that women are the sex hormonally primed for parenthood. This notion is so generally accepted that it escaped the fact-checker's scrutiny. Like much of the conventional wisdom about the hard-core nature of maternal versus paternal parenting, it's also misleading.

Men undergo their own neurobiological experience as their babies-to-be gestate. Throughout the prenatal period, men in close contact with pregnant partners are physiologically primed to care for infants. Expectant fathers experience a rise in the levels of the pregnancy-related hormones prolactin, cortisol, and estrogen in proportion to that of their baby's mother. Additionally, testosterone, associated with competition for mates, declines. Second-time fathers produce even more prolactin and less testosterone in the company of a pregnant partner than do first-timers.

The mechanisms for these changes in men remain unidentified; not so for the marmoset monkey. Research has established that the marmoset fetus sets off its father's hormonal shifts when its adrenal gland produces a glucocorticoid that's ultimately excreted in the mother's urine. The scent of that glucocorticoid readies the marmoset male to love and care for his infant. While it is unlikely that this occurs in men, cells in the human nose do show an electrochemical response to airborne estratetraenol, an odorless steroid found in the urine of pregnant women. (And here's something George finds amusing: Estratetraenol has also been shown to worsen men's moods.)

Throughout their children's lives, involved fathers continue to experience hormonal changes. In North America, men in long-term relationships like marriage and fatherhood almost uniformly have lower testosterone levels than their single and childless counterparts. One five-year observation of men (twenty-one years old and single at the study's outset) found that those who became fathers experienced a significant drop in testosterone production relative to those who did not. The study's authors write, "Our findings suggest that human males have an evolved neuroendocrine architecture that is responsive to committed parenting, supporting a role of men as direct care-takers during hominin evolution." As anthropologist Sarah Hrdy observes in *Mothers and Others*: "Men are physiologically altered just from spending time in intimate association with pregnant mothers and new babies. To me, this implies that care by males has been an integral part of human adaptation for a long time. Male nurturing potentials are there, encoded in the DNA of our species."

Anthropologists also have a word for the process of becoming a male parent: "patrescence." *The New York Times* has not published an article about it. It garners only 264 Google hits versus 10,400 for "matrescence." Those with an interest in the formal study of fatherhood continue to note the relative lack of research in the field. In 2005, journalist Paul Raeburn was inspired to write a book he ultimately titled *Do Fathers Matter?** while attending a meeting of the Society for Research in Child Development. "I found hundreds of scientists describing research on children, families, and parenting, and only a dozen or so dealing with fathers," he recalls. "Nearly all the authors of these studies began their talks by noting how little research on fathers had been done."

Our pronounced cultural biases about which parent really matters have influenced the reach of scientific investigation, which then in turn underscores those biases. They also inform

---

* They do. Studies show better cognitive, behavioral, social, and psychological outcomes in children with involved dads.

social policy. In 1971 President Richard Nixon cited evolution as one reason for his veto of a bill that would have provided universal government-subsidized early child care. He feared it would disrupt nature's mother-centered plan.

In the social sciences as well, assumptions about special maternal biology have had a far reach. It was 1970 before psychologist Milton Kotelchuck questioned the orthodoxy of developmental psychology and asked what hard evidence existed to support the notion that children relate uniquely to their mothers. Kotelchuck used the "strange situation" research protocol—during which young children are observed as their parents enter and leave the room in the presence of a stranger—to upend then-prominent beliefs about the special and exclusive relationship between mothers and babies. He demonstrated that six-to-twenty-one-month-olds were just as likely to be calmed by the presence of their fathers as their mothers. "It did not seem reasonable that in a world where mothers often die in childbirth that we'd have a species where children can't adapt to other people," Kotelchuck said.

Late in the 1970s, Michael Lamb, a pioneer in the research on the importance of men to their children, was the first to look at the physiological underpinnings of fatherhood. Lamb monitored skin conductance, blood pressure, and mood among parents watching videos of crying or smiling infants. Mothers and fathers did not differ in any measures of responsiveness to the videos.

Around the same time, psychologist Ross Parke and colleagues studied fathers of newborns in maternity wards. For most of the behaviors his team measured, fathers and mothers hardly differed. Men spoke to babies in high-pitched voices and responded with sensitivity to infant cues during feeding. They also exhibited patterns similar to their wives in heart rate, blood pressure, and skin conductance when holding their children. The major difference Parke observed was that fathers, unlike mothers, took a step back from their child's care in the presence of their spouse. Their assumption that a baby primarily needs his mother limited their involvement, the naturalistic fallacy in action.

Sarah Hrdy speculates that, at the outset of a child's life, at least, the problem is not only that fathers believe they should step back but also that mothers may be slightly predisposed to step forward with more haste. In a study that measured response times and hormone levels in parents listening to infant cries, mothers and fathers were equally reactive to wails of distress (recordings of baby boys being circumcised). When the cries were fussy rather than pained, mothers' physiological responses and then also their reaction times were a little quicker than fathers', though fathers' responses were quicker than those of childless adults.

Long past our daughters' infancies but on the same continuum, George felt this difference play out between us. "You don't give me the chance to do things," he observed to me once during a long weekend out of town. It was dinnertime at a crowded family lodge, and there was a buffet for the kids. I got up to get the girls food as soon as we were seated—an attempt to curtail the whining of hungry children, cries that are fussy rather than pained. It had never occurred to me that George would step in if only I slowed down. I'd mistaken his sluggish pace for disinterest, his slow reaction time for inertia.

Hrdy supposes that men's marginally lower threshold for

responding to infant signals is likely innate, a result of the developmental trajectory of the mammalian brain (that is, females were caretakers long before males developed that neural architecture), but then asks, "So what? Who cares? And that's just the point. The act of caring has consequences—habits of mind and emotion. . . . The point is, consequences are magnified out of proportion to initial causes."

When one parent gets into the habit of quickly responding to an infant's needs, the other is likely to accommodate that habit by failing to respond. This pattern then calcifies over days and weeks and months and years. I heard similar themes in the musings of many of the mothers I interviewed. Erica in Portland explained, "When he's on, he's great. But it's almost like I have to remind him or take myself out of the picture for it to happen. If I say I need to be out of the house, he'll step up. But as long as I'm there, he won't." Emphasizes Hrdy, a mother herself who acknowledges big feelings about this issue, "A seemingly insignificant difference in thresholds for responding to infant cues gradually, insidiously, step by step, without invoking a single other cause, produces a marked division of labor by sex."

And Then There Is the Brain

The attempt to locate essential differences between men and women in the structures of the brain began in the mid-nineteenth century with tools like tape measures and sacks of millet grain. Findings were used to oppose women's suffrage and equal access to education. Today more technologically advanced approaches like neuroimaging can serve the same function. Since these studies' conclusions are often used to reify gender stereotypes, neuroscientist and author Cordelia Fine has dubbed this line of work neurosexism. She writes, "Remember that psychology and neuroscience, and the way their findings are reported, are geared toward finding difference, not similarity. Male and female brains are of course far more similar than they are different. Not only is there generally great overlap between 'male' and 'female' patterns, but also, the male brain is like nothing in the world so much as a female brain. Neuroscientists can't even tell them apart at an individual level."

When I call neuroscientist and author Lise Eliot to ask if there's an unavoidable, innate explanation she can think of for the problem I'm investigating, I can all but see cartoon smoke blowing from her ears. "I'll cut to the punch line," she says. "There's very little in human behavior that's innate. Most of what we do is shaped by our conscious and unconscious experience. Calling gendered division of labor 'innate' is a convenient way of maintaining the power structure, period."

Off the top of my head, I run a couple headline-grabbing female/male brain difference findings past Eliot, and she counters each with information to the contrary. Per her own research, for example, when corrected for overall brain volume, women do not have a larger corpus callosum than men, an apparent misrepresentation I remember reading about during grad school.

The corpus callosum is the structure that connects the two hemispheres of the brain. If women's hemispheres were more connected than men's (the technical term is "less lateralized"), the two sides would communicate more fluidly. This spurious finding has been used to explain women's supposed greater facility with multitasking as well as men's supposed greater capacity for STEM work. A handful of the mothers I interviewed referenced the former to explain why they naturally, if half-heartedly, take on more at home than their spouses. "Women are known to be better multitaskers," said Marla, a forty-three-year-old social worker in Chicago and mother of a six-year-old daughter, as she explained why she managed more of her daughter's life than her husband.

Eliot responds, "It's bullshit. Our brains get good at whatever we're faced with doing. Secretaries are good multitaskers. We're letting men turn us into secretaries." More tellingly, even if the corpus callosum difference had held up, the conclusions popularly drawn from it align more closely with retrogressive attitudes about the sexual division of housekeeping (and careers in the sciences) than with actual animal research, which suggests that creatures with *more* lateralized brains are better at simultaneously accomplishing multiple tasks. The inferences drawn from brain-difference studies are often, to use another Fine-ism, neurononsense.

In actuality, brain functions arise from distributed neural networks and a daunting complexity of connections, neurotransmitter systems, and synaptic functions. The brain's structural architecture alone doesn't provide much information of the kind that's being sought—and to be clear, as Fine jokes, here's the gold standard for exciting discovery: "I finally found the neural circuits for organizing child care, planning the evening meal, and ensuring that everyone has clean underwear. See how they crowd out these circuits for career, ambition, and original thought?"

Still, as Eliot explains, sex differences sell. "They always have this kind of outré, anti-PC overtone to them. 'Oh, look, we've been deluding ourselves when science is proving other-wise.'" Eliot, herself the mother of three grown children, tells me, "Everything we call a sex difference, if you take a different perspective—what's the power angle on this—often explains things. It has served men very well to assume that male-female differences are hardwired. It's been harmful for women to live that." Today, while popular "science" continues to underscore that patterns of behavior rooted in the brain are hardwired, or something one is just born with, real science has landed in a different place altogether. Contemporary neuroscience is all about plasticity, "the capacity of the nervous system to change its organization and function over time." Brains are not so much hardwired as constantly rewiring themselves in response to real-time experience.

A 2014 study out of Bar-Ilan University in Tel Aviv exemplifies this understanding. Researchers compared FMRI data in three groups of first-time parents: primary-care mothers, secondary-care fathers, and gay primary-care fathers raising babies without women. If an MRI is a still photo of a brain, then an FMRI is a movie. It allows researchers to look at brain function as well as structure. The brain activity of the three groups of subjects was not identical. In primary-care mothers, parenting behavior caused greater activity in the amygdala, the evolutionarily ancient structure involved in emotion processing. In secondary-care fathers, the same parenting behaviors went along with greater activity in the newer sociocognitive struc-tures of the neocortex. In both groups, parenting integrated the functioning of those two neural networks—and the more in-volvement fathers reported, the more integrated the networks were. The researchers also found that the primary-care men, those who'd devoted as much time to their babies as the mothers, showed activation in the amygdala that was comparable to that of the women, as well as greater activation in the sociocognitive structures similar to the secondary-care fathers.

The researchers concluded that the differences between the three groups were not so much a function of biological sex or genetic relatedness to the infant (the primary-care fathers had adopted) but, rather, of how much time the subjects had spent in intimate contact with their babies. They write: "assuming the role of a committed parent and engaging in active care of the young may trigger [a] global parental caregiving network in both women and men, in biological parents, and in those genetically unrelated to the child. Such findings are consistent with the hypothesis that human parenting may have evolved from an evolutionarily ancient alloparenting substrate that exists in all adult members of the species and can flexibly activate through responsive caregiving and commitment to children's well-being."

The secondary-care fathers were born to be partners, not helpers. But in a number of ways, assuming the secondary role stacks the deck against equality from day one—not due to so-called hardwiring but because of the failure to wire in the absence of experience. That is, the failure to learn.

The consequences of behavioral disparities that begin with very slight and possibly innate predispositions in the parents when the child is born grow larger as the baby does. When couples take the path of least resistance, the mother's depth and breadth of experience eventually outpaces the reach of the father. How many parent-teacher conferences and calls from the nurse's office and evites to birthday parties will a mother field alone before her expertise becomes unmatchable?

It was the fall of Liv's first-grade year before I understood that we'd hit a point of laborious return. The pope came to New York, and his visit disrupted the trains. It was a Monday, my late night at work, George's evening to pick up the kids. My husband sent me this text: "Not sure I'll make it home in time. We need an alternate plan." By "we" he meant me. Pickup was on him, and he had no alternate plan. For years I'd taken those on, in one form or another, and letting him try and falter now (as ever) was not an attractive possibility. If he failed, it was Liv and Tess who'd be waiting around, not to mention the staffs of their schools. Still, I might have demurred. George would have figured it out. But that felt wrong. We were supposed to be a team. I called another mother, and she said she'd get the girls. Despite our best mutual intentions, here George and I were, in the same place we always landed.

The Tel Aviv study offers: "[While] pregnancy, birth, and lactation . . . provide powerful primers for the expression of maternal care via amygdala sensitization, evolution created other pathways for adaptation to the parental role in human fathers, and these alternative pathways come with practice, attunement, and day-by-day caregiving."

April, a chief operating officer and New Yorker raising two children alongside her wife, was initially her family's secondary-care parent. That left her feeling less capable with her children. She said, "When you're not usually in the primary role and you're thrust into it for a day or two, you're terrible at it. I've been in that position. I'm horrible. I don't know where the kids are supposed to be, the kids are tense, and everyone's waiting for Jill to come back to make it better. When it's only squeezed into your life sporadically, you're set up for failure. In heterosexual couples, that seems to just exacerbate the theory that men aren't good at this."

Fathering, like mothering, is biologically and socially determined. It is the day-in-day-out experience of attending to children—and not biological sex—that encompasses what we now refer to as motherhood. The more we understand this as an experience available to either sex, the less sense it makes to characterize parenting as a particularly female talent. Such talk functions only to ensconce inequality, to reinforce for ourselves and then instill in our children the belief that mothers alone must bow under the weight of all tasks.

CHAPTER 3

We Are Raised to Be Two Different Kinds of People

My Husband Stopped at Walgreens, a Mothers' Group Chat

In late winter 2018, in one of the more active mothers' groups I had joined on Facebook, a spirited discussion about the contrasting social orientations of men and women was under way in the city of Chicago. It did not begin with, but seemed best surmised by, a woman named Arianne, who wrote: "I am 7 mos pregnant and I threw up on the way home from my son's swim lessons b/c my acid reflux was so bad. We literally had to pull off the road and I threw up in a parking lot. Then my husband had the audacity to stop at Walgreens to get nasal spray while I sat in the car waiting to go home. Men don't get it. They are often times oblivious to others' needs and only think of themselves."

The conversation went on to elucidate the different ways that women versus men considered the concerns of others. The women suggested strategies to get men to think about their needs (for example, with Post-it notes left on bathroom mirrors reminding them to "hug your wife" or "paint the bathroom") and to help them to feel women's pain (for example, by "going on strike" to make them "realize everything you do"). They also offered advice as to how a woman might more easily adjust to the unpleasant realities of heterosexual relationships—not only to the fact that men fail to imagine that their vomiting, pregnant wives might prefer to go straight home and not to Walgreens, but also to their lack of recognition of all the consideration their wives were routinely providing. "You probably don't mind doing all the things you're doing," wrote a woman named Kim in response to one emergency medical technician's announcement that, among other indignities, her husband had never gone grocery shopping in the course of their eleven-year marriage. "You just want to feel appreciated for doing those things. A simple thank-you goes a long way."

I, for one, enjoyed feeling appreciated, but I also wanted opportunities to be similarly thankful to my spouse. It's not that I never had them. George, for three years running and at great cost to his welfare, was the one to get up with Tess, never a good sleeper, in the middle of every night. After Liv was born, he became a champion swaddler, an origami-like aptitude that I never acquired, and which he revisited with Tess. Still, his tendency to overlook emergent needs—the nonroutine ones that were the patchwork of family life—never ceased to make my jaw drop to the floor. There was something very basic that I could not wrap my head around with my generally kind and hardworking husband: the capacity (and one he seemed to share with so many of his gender) to forgo keeping others in his mind.

One summer evening in 2018, we arrived home from a full day at the beach around the girls' bedtime. They hadn't eaten dinner, and in the car, we'd settled on chicken nuggets from our freezer. I started our sand-encrusted daughters bathing as soon as we got home, after watching George enter our kitchen. I assumed he was putting the nuggets in the toaster oven. When I emerged from showering and drying off my younger child maybe five or ten minutes later, he was only standing at the counter and drinking a cold beer.

I got out the nuggets, opened the box, put the pieces on the toaster oven tray. He watched me do this, failing to offer so much as an "oops." It had not occurred to him that he might have cooked the nuggets, that I might have expected that, or that our children were tired and hungry and all but ready for bed. It was not laziness. It was something I had no name for and nothing I could hope to understand.

Nurture

If gender essentialism makes a case for the innate, distinctive qualities of woman- and manhood, gender existentialism offers an alternative. Gender existentialists see gender as a social construct radically impacting the way we think, act, and see ourselves, linked to sex not by biology but by culture. More women than men are gender existentialists. In a recent Pew Research poll, of the 64 percent of Americans who believe that women and men have different approaches to parenting, 61 percent of women versus 41 percent of men believe these differences are socially (as opposed to biologically) determined.

Deanna, forty-two, the teacher and mother of two in San Diego, said, "It's so deep on so many levels. Culturally, the way we portray women; historically, the way we've treated women around the world for thousands of years. Women are seen as less important. I wasn't fully aware of that until the 2016 election. It became so clear to me then. I see it in jokes my friends make, in how I talk about myself. Women are disrespected more. Women matter less."

Deanna described how mattering less played out in her own life. She gave up the best job she'd ever had to relocate for her husband's career. She did not request that he curtail his weekly business travel even when she was pregnant with their second child, working full-time as a teacher, struggling with anxiety, and taking care of a toddler: "I felt all of it was my responsibility." Deanna's own parents had divorced when she was two, and she'd been raised by an often single mother focused on finding a man. "I remember her bad broken relationships, and her talking to me about what it meant to be a woman." Here is what it meant to be a woman: Keeping a husband was of utmost importance, and inasmuch it was a wife's job to always maintain his absolute comfort.

Gender existentialism holds that trying to fit into one or another human category gets in the way of living authentically. It's hard to imagine a person who has not felt encumbered by the mandates of group membership. Our preferences take a backseat to the rules of the gender system. I can't be the only grown woman who remembers sneaking time with Matchbox cars when none of my classmates were looking. Observational studies of toy choice among children demonstrate that three- and four-year-old boys spend 21 percent of their time playing with "girl toys" when they're alone; that drops to 10 percent when a peer is as much as playing nearby. From the get-go, girls are less tightly policed for gender violations, and they enjoy greater relative freedom with toys. Girls pick "boy toys" 34 percent of the time when playing alone and 24 percent of the time when another kid enters the picture. Hearts and minds allow for wider-ranging possibility than social pressures permit.

Gender socialization starts at birth. Parents have different expectations of boys and girls from infancy, and their perceptions of their children form alongside those expectations. Girl and boy babies reliably differ in only these ways: On average, male infants have a harder time self-regulating, and on average, they take longer to move from a unilateral to a mutually engaged state.

Even in the absence of any other objectively measured differences, parents of daughters are more likely than parents of sons to rate their children as softer, littler, finer-featured, and less attentive. When mothers and fathers are asked to watch a video of a baby they've never met, they describe the baby differently when they are told it is a boy than when they are told it is a girl. Mothers of baby girls consistently underestimate their daughters' locomotor abilities, while mothers of boys overestimate theirs. Stereotyped expectations influence the acquisition of gendered behaviors, turning expectations into prophecies.

Historical evidence suggests that as men and women have moved into more similar public roles, we've begun to highlight sex from birth (or before) more dramatically. In the era of separate spheres, toys and clothing were gender-neutral. Baby boys wore nightgowns. Today's gender-reveal announcements are not only an outgrowth of social media but also an effort to reassert the primacy of sex in a world where male and female roles are increasingly undifferentiated.

We classify people into two kinds. Each kind is expected to engage in specific types of thought, feeling, and behavior. These expectations are reinforced in endless small ways over the course of countless interactions across a wide range of settings. The expectations are universal and carry a moralistic bent, communicating directives, important norms of good behavior. Girls learn to behave in feminine ways that signal accommodation, and boys masculine ones that signal assertiveness.

Without much awareness, adults direct young children toward the "right" kind of behavior, and not even just in obvious ways like keeping dolls from boys. Take student-teacher interaction in preschool classrooms: In studies, thirteen-month-old boys and girls act the same, but adults don't respond to them in kind. Girls get more attention from teachers for gesturing and babbling, boys for whining and screaming. At thirteen months, kids are equally likely to grab, push, and kick. But teachers intervene to modulate girls' aggressive behavior only 20 percent of the time. In contrast, boys' aggression ends in teacher intervention 66 percent of the time. In learning theory terms, boys' aggression is reinforced more than three times as often as girls'. By the age of twenty-three months, the girls have become less aggressive and the boys more so. Both groups have learned to optimize the potential for adult attention by behaving in the ways that most reliably get them noticed.

Clearly, socialization contributes to gender differences in behavior. It has been shown, for one, that boys raised in egalitarian homes show the same amount of interest in babies as girls, while boys raised in traditional homes show less. It will never be possible to parse the relative inputs of biology and culture, and at any rate, the two interact. In her 1999 book *Why So Slow?*, Hunter College psychologist Virginia Valian explains, "Hormonal effects . . . are context dependent. Even in rats, the effects of sex hormones differ, depending on the sort of handling the animals receive, the type and amount of stimulation provided by their environment, and the kind of maternal care they receive. . . . [H]ormonal and environmental effects act together— they coact—to jointly influence people's and animals' traits and behaviors."

Maybe the differences that eventually manifest between boys and girls are partly the outgrowth of genes and hormones. Cross-culturally, anthropologists have identified seven behaviors that diverge consistently between boys and girls by the age of three no matter where they are raised. These include: Girls work more; boys play more; boys spend more time at greater distances from their mothers than girls; girls spend more time in infant contact and care than boys; boys engage in more rough-and-tumble play; girls play-groom more; and boys play-fight more.

While it's easy to assume that cross-cultural behaviors result from hardwiring, first consider that what almost all cultures worldwide share is that they are patriarchal ones—85 percent of them and rising, per a mid-twentieth-century survey. Second, despite the fact that there are almost no behavioral differences between girl and boy babies, parental behaviors toward infant daughters versus infant sons vary in consistent and measurable ways. There's a bunch of data on this, but for brevity's sake, I'll just say that, for one, parents of boys provide more playful physical stimulation than parents of girls. For another, mothers of girls engage in longer periods of caretaking touch than mothers of boys.

Propensities for rough-and-tumble or grooming play could be outgrowths of infants' earliest experiences. Nostalgia starts young. If warm emotional memory is associated with the physical experience of being either jostled or groomed, we are likely to re-create these experiences for ourselves as we grow. In line with this idea, gender scholars now speak of "the gender-enacted body" rather than one whose gender expression is simply formed by biology or society. In this model, gendered characteristics are not inborn traits or socialized givens but dynamic processes that depend on individual life history.

Nurture Is Self-Perpetuating

Social structural theory suggests that a culture's division of labor by gender drives all gendered differences in behavior—and then certainly the actions of men and women in family life. Historically, men's greater size and strength allowed them to pursue activities like warfare that gave them more status and power than women. Once in those roles, men became more dominant, and women's behavior accommodated.

Despite the contemporary irrelevance of sheer physical strength to achievement and status, this dynamic hasn't shifted much. In her 1994 book *The Lenses of Gender*, the late psychologist and gender theorist Sandra Bem explored why the declining focus on both childbearing and warfare in contemporary societies did not, over the long haul, lead to less stereotyped behavior in women and men. She suggested three tenets for the maintenance of gender roles: androcentrism, gender polarization, and biological essentialism. Androcentrism is the belief in male supremacy and the attendant higher status attached to all things masculine. Gender polarization is the organization of social life around two distinct and unequal halves of a population. Biological essentialism is the idea that gender differences are directly tied to chromosomal ones. In the midst of these, we are saddled with deeply ingrained cultural notions about what men and women are best at and how they should conduct themselves.

Men should do for and think of themselves (behaving "agentically"), while women should do for and think of others (behaving "communally"). While this has harmed men in meaningful ways—what has been called the loneliness epidemic impacts them disproportionately—it remains the precursor to status and success. As Australian philosopher Neil Levy has noted, "It is not an accident that there is no Nobel Prize for making people feel included."

Katrina, thirty-five, a social worker and mother of two in Chicago, describes being a (communal) woman married to a(n) (agentic) man: "I feel overwhelmed in general. I feel frustrated often. I got mad this morning when my husband strolled downstairs at 7:05 and I'd already spent half an hour managing the chaos of the morning alone. It makes me angry. Why can't he get up earlier and get downstairs and be available? Why does he sleep in on Saturday until eight? Why is that something that can happen?"

"Why is it?" I ask her.

"Because he doesn't get out of bed! I could sleep in, too, but then nobody's needs would get met, and the dog wouldn't get out."

I inquire further: "Do you ever ask that he get up?"

"If I did, it still probably wouldn't happen. Or I wouldn't be able to sleep in, and I'd get up. Or it turns into a nagging situation the morning of. 'Hey, get up! Get up! Get up!' I'm not his mom. So it's a hard situation. One morning I went to the gym early. I said, You need to get up at X time and get them ready and fed before eight so we can get to gymnastics. I came home at nine. They had not eaten breakfast yet. The dog was still in her crate."

Naturalists assume that the structure of parenting is biologically self-evident, that what is self-evident is instinctive, and that what is instinctive is inevitable. In contrast, a bioevolutionary perspective holds that women are primary parents now mostly because they always have been. The sexual division of labor was the starting point in the earliest human societies and has been perpetuated since. Feminist psychoanalysis expands on this idea. Noting that, "All children have the basic experience of being raised primarily by women," sociologist and psychoanalyst Nancy Chodorow outlines a process she calls "the reproduction of mothering," a social and psychological—but not biological or intentional—process in which female mothering reproduces itself cyclically.

In her book *The Reproduction of Mothering*, Chodorow writes, "Women, as mothers, produce daughters with mothering capacities and the desire to mother. These capacities and needs are built into and grow out of the mother-daughter relationship itself. By contrast, women as mothers (and men as not-mothers) produce sons whose nurturant capacities and needs have been systematically curtailed and repressed." In the earliest months and years of personality development, Chodorow theorizes, a girl feels connected to her mother by virtue of her sex, while a boy feels disconnected by virtue of his.

Accordingly, a boy's development involves the repression of the need for relationships and sense of connection and then also, eventually, "the reproduction of male dominance." Or, as the actor and author Michael Ian Black described it in a 2018 *New York Times* op-ed about young men and violence: "Too many boys are trapped in the same suffocating, outdated model of masculinity, where manhood is measured in strength, where there is no way to be vulnerable without being emasculated, where manliness is about having power over others."

The emphasis on masculine power among boys starts young. By nineteen months old, boys respond positively to other boys only when they're engaged in masculine-type activity. In contrast, girls react positively to other girls no matter their style of play. In *Why So Slow?*, Valian describes play studies of young children: "Masculine activities gradually acquire a superior status, initially through fathers' reactions to boys' choices of feminine activities and later through the disapproval of male peers. . . . [B]oys were especially likely to punish their male peers for feminine choices by ridiculing them or interfering with their play physically or verbally. Boys thus learn to devalue feminine activities and to shun them in order to avoid compromising their higher status. Boys cannot risk the stigma of being girl-like."

Then neither can some grown men. As Shannon, the Oklahoma City mother, explained to me about her husband's refusal to fold laundry: "You don't want your buddy to see you doing this stuff. They'll think you've given your pride to the woman." Though frustrated by what it means for her, Shannon also feels some sympathy toward her husband's social vulnerability. She swallows her pride in order to protect his, the ubiquitous feminine cost of masculine fragility.

Observational studies of two-year-olds in preschool classrooms demonstrate that while girls change their play behavior in response to the wishes of classmates of both sexes, boys do not allow themselves to be influenced by girls. Kids' social behavior becomes more sophisticated around age three, when they begin to try to control their friends' activity with increasing frequency. As attempts at influence increase with age, girls and boys begin to engage in different ways: girls with more polite suggestions and boys with more direct demands. Over time, boys become less and less responsive to gently delivered requests. And while boys continue to wield influence over all children, girls can generally influence only other girls.

Without intention or explicit direction, we do become two different sorts of people. From the age of three, half of us begin to ask politely and consider the preferences and feelings of others, while the other half assert demands and ignore friends' wishes, especially if those friends are members of the second sex.

If you dated men while in your twenties, you know how this plays out in young adulthood. And if you've read the work of psychologist and couples researcher John Gottman, you also know how this dynamic shows up in a marriage. In watching hour upon hour of video of heterosexual couples engaged in conflict, Gottman found that husbands frequently "stonewall"—remove themselves mentally and emotionally from the conversation—when their wives raise issues. As it's been described, "Stonewalling behavior makes it difficult for wives to influence husbands or even have a sense that their unease is being heard. Wives, on the other hand, tend to engage in their husbands' concerns."

In my own interviews with mothers about their inability to effect change at home, I heard some version of Queens mother Monique's sentiment over and over and over again: "How much convincing of the other person can you do?" It is no wonder that some research finds that among all gendered configurations of couples, lesbians have been found to co-parent most harmoniously.

When I ask New Yorker April, parenting with another woman, what she makes of this finding, she attributes it to the fact that same-sex couples tend to have more role flexibility in general. "At this point, we've both spent time slowing down at work and then being the primary parent. When you've done that, you really know what it takes and make sure to step up in other ways. I have a straight female friend whose husband has never been the primary, and it's clear that he doesn't get it." But it is female same-sex couples—and not male—whose relative ease with co-parenting is supported by the literature.

David, one of the gay fathers I interviewed, acknowledged that the issues he faces with his husband "are very similar to many heterosexual homes, and the main one has to do with mutual recognition." When two men raise children together, they may each be more likely to face the same struggles that women have when parenting with men, of the my-husband-stopped-at-Walgreens variety.

In her 2011 book *Joining the Resistance*, the psychologist and psychoanalyst Carol Gilligan looks at gender in middle childhood. Years after the processes described by Chodorow have been set, Gilligan sees boys' and girls' reproductions of masculinity and femininity in action. Boys cast off their softer parts, and girls, their more assertive ones. Those aspects of their personalities go underground. Psychologists call it dissociation, the failure to know what we know and feel what we feel. Dissociation results from traumatic experience, including intense feelings of shame. Gilligan believes it's no coincidence that boys are prone to depression around age eight, when expressions of tenderness and vulnerability become socially unacceptable. Girls, on that longer gender leash, are most likely to become depressed as they enter adolescence, the point at which they're expected to become young ladies, "silent in the name of feminine goodness." Gilligan writes, "[I]t is not surprising . . . that at times in development when children are initiated into the codes and scripts of patriarchal manhood and womanhood . . . it is not surprising that these times . . . are marked by psychological distress."

While gender differences are reinforced through social processes from the cradle to the grave, the arrival of a baby seems to intensify the usual behavioral prescriptions and expectations for women and for men. Motherhood has been called the most gender-enforcing experience in a woman's life. The home itself has been called a gender factory. The transition to parenting, despite its magnificence, is a time marked by emotional distress. According to the World Health Organization, about 13 percent of women who give birth each year have symptoms of postpartum depression, and recent data suggests that it is equally prevalent in men. Many believe these occurrences are underreported. Is the unconscious imperative to contort ourselves into these rigid male and female postures a contributing factor?

We work to maintain our rightful relative positions and feel discomfited when we don't. A recently divorced woman whom I know admitted with some surprise that she felt like she was "betraying" her sex now that her ex-husband has half custody—and, for the first time ever, is doing half the work. Vidya, forty-one, is a mother in Los Angeles. She reports doing less cooking and cleaning than her husband before noting, "I feel like I have to keep telling you I'm not a terrible cook!" She thinks about her impulse and concludes, "Not doing the housework casts doubt on my competence as a woman." Vidya didn't feel this way before she was married, though her housekeeping was just as minimal. It's only in relation to a man who does more than she does that something feels notably off.

Psychologist Eleanor Maccoby and others believe that it is not exactly socialization on its own that accounts for gendered behavior but, rather, the "social relational context." Women and men never behave so much like women and men than when they find themselves in each other's company. Maccoby says, "Sex-linked behavior turns out to be a pervasive function of the social context in which it occurs. . . . The gendered aspect of an individual's behavior is brought into play by the gender of others."

Gilligan concurs, writing, "[T]he good woman cared for others: she listened to their voices and responded to their needs and concerns." What she also observes is that men, up to and including good ones, do not get this memo. Maybe you've noticed in living with one. At first it feels disorienting, watching another human being move through the world in this foreign way, not compelled to notice others, to anticipate their needs.

My husband, sprawled across our bed in the evening, reading on his phone, does not move to make space for me when I enter the room. It's such a little thing, but acculturated to femininity, I am all but physically unable to lie still under the same circumstances. I've tried, and it feels wrong. In New York City, it's common to see men sitting with legs wide open on a crowded subway, taking up more than their fair share of seat. The practice has come to be called manspreading, and it's gained a notorious reputation. Women can hardly consider making themselves so comfortable at another rider's expense. We fume when we see it, our outrage at least partially displaced on to that sprawling, hapless man. He becomes every guy we've ever known, every male we're more reluctant to condemn.

Who wants to feel that outrage toward a person whom they love? Before kids, George and I had a biannual argument about cooking, which was my responsibility alone. "I'm perfectly happy to eat takeout," he'd say with great sincerity, but no regard for mutuality, whenever I protested this arrangement. Every time the discussion rose to the level of argument, he'd put together exactly one very nice meal and then never cook again until our next fight. Eventually, I gave up. How much convincing of the other person can you do? I like to cook anyway, I told myself; it's easier for me because I've been doing it longer; at least he cleans up.

It became harder to quell my frustration with rationalization once there were two more people in our home, both hungry for supper each night. I, too, wanted the occasional dinner prepared for me—though what I also half longed for was George's comfort with his right to enjoy but never provide that meal. Writing in *Glamour* in 2018 about the last years of her marriage, mother of two Lyz Lenz explained: "I stopped cooking because I wanted to feel as unencumbered as [a] man walking through the door of his home with the expectation that something had been done for him." I listened to the women I interviewed explain the fact that they did more of all varieties of caretaking even before they had children with statements like: "I was home more," "I cared more about how the house looked," "We were raised differently." They wrote off the most prominent factor of the last, which was not that they had parents with different standards and expectations but, rather, that they were raised to be women, and their husbands were raised to be men.

We immediately understand that motherhood and fatherhood are hardly one and the same. Mothering, the poet Adrienne Rich has observed, is ongoing; fathering is a discrete act. Men are not mothers because they are not women, and are not expected to take note of other people in the same way, denying themselves, as Zimbabwean gender equality activist Jonah Gokova has said, "the experience of being fully human." It is why none of the women I interviewed could imagine stonewalling their husbands in the way that they were often stonewalled.

"In the gendered universe of patriarchy," Gilligan writes, "care is a feminine ethic, not a universal one. Caring is what good women do, and the people who care are doing women's work." If men have been socialized practically from birth to maintain their higher position by differentiating themselves from women, how better to do that in a dual-breadwinning adulthood than by sleeping late and failing to cook and leaving the dog in her crate? To resist these gendered assignments to provide or withhold care is a task that neither mothers nor fathers are currently pulling off as well as they might.

It's Hard Work Fighting Nurture

Imagine my excitement when, early in my research, I came across the 2010 book *Equally Shared Parenting: Rewriting the Rules for a New Generation of Parents* by Mark and Amy Vachon. Here was the game plan I needed to move forward. Whatever George and I had been doing that had left me overly taxed, and him defensive in the wake of my anger, we could rectify it, and this was how.

Imagine my broken heart when the book's first and strongest suggestion was that aspiring equal sharers work only part-time. The Vachons write: "Equally shared [parenting] means purposefully choosing to optimize your life rather than maximize your paycheck." In theory, that was appealing. The Vachons recommend self-employment (check). But, like most couples raising two kids, George and I were in no position to work fewer hours. We'd scaled back a little over the years, but working less meant earning less, and none of our big expenses were discretionary. Canceling cable: That was the only cut we could ever foresee making to our budget, and it barely made a dent.

Inability to work part-time isn't a deal breaker for ESP (equally shared parenting's acronym), but the Vachons concede that when couples can't swing that, hiring out help becomes a necessity. Mothers with the luxury of affording that get it instinctively. The data shows that women in two-career couples who outearn their male partners benefit not because they are able to negotiate a more equitable division of labor with their spouses but, rather, because they use their resources to hire that labor out. Per the research, as women's income goes up, so does household spending on housekeeping services and eating out. The same cannot be said of the relationship between men's earnings and such spending. In fact, every additional dollar earned by a wife will matter more to her housework time than every additional dollar earned by her husband.

I had long since hired a woman to clean our apartment twice a month. I was all but in love with her. The points of consternation in our marriage-with-children, though, weren't about anything we could realistically pay to eliminate. There is a limit to what money can buy. I didn't want a personal assistant keeping track of all the emails from the school, even if I could have afforded such a thing. I wanted a husband who kept track of the emails with me (or, at the very least, didn't route them straight to his spam folder without as much as running that plan by me first)—one who spared me the trouble of needing to issue a dozen chirping reminders for every singular task he committed to take on.

The further I read into *Equally Shared Parenting*, the more my hopes were dashed. I'd had some idea, apparently, that such hard change might be accomplished casually, if only with proper instruction. This was, of course, naive. As the Vachons describe it, equally shared parenting is its own part-time job. Its four very sensible domains of equality—childrearing, breadwinning, housework, and self—require "willingness," "courage," "surmounting barriers," and prioritizing "living below one's means."

In a nutshell, they suggest scaling back two careers rather than one in order to minimize the need for outside child care, and to ensure that neither party feels alone with the pressures of family life. The challenge for men, they write, is to embrace more work at home and with the kids, while the corresponding one for their wives is to share the financial burdens while ceding their traditional control of the home. There is no call to divide tasks down the middle with a hatchet but, rather, to "care in detail about how the home is run and own the responsibility for making it a happy place to be. Both of you are committed to learning how best to care for your children and put that plan into action. You are equally invested in your careers and can be assured that the other has no intentions of bowing out of paid work just to escape the frustration or politics. We think this leads to an authentic life because no one is hiding behind fake excuses to avoid the real work of caring for your family, yourself, and each other." I was just as committed to my professional life and breadwinning role as my husband was to his. Ditto the women I knew. We simply hadn't secured the corresponding concern for our children and homes from the men.

Here is one example of what ESP takes. The Vachons introduce a couple named Marci and David. Neither of them "wanted a life that centered on the standard American dream—the possessions and social status that are emblematic of success and unconsciously direct so many of our decisions. As David described their core desire, '*We mostly just wanted to be equals.*'" (Italics mine.) So earnest, so sweet, but it struck a strident chord. Why should the establishment of what should be a given require such primacy of purpose? But it does seem to. Without that primacy, one risks a life stacked against the woman's self-interest. "Relationships don't *work out,*" a colleague of mine likes to say, "relationships are *a workout.*" That is all well and good. Marriage is hard. But please take a moment to let it sink in that it requires intense, concerted effort and a very special breadwinning arrangement for a woman and a man to live together as if they have the same value. *We mostly just wanted to be equals.*

Sitting close on the couch in their Massachusetts living room, Mark and Amy Vachon are warm and engaging, a couple I'd want to be friends with. They have an easy rapport and take turns answering my questions. They look well rested, like people who work part-time and no longer have young children. Their two kids have grown into teenagers, and Amy says their parenting workload has lightened in some ways. "We traded the physical work for the mental work. We're in that stage where we're the taxi drivers, trying to figure out ways to have meaningful conversations in the car. And we also have more time to ourselves."

Mark and Amy agreed on their first date to the kind of family life each wanted to build. Amy lost her father when she was eight, and she'd watched her mom do everything as a single parent. It looked lonely, and it made her carefully consider what she wanted in life from a young age. She says, "I thought, If I'm going to marry someone, I want to walk through life with that person, I want us to walk in each other's shoes. And if I'm home taking care of kids or I'm the main parent, it's a separation. For me, it's more that we can do these things together, get inside each other's heads. That is a good relationship. Mark said, 'Wow, that fits a lot with what I'd like. I'm afraid to get married to somebody and have them expect me to be their provider. I don't want a status male prescriptive job. I want a balanced life.' His big goal was to have fun. Neither of us wanted what we saw around us. So we were very conscious about it, we talked about it. We do a lot of talking. That's very important for couples, or else they find themselves by default falling into all this cultural stuff.

"It starts right away. You get into a social scene, people defer to the woman when it comes to kid stuff and baby stuff, and oh, isn't the dad wonderful, he's a hero if he does anything. That's seductive. Who wouldn't want to be called a hero? Dads start to think, 'Oh, I do a little bit and I'm awesome,' as opposed to 'Stop calling me a hero, I'm doing my job as a parent.' We have a president who brags about not having to change a diaper. So I don't think we've made progress. Our book could be written today and not say hardly anything different."

Says Mark, "We came up with two foundations. Equality, which is what Amy brought, and balance, which is what I brought. In the beginning, I wasn't looking for an equal partner. I just didn't want to lose the fun life I'd been cultivating as a single man. I was already working reduced hours before we were married. My friends were like, 'What are you doing? Climb to the corner office!' I was like, 'No, I like having Fridays off!' That's what I brought to the relationship. Let's find a way to enjoy our life."

Their commitment to balance and equality ultimately worked so well—and diverged so much from what they saw around them—that they wanted to share their ideas with the world. Recalls Mark, "It got me going, early on, when I'd hear people say, 'We're so lucky, Mom can stay home and Dad can work.' And I'm thinking, That's not luck." The Vachons interviewed fifty equally sharing couples in the process of their writing. Remembers Amy, "They were people who were just extraordinarily passionate about this and went to great lengths to make sure they could live this way."

Mark: "Engaging in it is challenging. That's what keeps people from doing it. It creates tension. It's easy to live the standard expected roles. It's difficult to work to try something different. We learn from early on. Girls are taught, as they're being raised, here's a doll, take care of it. Boys don't get the same kind of encouragement. They're allowed to be more physical, more active, grow up into strong adult men, instead of getting recognized for their nurturing capabilities."

Amy: "As our son gets older, I see it, the culture he's raised in has ideas about masculinity, and if he strays from those, he risks ridicule or being brought down a status peg. And he's seen a different model in action at home, but it's hard even for him."

Whatever they've accomplished in their own family, Mark and Amy know that more traditional gender roles permeate outside of it, and that these are indelibly part of their son's nurture as well. I was testament to this. My own father was a primary parent, at least from the time I was eight, when my mother went back to school. He never missed a band concert. He cooked most dinners for years. But I lived in a larger world, and I knew that my house wasn't normal. I loved my dad's attention, but I also wanted to be like the other kids on my block, with nominally present fathers and moms who got home early, took summers off, kept winter cupboards stocked with marshmallow Swiss Miss. From my perspective as a child, that breakdown looked really right.

It might have looked less right as I got older, but my eye was not on that prize. For most of my twenties, I was hardly thinking about marriage, let alone the raising of kids. I might have been well served to be. I came across Elizabeth, a thirty-two-year-old new mother in Northern California, after she responded on Twitter to a *Medium* article by journalist Jessica Valenti headlined "Kid Don't Damage Women's Careers—Men Do." Elizabeth tweeted: "If you have an equal partnership, having kids is awesome. If you don't you're pretty much screwed. I've seen too many friends pushed to the edge of exhaustion (and, real talk, depression) by uneven responsibilities. It 'just happens.' But it's completely avoidable." ("How have you avoided it?" I wrote back, explaining my research. "My trick: Marry a Swede," she replied before agreeing to an interview.)

It turned out that a decade earlier, toward the end of her time in college, Elizabeth had found herself in casual conversation with female classmates at Middlebury College about their career plans once they had kids. She was surprised that most of them were pretty sure they'd take a couple years off. This got her interested in family leave policy, which she learned was "absurdly terrible" in the U.S., which led to her and her friend Ingrid securing a grant that allowed them to travel around the U.S. and Europe interviewing young professionals about their work/ family plans. "This has been on my mind for a long time," she told me. "No one else probably decided at the age of twenty-two, 'This is really important to me, and I'm going to spend all this time looking into this, and every dinner conversation I ever have is going to be about this.' And then I went to grad school to study work and family."

When she and her husband got together, Elizabeth recruited him to join in her great mindfulness around equal sharing (as she noted, it did not hurt that he was from a culture where gender equality is more of a given—where men, for example, have been known to volunteer to pay for half of their girlfriends' birth control).

Elizabeth started graduate school during a period when her husband was traveling a lot for work. She began taking more care of the home and addressed it with him posthaste. "That's how it starts. It's the pattern we read about, the woman happens to be at home more, and so more household things start falling to her. Neither of us wanted that. I thought we should create an Excel spreadsheet to divide the chores. He wanted it to be more organic. It wasn't one thing that solved it, but we both kept starting that conversation often. And then before we had our daughter, we had the same level of thinking about it. Who was going to take how much time off, what were we going to do about child care, who will do drop-off, who will do pickup. It was just a constant conversation about the nitty-gritty of it.

"Ingrid and I, who'd been thinking about these things to a crazy degree since way before we were married, ended up with partners who really do their fair share, and careers that we're trying to make work. Our friends who thought we were being too intense are really struggling. We have two other close friends with kids. One of them is a stay-at-home mom. Both of them are exhausted and resentful. There are all these structural issues that could be better in the U.S., but it's a personal thing in the end, the decision to have those difficult and repeated conversations about expectations that a lot of people don't have because they think it will work itself out. I feel like I was saved by having those conversations."

Like the Vachons, Elizabeth offers a plan, and as with the Vachons, that plan entails a long-standing and steadfast attention to the maintenance of equality—the apparently necessary antidote to a history of so much less. Having spoken with all three, I could see where George and I had failed. We never once sat each other down to declare our mutual commitment to sharing—*we mostly just want to be equals.* Since we hadn't made sharing an unambiguous team objective from the get-go, my anger left us at odds with each other rather than placidly recalibrating to meet a mutual goal.

Elizabeth said, "Our attention to this has meant things

have worked out really well. It helps that I work for myself, so my hours are flexible, and my husband only works nine to five, which is a huge thing. But the people I know who are struggling—the socioeconomic class that we're talking about—they have choices. My friend who is having the hardest time, her husband is an ER resident. It's a tough job, but he's also chief resident. You don't have to become chief resident. They have a toddler, and she's pregnant, and he's training for a triathlon. He's actually also one of my closest friends. I've called him out on this. He feels like he deserves it because he works really hard. I think it started with, she was breastfeeding, and they didn't want to sleep-train, and because he works nights so he would sleep in another room, so she took on all of the waking up at night. Once you do that, it's really hard to get back to 'We're equally responsible, and we really have to watch out for each other's needs.' She has to be home more, so he just takes a little bit more and a little bit more for himself. It's not malicious. But it's hard for me to say he doesn't know what he's doing. He tries to say things like, 'Once I'm done with residency, it'll be better,' but I just think you cannot say it will be different later. You have to do it when it's hard, because it's always going to be hard."

And So You Might Not Want To (Fight Nurture)

In the first season of the Netflix series *The Crown*, a dramatic re-creation of the early years of Queen Elizabeth's reign, the queen's husband, Philip, bitterly laments the costs of marrying a princess-turned-sovereign. After Prime Minister Winston Churchill and the queen grandmother agree, against Elizabeth's wishes, that the couple's children must take her last name, Philip explodes at his young wife, "You have taken my career from me . . . you have taken my name. What kind of marriage is this? What kind of family?" The duke's rage is palpable, and for a minute I feel for the guy. But then, of course, it hits me that it's exactly the kind of union that women have long been required to accept. Those age-old rules around relinquishing one's name and ambitions feel so viscerally unacceptable when the gender roles reverse.

On the show, at least, Philip spends the next few years resenting Elizabeth, neglecting his marriage, shooting whiskey, and (maybe) sleeping around. Elizabeth is punished for her powerful position, and it wasn't even one she chose. Backlash theory suggests that consequences like these await women who fail to conform to gendered norms. You don't have to read Susan Faludi's classic *Backlash* (though you should) to know the shadows that descend upon women who don the most forbidden crown of agency.

It does remain forbidden. While attitudes about women at work have become increasingly liberal in the last half century, attitudes about women's role in the home have actually been moving in the opposite direction. Since 1975, the Institute for Social Research at the University of Michigan has surveyed high school seniors about their values. In 1976, 82 percent agreed that women should be considered as seriously as men for jobs in business and politics. That went up to 91 percent by 1994, where it has remained. In 1976, 76 percent agreed that women should have exactly the same job opportunities as men. By 1994, that had risen to 89 percent and has likewise held constant. In the same data set, positive attitudes toward working mothers continue to climb.

In sharp contrast, though, endorsement of gender equality in the family peaked in 1994—the very year I left college, so optimistic about a husband who would share—and has been on the decline ever since. In 1994, for example, when presented with the statement "It is usually better . . . if the man is the achiever outside of the home and the woman takes care of the home and family," 58 percent of high school seniors disagreed. But that was domestic egalitarianism's pinnacle. By 2014, the disagreement fell to 42 percent, back down to where it had been in the mid-1980s. Similar sentiments saw virtually the same trajectories and in other surveys as well. The University of Chicago–based General Social Survey, assessing American attitudes annually since 1972, reports that millennials remain progressive on the work front but endorse increasingly traditional attitudes about the home.

Why would this be? Writing in 2017 for the Council on Contemporary Families, sociologists Joanna Pepin and David Cotter assert that these slippages defy expectations and can't be accounted for by variables like race, region, religiosity, family structure, or mother's employment and education. Instead, they hypothesize that "egalitarian essentialism"—the belief that men and women are entitled to the same opportunities but will ultimately make different life choices because of biology—is the ideology that has replaced the mandate of separate spheres. They explain, "In the 1980s and early 1990s, people seemed to be moving toward the idea that women and men could work equally well in both the public and private spheres. Yet the narrative that eventually emerged became a hybrid of . . . two approaches, promoting women's choice to participate in either sphere while trying to equalize the perceived value of a home sphere that was still seen as distinctively female. The egalitarian essentialist perspective mixed values of equality (. . . gender discrimination is wrong) alongside beliefs about the essential nature of men and women (men are naturally . . . better suited to some roles and women to others)."

Since 1994, high school seniors have become increasingly likely to agree that "the husband should make all the important decisions in the family." The dismantling of the patriarchy will not proceed in a linear fashion. Pepin and Cotter reach a conclusion that is at once obvious and startling: The rising status of women outside the home has actually increased our inclination to reinforce male dominance inside it.

According to the census bureau, 28.8 percent of employed wives earned more than their employed husbands in 2017, down from a high of 29.4 in 2013 (this doesn't include the households with an unemployed male partner—which was 7.1 percent in 2015, according to the Bureau of Labor Statistics). But women who make more money than their spouses remain reluctant to highlight this fact. Researchers at the U.S. Census Bureau compared self-reported income on census forms to employer filings with the IRS. They found that in couples with higher-earning wives, both men and women exaggerate the husband's income and diminish the wife's.

In the 1980s and 1990s, relative resources theory posed that women did more unpaid labor only because they brought in less cash. Today that theory has been upended. Sociologist Veronica Tichenor, who wrote the book on women who earn more than their husbands (2005's *Earning More and Getting Less: Why Successful Wives Can't Buy Equality*), told me, "The women

I interviewed hinted that they didn't ask for more at home because to try to exert power over your husband is not to be a good wife. Some said, 'I don't want him to call me a bitch.' We let men do that. Every time women show dominance, it's unattractive. It's unfeminine. Un-wife-like." Rather than using their earning power to balance any scales, high-earning wives chose to demur to masculine prerogatives. *The rising status of women outside the home has actually increased our inclination to reinforce male dominance inside it.*

This inclination rears its head in a variety of ways. In a 2016 YouGòv survey of British adults, 59 percent of women and 61 percent of men expressed a preference for female surname change upon marriage. This preference was stronger among the youngest group of women (ages eighteen to twenty-nine) than it was among their older sisters (ages thirty to forty-four)—59 to 55 percent. In a 2010 survey of twelve hundred American adults, over 70 percent of respondents expressed the belief that a woman should take her husband's last name upon marriage, while half of those surveyed said that female name change should be required by law. The most common reason cited was the belief that women (but not men) should prioritize their marriage and their family ahead of themselves.

To put those pieces together, if loosely: In the year 2010, 50 percent of American adults believed that women (but not men) should be legally bound to put their marriages and families ahead of themselves. In a nod to backlash theory, the study also looked at the potential ramifications of a woman's failure to give up her name. After reading brief vignettes about women who had or had not, some groups of men expressed harsher attitudes toward the fictional women who had kept their birth names upon marrying.

Even among couples who defy tradition and maintain different last names upon marriage, only a minority favor bestowing the wife's name upon the child. In the YouGov study, only 12 percent of the men whose wives had kept their own names and 18 percent of women who'd kept their own names endorsed passing down the maternal surname.

When Rich, born in Philadelphia in 1977, married Michelle, born in Kansas in 1973, he wanted her to keep her own last name. She remembers the couple's conversation at the time: "He said, 'I wouldn't give you my name, because it's the remnant of patriarchal society.'" When she gave birth to their son a few years later, "I wanted to give him both of our last names, but Rich said, 'No. That's confusing. If we have a girl, she can have your last name.' There was a hole where I used to have a vagina, and I wasn't in a good state of mind, so I just agreed. At the end of the day, I'm not upset about it, but it was so surprising. It's interesting that these things come up that you would never expect. Some things are so culturally ingrained, they come out when we're not even aware."

Few men consider taking their wives' names. The YouGov study found that only 1 percent of men and 2 percent of women favored a husband changing his name. In the U.S., research out of Portland State University found that in a nationally representative sample of 877 married, heterosexual men, under 3 percent had taken their wives' names (earning the phenomenon the title of "micropractice").

Men who've engaged in this particular micropractice report

social consequences from strange looks and ridicule to the refusal of relatives to attend the wedding. In 2009, California became only the seventh state in the nation to make name change after marriage as simple for men as it is for women. Six years later, *Business Insider* editor James Kosur (né McKinney) described the process he had to go through in Illinois to take his wife's name after the birth of their child. Once he'd filled out paperwork and received a letter of intent from a court, he was required to take out an ad in a newspaper for three weeks to announce the proposed change (a very old law intended to preclude attempted fraud). When no one came forward to protest his new name, he finally appeared in front of a judge. Kosur wrote, "If I was a woman who had been recently married, I would have presented my marriage license to the court, paid a name-change fee, and moved on with my life."

New York University sociologist Paula England writes, "What is more striking than the asymmetry of gender change in the [home] realm is how little gendering has changed at all in dyadic heterosexual relationships. It is still men who usually ask women on dates and initiate sexual behavior. Sexual permissiveness has increased, but the double standard persists stubbornly. Men are still expected to propose marriage. Children are given their father's name. Incentive to change these things is less clear than the incentive to move into paid work and into higher paying 'male' jobs. The incentives that do exist are largely non-economic." (Or at least are less obviously and immediately economic. Many metrics back up a Bloomberg Markets headline from 2017: "The U.S. Economy Would Be Better Off if Men Did More Housework.")

Nurture Is Winning

To the modern, involved mother, *The Journal of Marriage and Family* reads like a fortune cookie. Crack it open to find not exactly a prediction but an articulation of some circumstance. Here from a group of Australian social scientists in 2008: "[C]ultural expectations . . . point to . . . housework as women's work and a display of love for her family and subordination to her husband. Men, on the other hand, display their masculinity and reinforce their . . . power, by limiting the time spent in household tasks, particularly those that are female typed."

We've assigned and continue assigning different responsibilities to male and female parents, though it is unclear exactly what if any child care tasks are routinely assigned to fathers. A mother in my neighborhood named Ivy told me about a trip she was organizing with her husband, Davin, and their two young sons. The vacation involved a flight and staying with friends. As they planned what to do with the family they were visiting, there was a text chain between Ivy, Davin, and the mother in the other family. At one point in the long and ongoing conversation, the other mother texted: "Ivy, do I need to have car seats for the boys when I pick you all up at the airport? (Sorry to bother you with this Davin!)" Ivy was her family's sole breadwinner at the time. Davin had long been as committed as Ivy to their sons' vehicular safety.

Even in the era of the modern, involved father, public discussions about balancing breadwinning and caretaking focus on women and not men. Mothers who travel for work note that they are invariably asked who is watching their kids, while fathers all but never hear the same question. Climate scientist and mother Zoe Courville recalls these words from a male colleague who, like her, was often in the field: "He said, 'I was always grateful that my wife stayed home with the kids, because kids need their mothers.'" Courville, who already felt guilty about leaving her child, explains, "He very pointedly wanted to let me know he thought that was important."

Combining work and family is conceptualized as a female problem rather than a human one. In 2018, novelist Lauren Groff "respectfully declined" to answer a reporter's question about work-family balance, "until I see a male writer asked this question." (The Internet met her refusal with virtual mass applause.) In a speech at a Women in Hollywood event in 2014, actress and mother of three Jennifer Garner noted that she was asked about pairing work and child care in every single interview she did, while her then-husband, also in show business, was asked nary a once.

Men, however, may still be called upon as experts in the work-family balance arena. I attended a seminar on it at an American Psychological Association conference in 2015, and I sat agog in a roomful of mostly young women in my female-dominated field as the male presenter informed us that sometimes he had to turn down writing opportunities to help his stay-at-home wife with their (six!) kids, but that he made time to train for triathlons.

I swallowed my discomfort as an old friend, whose college-age daughter was applying to medical school, thought aloud about the family-friendly specialties her child could comfortably choose. It was a reasonable conversation but one I knew we wouldn't be having if the matter concerned her sons. To hear my friend so breezily ceding her daughter's options—without a second thought, and despite her obvious pride in her eldest's accomplishments—made me despair for all the girls who came before her. None of it was any of my business, but I couldn't help hoping that her daughter would only sigh and roll her eyes in response to maternal concerns she deemed antiquated.

Though how would she? It remains true that girls are the ones implicitly instructed to consider marriage and family from early on. This is one more part of nurture, and not an insignificant one. "Mom, when do I need to start worrying about having a boyfriend?" Liv asked me when she was six. "Never," I answered, taken aback by the question and regretting all the *Barbie: Life in the Dreamhouse* episodes I'd been letting her watch.

As the novelist Chimamanda Ngozi Adichie writes in her nonfiction *A Feminist Manifesto in Fifteen Suggestions*, "We condition girls to aspire to marriage and we do not condition boys to aspire to marriage, and so there is already a terrible imbalance at the start. The girls will grow up to be women preoccupied with marriage. The boys will grow up to be men who are not preoccupied with marriage. The women marry those men. The relationship is automatically uneven because the institution matters more to one than the other. Is it any wonder that, in so many marriages, women sacrifice more, at a loss to themselves, because they have to constantly maintain an uneven exchange?"

Research from the late 1990s suggests that a woman's psychological well-being is more shaken than a man's by marital dissolution. Even when controlling for socioeconomic status, women are more likely than men to become increasingly depressed after divorce. The same is not true for women after other losses, such as a layoff from a job or the death of a spouse. In fact, women are the more resilient sex in widowhood. If women are conditioned to see marriage as an achievement, as a crucial marker of success, and men are not conditioned to see marriage the same way, it makes sense that the end of a relationship through divorce but not death would have greater impact on a woman's well-being. Divorce brings pain to a woman in a way that a partner's death, with all its profound despair, does not. It confers the shame of failure at her most important task.

While racial disparities generally have not been found in studies of either the uneven distribution of care work within couples or the psychological impact of divorce (and researchers have looked), writer Tamara Winfrey-Harris, author of *The Sisters Are Alright: Changing the Broken Narrative of Black Women in America*, suggests that dictums around gender role conformity in the home are even stronger in the black community than in other communities in the U.S. "Black women have a particular history that, I think, makes it worse—we are given advice not about how we become more ourselves and how we seek happiness in relationships, but about how do you make men happy so they will choose you and not leave. A whole industry has cropped up in the last decade especially, telling black women how they need to be smaller and more feminine and more submissive to their husbands in order to restore the black family. It's not just 'Do this because that's what *women* do,' but 'Do this because healthy black families rest on black women.' What we need is a new paradigm for committed adult relationships that recognizes the humanity of both partners. We cannot save our communities with a template that only allows half of us to be free."

Adichie advises in her manifesto, "Never speak of marriage as an achievement. Find ways to make it clear to her that marriage is not an achievement, nor is it what she should aspire to. A marriage can be happy or unhappy, but it is not an achievement." Maybe this cannot be repeated enough. Consider the professed career aspirations of single women in 2016. In a study at an Ivy League university, newly admitted MBA students were asked about their job preferences. Some students were told that the information would be kept private. Among those, men, women in committed relationships, and single women answered similarly. Other students were told their answers would be public, shared with classmates. Under this circumstance, single women (but not others) reported wanting lower salaries, less work-related travel, and less demanding schedules than the other groups. They also renounced their own ambition and desire for leadership roles. During the semester that followed, while these single women performed just as well on exams and assignments, they ultimately had lower marks for class participation. Presumably under some pressure to secure a male partner, these women felt compelled to hide their extrafamilial ambitions in the name of being appropriately female.

"What individuals internalize about gender and use to make sense of their personal lives does not necessarily support their own individual well-being," write sociologist Anne Rankin Mahoney and psychologist Carmen Knudson-Martin in *Couples Gender and Power: Creating Change in Intimate Relationships*. This is clear. Anne, forty-two, whom I met through the new mothers' group in my neighborhood, tells me, "If we're both home on a Saturday, he'll voice the fact that he's tired and get up and go take a nap for four hours. 'I am tired, I am going to take a nap.' I'm tired. I'm the primary caregiver. I remain tired. When he wakes up, he tells me I should nap, but that never happens. What I've done is I have No-Mom Thursday. Every Thursday after work, I take time to myself, even if that means just sitting in the office cleaning out my inbox. But he gets all the other days. Including weekends."

As author and social activist bell hooks has noted, "[A]ll of us, female and male, have been socialized from birth on to accept sexist thought and action. As a consequence, females can be just as sexist as men." So we are sexist against our very selves, and alongside our equally sexist husbands, we live in our families in ways that affirm and reproduce that sexism. "Why does Daddy always drive?" Tess asked me when she was four, at which point I began making a point of getting in the driver's seat more often. I battled with Liv for years over brushing her messy hair, all the while wondering if I would've gone to the same trouble with a boy. At her request, George bought Liv a makeup kit for her seventh birthday. ("The reviews on Amazon said it was perfect for little girls," George informed me upon the delivery of a multi-tiered, butterfly-shaped assortment of eye shadows and lip colors my grandmothers would have died for.) "Making yourself look pretty is not an activity!" I'd holler at Liv each time she asked to use it, though she was equally likely to make her sister up as some kind of green-faced zombie.

Women not only monitor the emotional temperature of the home, keep the mental lists, and perform the bulk of routine housework and child care; they also feel more responsible than men for this work no matter their income, outside commitments, or ideology. Woman after woman acknowledged this to me. But to acknowledge it without trying to alter it is to perpetuate what has already been perpetuated. I do it myself all the time.

DC-area writer and mom blogger Dara Mathis said, "I hear

from a lot of people I know who are mothers—they tend to feel more burdened themselves. Even if they know their spouse is open to taking on more of a share, they feel more burdened to make it easier for him. That's how I felt." Men have been known to share this attitude toward having things made easier for them. The British cultural critic Jacqueline Rose, author of *Mothers: An Essay on Love and Cruelty,* has noted that while women feel that parenthood creates a surfeit of burdens, men experience those same burdens not as an excess but as a deficit— as activities that take something better (and deserved) away from them.

Women go along with the moral story (or the oppressive one, you choose), the one that would actually be quite lovely if it applied to more than half of us. Penn State sociologist Sarah Damaske, who studies families and labor, says, "I find in my research that women feel obligated to frame things as if they're doing them for their kids. It's more culturally acceptable to say, 'It's good for my daughter to see me in the workforce' than it is to say, 'I'm in the workforce because I want to be, and if it's good for her, that's a nice side benefit.' I argue that in some ways that framing has been good—it's allowed women to push against these cultural demands about self-sacrifice while creating space for themselves. But it's also bad, because it hasn't changed that narrative of obligation to family first, over asserting one's own desires and ambitions."

Though shifting socioeconomic conditions do necessarily serve to modify cultural attitudes around gender, the beliefs that underlie them aren't easy to erode. As sociologists Ridgeway and Correll have written, "The gender system will only be undermined through the long-term, persistent accumulation of everyday challenges to the system resulting from socioeconomic change *and individual resistance.*" (Italics mine.)

Individual resistance (see the Vachons and Elizabeth) is no small thing. It involves many effortful conversations on a to-do list that is already lengthy. The toll of just barely trying may also be high. Carissa, the woman in Seattle who'd just had foot surgery, sees the conundrum like this: "My husband and I will be fine. This for me is a bigger issue. I have two daughters, and we're not setting the example I want for them. In my worst moments, I say things out loud after he walks out the door. In irritation. My daughters know. They say things to both him and me. 'Why does Mommy have to do that?' They'll want me to do something, and I say, 'No, I have to finish cleaning the kitchen'; they'll say, 'Why can't Daddy do that?' It's not healthy. What happens next?"

CHAPTER 4

The Default Parent

Paternal Participation Is Flexible and Discretionary

Once I started looking, I found there are an almost infinite number of ways to measure family commitment and the gradations of that commitment by sex. In 2008, University of Cincinnati sociologist David Maume arrived upon the Urgent-Care Question. He boiled parental responsibility in dual-breadwinner couples down to one metric: If your kid gets sick, who takes time off of work? Using data from the National Study of the Changing Workforce, a survey of U.S. workers, he found that 77.7 percent of women and 26.5 percent of men report that they are the sole bearers of this responsibility (the survey looked at individuals and not couples, hence the greater than 100 percent sum total). Maume concluded that not much had changed since family researchers in the late 1980s wrote that men "accept" child care responsibilities when they are away from work, but women "adapt" their work arrangements to their husbands' schedules and the needs of their kids. In more cases than not, women remain the default parent.

In 2009, a group of researchers at Utrecht University in Amsterdam looked at the same issue through a different lens. They began with a gender-neutral hypothesis they called the demand/ response capacity approach. This approach posited that involvement in child care uniformly depends on the demand made on the parent, and the extent to which the parent is free to respond to this demand. Having an employed partner and young kids increases family demands. Work obligations restrict the capacity to respond. They looked at 639 Dutch couples with children to test the theory that if either partner is unable to engage because of work obligations, the other will make up for this lack.

What they found was not gender-neutral at all. While mothers and fathers differed little in their reported commitment to waged work, mothers were going to greater lengths to prevent their jobs from interfering with their family lives. The demand/ response capacity approach only applied to dads. The time mothers spent with their children was barely affected by their own or their partner's workload. The researchers write, "Our study shows that mothers in particular experience low flexibility with regard to parent/child time. As a result, work demands may be met at the expense of other activities such as individual or couple leisure time without children. Fathers use their time for fun rather than basic care tasks. . . . The general pattern that emerges from our study suggests that fathers have more discretion than mothers with regard to child-related activities. Mothers feel a greater sense of responsibility."

Miranda, thirty-eight, an environmental planner with two kids in elementary school in Vermont, has found: "When it comes down to time crunch, if we both have stuff going on, I'm much more likely to say, 'I'll let work slide.' In different jobs we've had, Lowell has had more responsibility at work, and he's made it clear that he can't leave. Sometimes that has been true, but it's also been true that I have very limited leave. He gets a lot more time off than I do. So I'll say, 'If I take this day off to do this thing for whoever, I'm down that leave and I don't have it,' whereas he can take it off and it doesn't matter. But that never plays a role in our decision making. It pisses the hell out of me."

Miranda's dilemma, her ambivalence about her role as the default parent, grows out of the bad fit between the nineteenth-century middle-class shift into separate gendered spheres and the late twentieth century's changing labor patterns. As historian Stephanie Coontz has noted of America in the 1800s, "Female domesticity and male individualism developed together, as an alternative to more widely dispersed social bonds, emotional ties, and material interdependencies." Once both work and extended family moved out of the home, it was left up to the public and the private sectors to assimilate those changes, and we all know how that worked out. Mothers took charge of caring for others, fathers embraced personal autonomy, and, in the U.S. at least, society removed itself entirely from the equation. Writes Coontz, "Self-reliance and independence worked for men because women took care of dependence and obligation." The more things change, the more they stay the same.

Sociologist Annette Lareau observed fathers in families sending kids straight to their mothers when they needed help with their homework—even as those mothers were also making dinner. "When men do work, it tends to be because women are [physically] unavailable," she tells me. Family studies professor Claire Kamp Dush notices herself excessively validating her husband when he picks up slack at home. "When it comes to husbands, I hit the jackpot. I give him credit. But sometimes he wants credit just for not being an asshole, when really, he's simply doing what a parent is supposed to do." Developmental psychologist Holly Schiffrin feels conflicted about her lack of gratitude. "My husband is a very involved dad, more than average, and when I complain to my mom, she says, 'Oh, he is so wonderful.' She's comparing him to my dad. I'm comparing him to me, and I know that I'm doing more!" And developmental psychologist Sarah Schoppe-Sullivan watches her husband stare at his phone while their eleven-year-old daughter competes for his attention. "He's a great dad in general, but I see that and think, This is not good. He's oblivious to it. If I were to do that, my daughter would be upset. 'Mom, don't ignore me!' She doesn't have the same expectation of her father."

It's been twenty years since social psychologist Francine Deutsch published *Halving It All: How Equally Shared Parenting Works*, a study of 150 dual-earner couples. Like other writing in the field, Deutsch's project grew out of her own experience as a woman raising children with a man, the fact that "when motherhood hit, egalitarian ideals went out the window."

Deutsch identified the unequal families among her subjects, the ones in which the women were the default parents. She divided the husbands in these pairs into three categories of secondary caregivers: helpers, sharers, and slackers. For example, as one mother related, "Eric will do stuff, but he wants to be asked. He wants to put it on his list. It's not something that he's thinking about unless I get him thinking, although he's really helpful." Eric is a helper. Sharers are fully involved in parenting, but only when other commitments to work or leisure aren't getting in the way. Slackers relax while their wives work a second shift at home. In all the unequal families Deutsch studied,

"There's an assumption that women's schedules are freer. It's always easier to infringe upon mother; mothers are supposed to be infringed upon."

Carissa in Seattle told me, "One problem is all these unspoken assumptions about who's going to deal with things. My husband will go ahead and make plans on a Friday with friends. He assumes he can do that. If I want to do something, I know I have to get him on board first, so I can have him home in the house. He's not a party guy. He's not doing anything he shouldn't be doing. But he gets that time. I don't get that time."

Meg, twenty-four, a security guard and mother of two-year-old twins and an infant in Las Vegas, Nevada, works graveyard shifts, midnight to eight a.m. Her husband works the same hours as a taxi driver. Meg comes home, relieves the babysitter, and sets up the day for her children: baths, meals, toothbrushes, clothes. Her partner arrives home and heads straight to bed. She says, "I'm pretty much by myself. He's barely learned to be a dad." I ask Meg when she sleeps. "Never," she replies.

Mothers avoid not only interpersonal conflict but also a more internal one when they resist forcing their partners' hands. When men decide to become equally sharing fathers, they may give up money or status, but in exchange for something more virtuous, the elevation of family life. When women reject their role as default parent, they're not taking on that same goodness. They cannot bask in its treacly moral glow. They are faced with relinquishing their virtue in the name of self-interest, or even just the occasional nap.

This is not an indulgence we take kindly to in women. One recent study out of the University of California, Irvine, for example, found that subjects presented with vignettes about parents who left their children unsupervised to tend to work concerns judged fathers less harshly than mothers. A father who takes on equal sharing may face criticism from the outside world for dialing back the traditional male role. The mother in that pair is left wrestling with moral ambiguity—both societal disapproval and its outgrowth, the fear that any wish for autonomy can be realized only at some cost to her kids.

Parental Consciousness and the Morality of Motherhood

In early 2018, a tweet from a woman I didn't know caught my eye as I procrastinated on Twitter one winter afternoon: "Arranging for summer camps is a fucking nightmare and that's even if you have every privilege. ATTN AMERICA: WOMEN WORK NOW." A parent named Deb offered empathy, responding: "the bane of every mother's existence from feb through march" before a third female tweeter chimed in with "and why is it not the bane of every *father's* existence from feb through march?" It struck me as a valid question, so I wrote to all three asking for their thoughts. Deb answered: "Dads don't consider, moms don't insist. Fathers quickly lose touch with the million details and logistics of their children's lives."

In the language of family studies, women and men do not develop the same "parental consciousness" when they transition into mother- and fatherhood; they continue on separate and unequal paths of knowing or not knowing as their children change and grow. Parental consciousness is the awareness of the needs of children accompanied by the steady process of thinking about those needs. Women have come to call it the mental load, and in those relatively egalitarian households where men share day care pickup and put away clean laundry, it's the aspect of childrearing most likely, as Skidmore sociologist Susan Walzer has put it, to "stimulate marital tension between mothers and fathers."

Francine Deutsch found: "Sometimes even when both parents tried to live up to principles of gender equality, mothers and fathers didn't experience parenting the same way. That meant mothers did more. [T]he mental work of parenting was all hers." Other researchers have noted that even men who put a premium on fatherhood usually remain mothers' assistants; their vast potential for parental consciousness lies dormant.

Molly, twenty-seven, the foster care worker in Tennessee, told me, "We can't afford full-time child care, so we're somewhat tag-teaming in terms of who manages the day, but when it comes to scheduling, it's me. My husband is never going to sit down and say, 'Let's look at the plans for the week.' If we want something to happen, I'm going to have to be the one to take initiative. It gets exhausting. I'm the household manager. He'll do what needs to be done, but not without some sort of prompt. If I bring it to his awareness, he's like, 'I get it.' He sees it when I bring it up, but it's not a continual awareness. And then he'll be like, 'How can I help?' and I don't even know how to hand it over to him."

Christine, a forty-one-year-old accountant with a baby and a six-year-old in Illinois, said, "I can't trust him to actually remember the minimal things I ask him to do. I have to remind him to do it. Whatever the activity is, I still feel like it's on my list. So asking him to do things does not relieve any stress for me or any responsibility. The whole idea of just having a list to start out with . . . of course he doesn't have a list. My son would not have what he needed if ever I woke up one morning and was sick or something."

One problem with consciousness is that you cannot see it. The mental load's relentless invisibility makes it hard to co-manage for two unequally motivated parties. It also makes it tricky to illustrate, and so a cartoon that accomplished this (*"Fallait Demander,"* translated as "You Should've Asked," by French artist Emma) quickly went viral in 2017.

The cartoon featured a plainly drawn everywoman laying bare the effort that goes into default parenting: "The mental load means always having to remember. Remember that you have to add cotton buds to the shopping list, remember that today's the deadline to order your vegetable delivery for the week, remember that we should have paid the caretaker for last month's work by now. That the baby grew another 3 cm and can't fit into his trousers anymore, that he needs to get his booster shot, or that your partner doesn't have a clean shirt left. . . . So while most heterosexual men say that they do their fair share of household chores . . . their partners have a rather different perspective: 'He always puts on the washing machine but never hangs the washing out to dry.' 'The sheets could be standing stiff before he thought to change them.' 'He's never cooked a single meal for the baby.'"

Social psychologists have their own name for the mental load. They call it mnemonic work. Studies have established that couples intuitively, rather than consciously and explicitly, divide the work of planning and remembering. And just as intuitively, it mostly falls on wives. In the world of co-parenting, the word "intuitive" is actually code for "mother takes it on"; co-parenting intuitively rather than consciously is how modern couples get into this predicament.

Psychologist Elizabeth Haines and her colleagues at William Paterson University in New Jersey asked men and women to think about the tendency to help others remember their personal obligations, needs, and commitments versus the tendency to rely on others for those reminders. Both genders reported the assumption that it is women who do the reminding and that men are the beneficiaries of this effort. In the estimations of men and women, men are simply not held accountable for that kind of thing.

When asked to illustrate the mental load in their own relationship, 64 percent of women gave an example in which they were the reminding one. Upon being asked the same question, almost the same percentage of men likewise cited an example in which their wives were the mental laborers. Additionally, in the rarer case that men were executing the mnemonic work, it was usually because they directly benefited from the task (for example, "I reminded my wife that she said she would buy me a jacket"). The psychologists conclude, "Doing more mnemonic work is one way in which women's tendency to be communal manifests. . . . The prescriptive aspect of this stereotype would then denote that women and men are held to different standards—wherein the societal standard for men to engage in this type of work is more relaxed than it is for women, thereby resulting in men actually doing less mnemonic work than women do."

Vanessa, a thirty-four-year-old Queens, New York, parent with two young children who started her own business when her job in corporate America proved incompatible with mothering, told me, "With my husband, it's hard to be on the same page. He's good at a lot of things, but he's not good at the day-to-day. If we need basics, if the kids need to be fed, I have to give him road maps, instructions, management. There's not the intuition of anticipating needs. That's not even remotely in the realm of possibility. I've stopped expecting it. My daughter's first birthday party is tomorrow. He's done nothing. He says, 'Tell me what I need to do tomorrow morning.' I have to lay it out. It's frustrating to plan, manage, and execute everything. That's five people's jobs."

Smith College philosophy professor Meredith Michaels co-authored 2004's *The Mommy Myth: The Idealization of Motherhood and How It Undermines Women*. She came to the idea after confronting how much the zeitgeist of motherhood had intensified between the births of her first child in 1972 and her fourth in 1989. She described interacting with her grown son around his parenting responsibilities today. "He lives nearby, and I do a lot of child care. I'll ask him, 'Who is picking up so-and-so?' He'll reply, 'Ask [my wife]. That's not my area to know who's doing what and where.' And I think, Why is that? And what are you doing to make up for fact that it's not your area? What *is* your area?'"

In the late 1990s, Skidmore's Walzer interviewed twenty-five middle-class, heterosexual couples with babies in upstate New York to try to get her head around so-called parental consciousness and its development—how do children fill their parents' minds, and how do parents judge their thoughts about their kids? In the book chronicling her work, *Thinking About the Baby*, Walzer notes, "[T]he parents I interviewed carried particular images of what mothers and fathers were supposed to think about—what their responsibilities and feelings were supposed to be—and they were accountable to these images." The fathers in her study spoke primarily about financial responsibility, while the mothers (also breadwinners) reported the belief that they were supposed to have their babies in mind at all times, no matter what.

One woman with reliable child care said that while she wasn't actually worried about her baby while she was at work, she felt like she had to behave as if she were. To do otherwise would make her look—to herself and to the world—recalcitrant and immoral. Walzer writes, "Worrying was such an expected part of mothering that the absence of it might challenge one's definition as a good mother. . . . Fathers do not necessarily think about their children while they are at work, nor do they worry that not thinking about their child reflects on them as parents." As British cultural critic Jacqueline Rose has noted, "The expectations that are laid on [mothers]" are laden with "adulation and hatred, which of course so often go together."

Worrying to no purposeful end is unfortunate, but productive worry stimulates action: the scheduling of well-child visits, the installation of outlet plugs, the introduction of solid foods. The fathers in Walzer's study both pathologized their wives for their vigilance and connected it to their babies' well-being. It is not, however, connected to a mother's well-being. Research has shown that family-to-work "spillovers"—thinking about family matters while one is technically otherwise engaged—are associated with increased stress, depression, and general psychological upset. Research shows that the transition between thinking about family and thinking about work can lead to difficulty concentrating, as well as negative self-appraisals that make people—mothers in particular—feel that they are failing in both roles at all times.

The idea that a mother should always be thinking about her children isn't new, but neither is it very, very old, and as Meredith Michaels experienced while mothering from opposite ends of two decades, it ebbs and flows with time. In the colonial period in the U.S., fathers were assigned one crucial task of childrearing: building their children's character. There was less emphasis on the special and exclusive relationship between mother and child. This began to shift with industrialization, after the American Revolution, in the early half of the nineteenth century. University of Wisconsin–La Crosse historian Jodi Vandenberg-Daves, author of the 2014 book *Modern Motherhood*, explains, "The differentiation between mothers and fathers accelerates in the 1820s and '30s. You see it in the women's magazines' ideal of the sentimentalized mother who is available, domestically defined, and selfless.

"The selflessness piece became really important to the cultural construction of motherhood. In flowery nineteenth-century language, it's there everywhere. Women were to teach morality by being the more moral of the two sexes. Men could go out into the world and be rough-and-tumble, because women would maintain that sphere. All of this was happening during slavery and industrialization, which of course exploited many mothers and children, and made a sheltered domestic life impossible. But by behaving as selfless 'moral mothers,' white middle-class mothers were thought to be making a social contribution. They got a compromised idea of citizenship: You don't get to vote, but you get to raise the sons that will keep the republic going." So-called moral motherhood is an ideology that vested moral authority in women as mothers but denied them political or economic authority. It was also child-centered, commanding women to put their children first and confining them to the home. It endowed what is actually the world's oldest profession with an ethical imperative that has since wavered, but only in degree. And it did not proffer the same for men.

Mothers and fathers butt heads in this mismatch of ideas about what makes an adequate parent. If I believe in my bones that being a good mother means thinking about my children's needs a hairbreadth short of all of the time, and my husband does not believe in his bones that being a good father means thinking about his children's needs a hairbreadth short of all of the time, we are reaching for different rings. I am bound to be baffled when our divergent internal pressures show their outlines—when he fails to register that spring break is approaching and we will need child care, or that the babysitter is coming and the kids will need dinner, or their teeth cleanings are months overdue. Walzer writes, "[S]ocial norms make it particularly difficult for mothers to feel that they are doing the right thing. I call this mother worry, and it is generated by the question: Am I being a good mother?"

Does a father ever deign to ask that question? Is a mother ever free to let it go? The world does not conspire to lessen her concern. Sociologist Claire Kamp Dush remembers a text message received by a female friend of hers from preschool when the friend was out of town for work: "We miss you!" they wrote, above an attachment of a photo of her son dressed and dropped off by his father in wildly mismatched clothing and two different shoes. "The school did not say anything to the father. They just took a picture and texted it to my friend. The suggestion was that it was her fault. She told me and our other friend, and we were like, 'Was the kid alive and at day care? Good enough.' There's that pressure society puts on women. If your mother-in-law comes to your house and it's dirty, she's blaming you."

Meredith Michaels says, "Even in countries with more social support like Sweden, I think the sexual division of labor is still pretty codified along traditional lines. To be a good father does not include putting in the hard labor of knowing your children in that kind of intimate way. It doesn't. Some men do, but it's against the grain of everything that is culturally there. There's this cultural overdetermination. When his mother died, Henry James said something like, 'And she gave herself to her children as mothers should.' Really? Huh. So you give yourself. I think that still prevails. I see young mothers now who basically operate under that rubric. I'm giving myself to my children. I'm not doing xyz for myself because my children need me."

Whether or not they operate under that rubric, mothers today remain mindful of the rubric's imperatives. Despite my own deeply held beliefs about what makes a decent parent—reinforced by a doctorate's worth of reading on psychoanalyst D. W. Winnicott's "good enough mother," a theory that centers on emotional attunement to one's baby and not a never-ending diet of self-sacrifice—I often felt pressure to appear as if I were, as Michaels puts it, not doing xyz for myself because my children needed me. When our daughters were very young, on the rare occasion when George and I had time to go for a drink between work and preschool pickup, I'd rush him as the clock moved toward five-thirty, to his disappointment and dismay. School closed at six, but I hated to arrive last-minute. I feared looking immoral, like a mother who didn't care. This had nothing to do with my children's happiness. When I managed to arrive markedly early, they only asked to stay later to play.

As the psychologist Alice Miller writes of this narcissistic preoccupation with looking like a virtuous mother, "I cannot listen to my child with empathy if I am inwardly preoccupied with being a good mother; I cannot be open to what she is telling me."

Some years later, this preoccupation got old. Its pull manifested differently, in feelings of mild rebellion when I turned down, say, Liv's request to be her third-grade class parent. By elementary school, it was liberating to decline a mothering ask. I could have yelled it from the heavens: "I don't want to come up with healthy, thematic snacks and grade-appropriate crafts for the Halloween party!" And by the way, Liv never raised the issue with her father, who also would have said no, and felt only a momentary tinge of regret for the personal loss.

I am the default parent, though Liv adores George and knows that he always helps. Walzer concludes, "Embedded in the use of the verb 'help' is the notion that parenting is ultimately the mother's responsibility—that fathers are doing a favor when they parent. The default position, which is a factor in mothers' parental consciousness, is that the mother is on duty unless she asks for or is offered help. This is a state of affairs that creates dissonance for some of the couples I met, and wives especially, who expected their marriages to be partnerships."

The Pitfalls of Unequal Knowing

One Thanksgiving not so many years ago, Brigid Schulte, a Pulitzer Prize–winning journalist, mother of two, and author of the book *Overwhelmed: Work, Love and Play When No One Has the Time*, resolved to divorce her husband. They'd invited eighteen guests for dinner. She'd spent the week making multiple trips to the grocery store and ordering special tablecloths. The couple ran their local Turkey Trot that morning, and upon arriving home, Schulte commenced chopping produce and assembling casseroles. By two that afternoon, the kitchen was a mess of vegetable peels and stained cookbooks, and Schulte was still in her running clothes. Her husband entered the kitchen and opened the refrigerator. She assumed he was going to take out the turkey. Instead, he grabbed a six-pack and headed out the door. She recalls, "I had a knife in my hand as [he] walked out. I wished I had been a carnival knife thrower 'cause I just wanted to like [swish sound] right at [his] head cause I was so angry." She spent the time that he was out mentally dividing their possessions: He could keep the couch. (Her husband, Tom, later conceded, "I'm not sure what I was thinking.")

But it wasn't just holiday meal prep that got Schulte to that point. At the time, she later recalled in an essay for *Slate*, "My husband didn't know who the kids' dentist was, had never made summer camp plans, never bought toilet paper, or filled out all those damn school and Girl Scout forms. He'd never clipped baby fingernails, nor had he been the one to figure out how to get work done when a snowstorm, strep throat or unexpected barf threw the whole jerry-rigged system of work and child care into disarray."

In the weeks that followed, instead of finding a lawyer, Schulte employed the tools of her trade. She pulled out a notebook and started interviewing Tom. They'd gone into their marriage with the presumption of equality. How had they gotten off course?

She told me, "You have to ask yourself, is it really worth destroying love and partnership, your desire for sharing your life together? Instead, we decided to think about how to equally share raising our children. Day-to-day, nobody wants to do drudge work. Mental labor is exhausting. My husband had no idea what I was keeping in my head. I was scurrying around and getting everything nice before he came home. We were caught up in traditional norms, what a good mother is. It was a failure of imagination. We both had to recognize that social pressures were policing us in a certain way. We needed to hold each other accountable. It's important to automate as much as you can so that you don't need to renegotiate and argue. Set a big vision. Experiment as you go. Because arguments over housework are not insignificant. The unfair division of labor is a big reason for the breakup of marriages." (The third-most-cited reason, actually, after adultery and growing apart.)

By that Thanksgiving, Schulte had reached a "threat point," defined in the social science literature as "the contribution threshold below which an individual may abandon the marriage rather than compensate for lowered partner investment." Threat points grow out of bargaining problems, how two actors share a surplus that they alone generate. These come from game theory, the study of mathematical models of conflict and cooperation. Threat points are often associated with resources like money or physical attractiveness—or the very lack thereof.

Tracy, the domestic violence advocate in Washington State, explained her inability to negotiate better for herself: "My husband is a software engineer. He thinks my work is not as hard, despite my job, the six loads of laundry I have to fold, and the dog I have to walk. I have a high school education and a fifteen-dollar-an-hour job. If he stands up and says, 'If you don't like it, hit the road,' what am I going to do?" How well either spouse might fare outside of the marriage because of their respective resources contributes to the estimation of threat points (for example, "The better able I am to support myself or find another spouse, the more I might demand from my partner in order to stay").

Threat points are also colored by cohort-specific gender expectations. For couples married before 1975, wives' employment was associated with greater risk of divorce. That is no longer the case. Similarly, wives' household labor responsibility is no longer linearly associated with greater marital stability— but men's willingness to contribute is.

Schulte related the story of a female friend with a nine-month-old baby who got so fed up with her husband that she simply walked out. "She said, 'We have the same job. Why am I doing so much more than you?' Then she left for twenty-four hours. He got it together."

SUNY Polytechnic Institute sociologist Veronica Tichenor, author of *Earning More and Getting Less*, explained what she heard from the women she interviewed. "Everyone around them is experiencing the same thing. They can laugh and commiserate about how tough it is and how incompetent their husband is. One woman in my book had two young daughters and complicated caretaking arrangements. She joked that if anyone in her life were going to walk out on her, it would best be her husband. 'If your day care person leaves you, now, that's a problem.' She was only half joking. 'I could get along without him. He does so little.' That's a risk for men."

And here's the rub: This risk just does not equal the reward.

Or, more precisely, there is no clear-cut reward for "doing so little" in a marriage. In 2010, researchers from Dartmouth College, the University of South Carolina, and Indiana University looked at the emotional costs of inequity in the household division of labor. Prior work had established that this inequity fuels depression in women. The group wanted to establish a more nuanced take on the variation in feeling that it might create in both partners. Equity theory proposes that perceived unfairness in all manner of scenarios results in emotional upset—no matter which side of the equation one finds oneself on. Regardless of who is getting or doing less or more, both participants are likely to experience distress. Using data from the emotion module of the General Social Survey, they determined: "Consistent with equity theory, individuals who perceive themselves as either overbenefiting or underbenefiting with respect to housework report significantly more negative emotions than do their counterparts who judge the arrangement as fair to both parties. . . . The influences of under- and overbenefiting on negative emotions are approximately equal."

Equal but not the same. The group found that perceptions of inequity to self were linked to anger and rage, while perceptions of inequity to other were linked to fear and self-reproach (a concise articulation of a dynamic in my own marriage if ever there were one). Furthermore, positive emotions take a hit in the face of inequity. Tranquility specifically goes down for both members of a couple as their perception of unfairness goes up. To be sure, unequally shouldered workloads are carried at great cost. But here's another difference between women and men: Women are more emotionally sensitive to overbenefiting. They feel worse when they're the ones doing less. In contrast, men are more emotionally sensitive to underbenefiting. They may feel chagrin while resting as their wives pack all the lunches, but their hackles go up faster and higher in the event that this scenario is reversed.

Erica in Portland noted, "I have a couple girlfriends who are married to stay-at-home dads. But they're overly accommodating as far as their husbands having time to themselves. In the end, they're working *and* they're doing more at home. I have a stay-at-home-mom friend who never gets a break."

Vidya in Los Angeles told me, "Weirdly, even when my husband wasn't freelancing much and I was working full-time at a job, I felt guilty that I wasn't doing half the housework. It was important to me that I be doing half at home, even though I was working way more hours than he was overall, and also basically supporting us." She felt better underbenefiting.

DC-area writer and mom blogger Dara Mathis describes efforts to avoid overbenefiting. "I do the cooking and he does the dishes. But we're trying to sleep-train our fifteen-month-old, which is going terribly, and it takes longer for us to put her to bed. So I will do the dishes for him. In my mind, even though I had cooked and was with the baby all day, it was unfair to him to expect that he would do the dishes and then go directly to staying with the baby for thirty minutes."

Men's Refusal of Responsibility and the Cult of Female Sacrifice

Women's greater relative comfort with underbenefiting juxtaposed with men's greater relative comfort with overbenefiting sets the course for men to refuse responsibility and for women to comply with their refusal. Men opt out in a handful of categorical ways. SUNY Stony Brook sociologist and gender scholar Michael Kimmel described discussions he's had with them on the topic: "Men often tell me, 'My wife gets on me all the time because I don't vacuum, and I'm watching a baseball game, and she comes in and says, 'At least you could vacuum.' So I do, and then she comes back and tells me I didn't do it very thoroughly. So I just figure I won't do it anymore.'" My own reluctant impulse to endorse this position runs so deep that Kimmel's retort to these men delights me. "I say to them, 'Well, that's an interesting response! If I were your supervisor at work and I assigned you a report, and I wasn't happy with what you turned in, and I told you so, would your reply be, 'Well, then, I'll never do *that* again!'?"

Kimmel is describing a refusal-of-responsibility strategy that has been called "adherence to inferior standards." Miranda in Vermont talked about it like this: "Even when we were first living together and trying to figure out who does what, I remember Lowell saying, 'If you feel like things need to be cleaner than they are, then you have a different threshold than I do, and you have to do it yourself.' So now I do almost all the cleaning and most of the cooking. Neither of us likes to cook, but I have more experience with it. He does almost all the dishes. That's how we've dealt with that. But his idea of doing dishes and mine are different. He throws them in the dishwasher, the counters are still disgusting, and the table has food splattered all over it. I clean up after he cleans up."

Other strategies include passive resistance, strategic incompetence, strategic use of praise, and flat-out denial. The parents

I interviewed all spoke obliquely to these categories. Yana in California has three young sons and a stay-at-home husband. She described his passive resistance like this: "We tried at some point to divide things more equally. We had a schedule of who would put the kids to sleep. I take the baby, you put the others to bed. Then I'd be upset because he was taking so long. So now I put everyone to sleep. In part, I guess this is mutual. But I'd say, 'Please do homework with the kids by the time I get home.' I'd get home, and he hadn't done it yet. So I took over, and now I do it myself. I just figured at some point that if I want things done, I have to stay on top of them." Yana's husband never explicitly turns down her requests—but he routinely fails to fulfill them.

Strategic incompetence looks like this: Nicole in Portland told me, "I cook because I have specific dietary needs, and he's not into it. I believe in the health of my kids. If I left it up to him they'd eat Hamburger Helper." Strategic use of praise like this: Meredith, from the new mothers' group in my neighborhood, said, "He'll look at me and say, 'Am I doing this right?' I have mixed feelings about it. Like, 'Oh, there's something I can do better than you, and you're respecting that!' On the other hand, it's like, 'I wish you spent enough time with her to know all these things as much as I do.'"

And finally, denial (that his behavior gives shape to her options): Mark, Nicole's husband, said, "It has to do with my wife's personality. She always has to stay busy. No matter what day of the week it is, she has the need to be doing something!" And Lowell, Miranda's husband, told me, "I do laundry when I need it. I operate on my time scale. As long as there are clean clothes, I don't prioritize that. We have different comfort levels about letting it build up. I could do it more often, proactively, but that's not my default nature. So she tends to be the one that falls to." Occidental College sociologist Lisa Wade summed up what she has seen like this: "Men find ways of being so difficult that it's not worth it. You do it yourself."

We play it as it lays. Wade said, "When inequality is what we're used to, inequality looks like equality. If you do an experiment and show subjects a room that is fifty/fifty male/female, people see a preponderance of women over men. We're so used to seeing rooms dominated by men that our vision is warped. I wonder sometimes, if men were doing half, if it would feel like they were doing two thirds. Now they can do a third and it feels like half."

Men refuse because they've seen other men refusing. It almost looks like equality. Studies on women and leadership have underscored that exposure to one gender or another in a particular role tends to be self-reinforcing. When business-people are asked to draw an effective leader, for example, they almost always draw a man. Even when sketches are (rarely) gender-neutral, adjectives used to describe a drawing are male-typical. And studies of emergent leadership find that men, but not women, are recognized as potential leaders when they offer ideas to their colleagues. We use stereotypes to size up situations. Our assessments feel based on the present but are actually drawn mostly from the past. The tendency to go along like this is called the confirmation bias. Quick—draw some-one doing a good job cleaning a table or putting a child to bed. Draw a parent alone in a room.

In the U.S. and other nations without strong family policy, men's resistance strategies undergird women's tireless immer-sion, what journalist Jill Filipovic has called the cult of female sacrifice. But in some countries things look, while not exactly egalitarian, different. Where there is state-sponsored universal child care—as provided in, let's say, Denmark—time-use studies show that fathers spend the same amount of time with their children as fathers in the U.S. But the ratio in father's to mother's child care time is much smaller in Denmark because Danish mothers (with some help from institutions) are left to do that much less.

While living in Paris, journalist Pamela Druckerman observed that mothers in France—where high-quality, state-subsidized child care is also widely available—express much less anger toward their husbands than their counterparts in the States. In her book *Bringing Up Bébé*, Druckerman writes, "France has less feminist rhetoric, but it has many more institutions that enable women to work. There's the national paid maternity leave, the subsidized nannies and crèches, the free universal pre-school from age three, and myriad tax credits and payments for having kids. All this doesn't ensure that there's equality between men and women. But it does ensure that Frenchwomen can have both a career and kids." Frenchwomen may not have equal partners, but other support is available should they choose to take advantage of it, which female primates have been doing for centuries. University of Nevada, Las Vegas, anthropologist Alyssa Crittenden tells me, "Those of us who study family formation and the evolution of cooperative breeding, we don't prioritize one caregiver over another. Distributive care is the most important thing. How that shakes out cross-culturally has to do with norms of the social group."

The so-called cult of female sacrifice was necessarily reinforced during the Cold War, when social groups in the West who decried feminism's goals aligned with the Red Scare. After the Bolshevik Revolution in 1917, the newly formed USSR declared state-sponsored early child care an important tool for indoctrinating children, or for helping them grow into ideal Soviet citizens. In the decades following, American opposition to government-subsidized early child care often centered on the premise that only mothers, and not state-funded preschools (or—and this didn't even warrant mentioning—fathers), could raise warm-blooded American citizens.

Lecturing across the country on egalitarianism in the 1970s, husband and wife psychologists Sandra and Daryl Bem acknowledged, "Middle class people were not open to the idea of providing child care outside the child's own home. As hard as this may be to believe, on those few early occasions when we tried to talk about day care, even our college audiences branded it as 'communist.'" As we added "under God" to the Pledge to differentiate from the godless Soviets, we solidified society's distaste for the collective contribution to rearing healthy kids. The indoctrination that materialized in the U.S. was subsequently aimed not at children but, rather, their mothers. As Betty Friedan noted in 1963's *The Feminine Mystique*, "fulfillment as a woman had only one definition for American women after 1949—the housewife-mother." Friedan's best seller chronicled simmering ennui among the period's housewives. The book owed its success to the permission it gave midcentury women to admit to the idea of wanting other things.

But the fear that just maybe they shouldn't was not so easily shed. And so writing over fifty years later, in 2017's *The H-Spot: The Feminist Pursuit of Happiness*, Jill Filipovic observed, "Women who think they're entitled to pleasure and happiness for themselves alone are cast as selfish or immoral. . . . Women who pursue the pleasure of achievement are overly ambitious careerists, and if they're also mothers, then they're probably paying someone else to raise their children. Women who put their own desires even temporarily ahead of someone else's—especially, god forbid, their children's—are unfit parents and bad people. This cult of female sacrifice, often masquerading as love, has real consequences . . . women get the head-patting platitude that 'motherhood is the most important job in the world.' It should come as little surprise that, contrary to the clichés and the promises, having children tanks women's happiness." See journalist Jennifer Senior's *All Joy and No Fun: The Paradox of Modern Parenthood* for lamentations on that particular research finding.

The cult of female sacrifice takes on varied forms in different cultural subgroups but always ends with one consistent message. In *Raising the Race*, Yale anthropologist Riché J. Daniel Barnes describes the "strong black woman framework" that requires African American mothers to—sing along with me now—do it all. Black feminist scholars are leery of the framework, which, they assert, masquerades as an accolade while really just maintaining the patriarchal order. Barnes writes, "Despite critiques by black feminist scholars, the black community continued to celebrate black women whom they represented as managing it all—work, children, and economic, political, and social insecurity—alone. . . . 'It is a badge of honor,' I was told, and one of the few stereotypes of black women that is actually positive. For black professional women, however, this myth, encouraging them to be superwomen who are beholden to their careers, spouses, children, families of origin, and the larger black community, increasingly comes at a cost the women are not willing to pay."

DePauw University sociologist Tamara Beauboeuf-LaFontant asserts that maintaining the myth of the strong black woman is a "costly performance." The professional women in Barnes's study were doubly stymied—not only by sexism but also by racism. They "still contend with the idea that they, as a group, are undesirable; their status as wives is much more precarious than their status as mothers and career women, and therefore all, or at least the majority, of their efforts must go into maintaining the marriage." Their threat points raised by the conventional wisdom, these women appeared reluctant, according to Barnes, to ask for or even acknowledge their desire for more from their husbands.

In *Feminism Is for Everybody*, bell hooks writes, "When women in the home spend all their time attending to the needs of others, home is a workplace for her, not a site of relaxation, comfort and pleasure." To test the hypothesis—also laid out by Arlie Hochschild in *The Second Shift*—that mothers feel burdened in their homes by the writ of female sacrifice (or the one of the strong black woman, take your pick), Penn State University labor and employment professor Sarah Damaske asked both men and women about their levels of happiness at home versus at work. When we spoke, I wondered if she'd found gender differences upon final analysis. "Yes," said Damaske, who is herself a mother. "Women are happier at work, and men are happier at home!" She laughed uproariously for a good minute before continuing, "It makes a lot of sense. Men have less responsibility at home. It's more of a haven for them than for their wives." Her team also took saliva samples and measured the stress hormone cortisol. Damaske said, "People's stress hormones decreased when they went to work. Everyone's. We think of our homes and these wonderful family moments, but home is also the daily chores of the dishes and saying, 'Can you pick up your toys,' and no one thanks you for cleaning the toilet. I think when you go to work, there can be this release of some of the daily stress of that labor."

Natalie, forty-one, a special education teacher and mother of two teenagers in the suburbs of Los Angeles, remembers, "Some years back, I was trying to find more time for myself. I was getting really angry and really negative. I just was not pleasant to be around. It seemed like because I put myself last, the thought of hanging out at my house, I didn't want to be there. It brought me so much stress. I'd go to yoga and feel relaxed, but I'd come back home, and that feeling would go away—as soon as I stepped in the door. My family could tell. I was carrying that load and not expressing myself. I was trying to be this perfect mom, wife, career woman, without taking anyone's help. Or even expressing 'I can't do this all on my own.'"

Add These Things Together and You Cannot Have It All

Natalie said that she reached a breaking point and decided to make some changes. She and her husband, Rob, pulled their kids from school, sold their possessions, and spent a year driving cross-country in an old camper van. As they traveled, she considered how she'd made her own bed, but Rob never examined his part. She told me, "It's interesting. We have these conversations.

He says, 'It's the whole feminism movement. If you guys didn't want everything, you guys would probably have it a lot easier.' I can see that to some extent." Feminism often plays the straw man in these discussions, as if the very desire for equality were problematic, rather than the fact that equality has yet to materialize.

Here's another question that men do not have to ask: Can *we* really have it all? Why ask if the earth is round—if cars are made from steel? And so women are stuck with it; I've seen it on Facebook. In 2017, Raquel, a woman in one Midwestern mothers' group, responded to a question about having it all from a member who'd recently been promoted: "I dislike the phrase 'have it all.' I am self-employed. Can I hustle 60 hours a week and spend tons of time with my family? No. Can I find success and fulfillment in my career and get to spend plenty of time with my kids? Absolutely! Does it suck that my husband never even has to think about this in his career, even though we work hard to have an equal relationship? A million times yes." The Twitter account @manwhohasitall highlights this particular brand of gender-role ridiculousness, posing questions like "Can you have a successful career AND be a good dad?" and "Is it too risky to hire attractive men?"

Like Natalie, Rob is a teacher. He could not assume the financial responsibility of supporting their family alone, though it would have been his preference. Absent that traditional (and ever more unattainable) male capacity, he nevertheless continues to expect his wife to be the traditional default parent. He blames feminism for giving Natalie big ideas—social justice movement as creator of mirage. He never questioned his right to the very same big idea: the ability to have a family, a work life, and also some time to himself.

Vanessa in Queens has her own business, two young children, and a husband who admires her ambition. Still, helping her to have it all has not been in his wheelhouse. She said, "My husband is totally accepting and supportive of strong women. The actual functioning of our life is a different thing. On paper, it sounds great. But in actuality, he lets eighty-five percent fall on me. He decided to buy a gym after our second child was born. He decided to begin the most grueling training program on the planet two months after she arrived. It didn't feel like the right time to take on something that would take him away from the family, but he didn't make that connection." So while he pursues his dreams unfettered, her possibilities narrow. "I have to make some decisions. I don't work out the way I used to. My husband goes for a run every weekend. I don't have the luxury to do that. I don't get to relax. I have to decide what needs to be done in a day and what can be tabled. It sucks, but I have to boss him around. He's a great father. If he were only that good of a husband."

The ABC sitcom *Splitting Up Together* features a newly divorced couple with three kids who decide to continue living in the same house for the good of their offspring. A montage sequence in the pilot's first minutes outlines the circumstances of the breakup in broad strokes. The father, played by Oliver Hudson, is on his way out the door for a run. The mother, played by Jenna Fischer, comes downstairs in a ponytail and glasses, carting a basket of laundry. He says, "I was just going to go for a quick run before work." She replies, "Cool. I was just going to do the laundry, vacuum, plunge the upstairs toilet, call a guy about the broken sprinkler, go to work, come home, and make dinner."

"Cool," he says. "What's for dinner?"

Boston College psychologist and psychoanalyst Usha Tummala-Narra reiterates that women receive positive reinforcement for caregiving from a young age. "You see what behavior gets you ahead, and that's internalized. This is what works, this is how I can exist in society and be seen, acknowledged, recognized. Conversely, for men, they're still recognized for masculinity and how much they're able to earn. So external social markers of success are still driving women and men today in terms of how they make their choices. I see it as adaptive. You adapt in order to survive within a framework. But the framework doesn't seem to be changing. The problem becomes, then, that the framework *doesn't* change. It's the framework, and not the behavior, that is pathological. Men are not socialized to feel guilty for having freedom or for not being there for other people. From the beginning, you've been internalizing the idea that this is the most important thing you can do. Being at work is great, but not 'the most important thing' you can do."

Thus, men feel entitled to have it all, though to call it that implies that it is something out of the ordinary, and of course, it is not, if one is a man. In *The Audacity of Hope*, Barack Obama writes about the problem in the early years of his own marriage: "By the time Sasha was born . . . my wife's anger toward me seemed barely contained. 'You only think about yourself,' she would tell me. 'I never thought I'd have to raise a family alone.' I was stung by such accusations. I thought she was being unfair. After all, it wasn't as if I went carousing with the boys every night. I made few demands of Michelle—I didn't ask her to darn my socks or have dinner waiting for me when I got home. Whenever I could, I pitched in with the kids. All I asked for in return was a little tenderness. Instead I found myself subjected to endless negotiations about every detail of managing the house, long lists of things that I needed to do or had forgotten to do, and a generally sour attitude." Later on, Obama takes a more sympathetic position toward his wife, but here he sounds like the new fathers I see in my practice, not to mention my own loving husband. While the mothers I work with are almost universally angry with their partners for their lukewarm parental consciousness—for being helpers, sharers, and slackers—the men I work with mostly seem as puzzled by their wives' frustration as Barack was by Michelle's, as George was by mine. I love her. I pitch in. What gives?

Michelle Obama, for her part, ultimately accommodated her husband's entitlement. During his first campaign for president in August 2007, journalist Rebecca Johnson reported in *Vogue*, "As bad as the time crunch is now, it was worse when the children were smaller. Both the senator and his wife have been frank about their marital troubles during those years, when the bulk of child rearing fell on her shoulders, even as she tried to maintain her demanding career. 'If a toilet overflows,' she likes to say in one of her standard 'stumps,' 'we women are the ones rescheduling our meetings to be there when the plumber arrives.' . . . 'I like to talk about it,' she says, 'because I think every couple struggles with these issues. People don't tell you how much kids change things. I think a lot of people give up on themselves. They get broken, but if we can talk about it, we can help each other.' Instead of quitting her job or divorcing her husband, Michelle decided to make peace with the situation. 'I spent a lot of time expecting my husband to fix things, but then I came to realize that he was there in the ways he could be. If he wasn't there, it didn't mean he wasn't a good father or didn't care. I saw it could be my mom or a great baby-sitter who helped. Once I was OK with that, my marriage got better.'" Despite the obvious pragmatism of her choice, which I respect, my heart sank when I read this last bit. If that was the best even Michelle Obama could extract from her marriage, what audacious hope remained for the rest of us?

With the Obamas as the platonic example, it's clear that it was not the then-senator's disregard for women or commitment to traditional family roles that tripped the couple up. Clearly, when we've concluded that egalitarian values and feminist-leaning partners will produce equally sharing fathers, we've been missing some crucial information.

That information is in part about implicit biases. Implicit bias—the attitudes and stereotypes that affect our actions in unconscious ways—is thought to explain all sorts of unintentional discrimination, from the disproportionate hiring and promotion of men to the police shootings of unarmed African Americans. It is also in heavy rotation in the gendered distribution of labor in the home. One may have a conscious belief that men and women should be equal while simultaneously maintaining a less conscious commitment to the primacy of male desire.

Metacognition, the capacity to reflect more deeply on automatic and unconscious beliefs, is an important counterweight to implicit bias. In the pre-employment screening of police officer candidates, for example, psychologists today routinely examine metacognitive competence—not whether applicants are racist (most people wouldn't label themselves such) but whether they can think long and hard about how they've been impacted by living in a racist society. "You really need cops who get this," psychologist Dave Corey, founding president of the American Board of Police and Public Safety Psychology, told me.

Joan Williams at the Center for WorkLife Law expressed a similar sentiment about male partners. She explained that egalitarianism (the belief that one is not sexist) is not enough precisely because even men who don't realize it typically continue to feel at complete liberty to put their own personal autonomy ahead of their wives'. She said, "My strongest advice to young women: Don't just try to find a man who's supportive of women. That's a threshold. But consider, what is his attitude toward himself and ambition? That's what determines your future. If he's ambitious *and feels entitled to that ambition*, you're going to end up embattled, marginalized, or divorced." Like Corey, Williams suggests a sort of pre-employment screening. Can a candidate for co-parent think long and hard about the impact of growing up in a sexist world?

Summer, a forty-one-year-old lawyer and mother of a three-year-old in Chicago, laid out the toll of implicit bias for me. "At the end of the day, it's always the wife that has to make the choice, a limited career or a limited family life. My husband wouldn't say this outright, but his attitude has always been, 'We have to look toward my career path.' I was offered a job in Atlanta, and they were going to create a position for me, double my salary, and there's a lower cost of living there. Even though he's a consultant, in the office once every two months, he was like, 'It would be a career-limiting move for me.' I've turned down a lot of opportunities. I had to take a position I was overqualified for. It's frustrating to report to somebody I'm more qualified than. I explain stuff to him and his bosses. All of my female friends at work have taken flexible arrangements, passed up promotions, or weren't promoted because they had the flextime. All the men who were once at my level have higher titles and salaries than me now, no matter if they have kids—my male boss has three. I read *Lean In* before I was pregnant, and I was like, 'This is great.' I read it again after having a kid, and I was like, 'This is bullshit.' It's unattainable unless you have a bevy of resources financially and emotionally." Summer fails to mention a third resource, the one that Joan Williams espouses: a partner who can give thought to—and then is better positioned to surrender—an unbridled entitlement to his own uninterrupted pursuits.

Women who are not professionals find themselves bearing the weight of multiple biases, implicit and otherwise. While high-earning mothers may ultimately scale back their market labor because of time constraints and their husband's unwillingness to compromise, mothers on the lower end of the income scale may be forced out of work altogether not only because their wages come in at less than their male partners (and below the cost of child care) but also because their work is disparaged.

The partners of pink-collar women often feel little respect for low-wage "women's work." Sociologist Sarah Damaske, who did the cortisol study, has interviewed working-class women with transient work in low-paying sectors. She said, "They don't have access to the same work that men do, and make less money than their husbands. A lot of women I interviewed found their spouses to be dismissive of their work. I interviewed a woman who said, 'I work at Kmart, so my husband says I should just quit my job, that it's not worthwhile.' That's not a challenge middle-class women face—they might also make less money, but they work in positions that are more respected. Working-class women talk about cooking or cleaning or doing hair, work that takes skill. The woman at Kmart said, 'I have to be able to always be polite and help the elderly person shop and the cranky person who wants to rush out the door.' No one acknowledges that these jobs demand ability. Academics play a role in that, calling those jobs semi-skilled. It's a real devaluation of that work. And that has an impact on the home."

Baby Bust

Faced with the knowledge that they cannot have it all, women in Japan have approached the problem by losing interest in marriage and procreation altogether. A 2011 report from Japan's population center found that 49 percent of women between eighteen and thirty-four were not in romantic relationships, and 39 percent of women in that age group had never had sex at all. Experts there call this Japanese trend "the flight from intimacy" and believe it stems from the juxtaposition of a highly developed economy and a barely developed equity between the sexes in the home.

In 2017, the World Economic Forum ranked Japan 114th of 144 countries in gender equality; in the same year, the U.S. was ranked 49th, the United Kingdom 15th. Traditionally, Japanese women have been expected to leave the workforce upon marriage. Those who don't are known as "devil wives." While the birth rate has been falling steadily in Japan since the 1950s, in 2014, just over a million babies were born there, a record low. This sets up what has been referred to as "a demographic time bomb"—rising longevity paired with plummeting birth rates. The economy shrinks, leaving far fewer workers to support a top-heavy system or a healthy GDP. Prime Minister Shinzō Abe is addressing this "critical situation" with measures that support relationship formation (for example, government-hosted speed dating and fatherhood classes for single men), as well as work-life balance for families in general (state-subsidized child care and time off for new dads). The government has committed to increasing men's time in child care from its current 67 minutes a day to 150 minutes a day by the year 2020.

Japan is an extreme example, but among the nations of the developed world, demographers have shown strong relationships between national birth rates and levels of domestic gender equity. Australian National University demographer Peter McDonald asserts that low fertility is the "result of incoherence in the levels of gender equity in individually-oriented social institutions and family-oriented social institutions." That is, in countries where women have equal opportunity in education and employment but remain the default parent, the birth rate has fallen to new lows (as it did in the U.S. in 2017). When child-bearing takes a disproportionate toll on "the human capital aspirations" afforded women, some of those women will decide not to have children at all (what English journalist Suzanne Moore has called "women's not-so-secret weapon. We could end humanity this way"), and many will decide to have fewer.

McDonald explains that this phenomenon becomes an issue especially for countries whose social institutions do not lend support to combining work and family, and also in those who still pay lip service to the logic of separate spheres. He writes, "The argument that state support for the combination of work and family is the key to sustainable levels of fertility was made in the 2005 European Commission Green Paper on demographic change. It has also been used to support work/family policy initiatives in various European countries. . . . It is a sensible approach for governments to increase or sustain fertility through support of the combination of work and family for mothers. If they are working they will pay taxes that can be used to pay for the services that they require. Furthermore, [it has been] shown that the association between higher fertility and higher GDP per capita . . . is not so much the result of wealth alone but of the higher labour force participation rates for women in the highest income countries. In turn, these are countries that have focused on policies that support the combination of work and family. This argument is supported by outcomes in the Nordic countries and in the English-speaking countries."

In contrast, demographer Thomas Anderson writes, "Where traditional norms regarding childrearing, household work, and male breadwinner roles prevail while institutional gender equity and female labor force participation increases, women are more likely to view having a family as being at odds with pursuing career aspirations . . . fertility falls to low levels."

Anderson and fellow demographer Hans-Peter Kohler have studied McDonald's work. Anderson tells me, "Peter argues that in places where there are high degrees of family gender equity within partnerships, you tend to have fertility near replacement rate or slightly under. One cannot dispute that correlation. You can look at the number of hours that men versus women spend in unpaid family work, and you find that where fertility is around replacement rate, the gap between men and women is smaller. In places where the gap is massive, fertility is low." The

U.S. actually falls into the first category, and though fertility has fallen below replacement rate, it still hovers around 1.77, which is higher than the 1.5 births per woman now formally considered "very low fertility"—in Japan, it is 1.42.

Anderson and Kohler wondered about the interaction of two things: 1) McDonald's correlation between birth rates and gender equity; and 2) research showing that husbands perform a greater percentage of unpaid labor in municipalities where sex ratios skew male—that is, the more men there are relative to women, the more likely men are to participate at home. The two began analyzing population data and domestic gender equality around the world since the industrial revolution. What they found was striking. As economies developed, birth rates fell. As each successive age cohort then became smaller, men—who tend to marry women four years younger than they are—found themselves in marriage populations that skewed toward female advantage (fewer women in the right age range to marry). As men sensed more limited possibility, or as women sensed an increase in their power in the marriage market, gender equity improved.

Anderson and Kohler called this effect "the gender equity dividend." Anderson says, "In households in Sweden or France, men are more willing to pitch in than in more traditional countries. A lot of people attribute that to top-down legislation— the government legislating toward that end. In the English-speaking countries, the government wouldn't go there. The U.S. speaks to that. They've got shitty, nonexistent policies on parental leave, but still, these days, men are doing more at home. There are multiple pathways to achieving higher gender equity in the household. It's hard to show on an empirical level why change has taken place. We believe the gender equity dividend is one more pathway. It greases the wheels. Today there are thirty-three million more men than women in China. My prediction: Massive change in gender equality is going to sweep that country."

This is how demography's findings play out in real time. Erica, the thirty-eight-year-old project manager in Portland, has had little success at making her husband an equal sharer. "If my kids are sick, I get called by the school. I have to leave work early. He's blissfully unaware of what's happening. He doesn't answer his phone. Occasionally, he'll joke, 'Things just get done.' When I try to point out that that's not the case, he's like, 'You're Mommy the martyr.' Birthday presents, vaccination records, dentist appointments. All the little things are things he has no clue about. I'll ask him to do something, he'll procrastinate and forget, and then I'm nagging. I buy their clothes, arrange play dates. He teases the kids, 'If it were up to me, you guys would be wearing potato sacks.' He makes a joke of it. But he's not doing a lot of those kinds of things. I take the kids to birthday parties while he gets time to himself. He gets a lot of alone time. Which I crave."

And so the birth rate in Erica's family is not rising. "We joked about that. People would ask, 'Are you going to have more kids?' I can't. I'd be booked into a psych ward. If I worked fewer hours or had family support, it might be different. Having two kids, I'm barely making it."

CHAPTER 5

24-Hour Lifelong Shifts of Unconditional Love

Intensive Mothering

"Kids are more important than grown-ups," Tess, in pig-tails and a skort, announced to me one day when she was five, a worldview emerging sharply like a new tooth breaking gum. I love proclamations like these, delivered with such declarative power by my daughters. But I often find their content disconcerting, like when Liv, at four, informed me that, usually, girls are nurses and boys are doctors, and I realized that months of six a.m. *Doc McStuffins* viewings had not quite hit their mark.

I was particularly struck by Tess's observation because of what I'd been reading. A fish can't see the water. Apparently, neither can I. My friends and I sometimes remarked that we didn't remember our own perfectly adequate parents going to quite the same lengths we often found ourselves caught up in. Full-time working mothers today spend as much time with their children as homemakers in the 1970s. I'd read that, but I'd never given much thought to the notion that modern standards of mothering were just that: some water we were swimming in. To give an idea much thought is to risk conscious conflict. To be conflicted is to contemplate change. To change is to jeopardize one's status as a good mother, a status to be maintained no matter its prohibitive cost.

The modern imperatives of mothering emphasize that the needs of (one's own) children are very, very important, while the needs of (one's own female) self are very, very not—especially when the latter diverge from the former. Kids are more important than grown-ups. What else was Tess to make of my relentless attention to the concerns of her and her sister, a way of structuring our lives that George often acquiesced to but never independently endorsed? Under my orchestration, our evenings were devoted to their homework, their dinner, their hygiene, and whatever mildly age-inappropriate twenty-two-minute show they were currently into on Netflix; our weekends to their entertainment, which often involved no more than the playground behind the school, but still. One winter Saturday, George and I watched the entirety of *Wonder Woman* on pay-per-view uninterrupted while the kids tromped around our building, and it was the best winter Saturday I ever spent. "Let's do this every weekend," we said. We never did it again.

In a 2018 *National Review* essay critiquing what she called the "motherhood is awful canon," journalist Heather Wilhelm notes, "Weirdly enough, the most common elements of torture invoked . . . seem largely self-imposed—the fruits of a particularly American earth-mother perfectionism, paired with a strange belief that good parenting involves making yourself as miserable as possible while sacrificing all sense of self. If you decide to co-sleep with your child in your bed until said child is two years old, for instance, you're probably not going to get much sleep for two years. If you decide against scientific evidence that baby formula is bottled hemlock and can never be used, ever—even when you're, say, sick in bed with strep throat—well, good luck to you." But even mothers who don't go to those lengths operate against that backdrop.

Miranda in Vermont half-heartedly rattles off a list of reasons why she'll never be a perfect mom. "I don't make everything from scratch. I use plastic containers instead of metal ones. The kids sometimes use the iPad when I'm by myself with them and trying to make dinner." What makes Miranda's list worthy of remark is that its items have less relationship to her children's well-being than to how willing she is to inconvenience herself. Mothering, as Miranda attests, is a task evaluated not only by outcomes (the general health and happiness of children) but also by how much deprivation a woman is willing to endure. Self-denial as a virtue; self-flagellation as a rule. "I was so good today," I remember the girls in my freshman dorm saying at day's end, recounting how little they'd eaten—a fixation author Naomi Wolf once postulated was not about female beauty but, rather, female obedience. "I am so bad," Miranda implies, having let her kids use the iPad so that she could prepare a not-from-scratch dinner in some peace.

The ideology of "intensive mothering"—a term coined by sociologist Sharon Hays in the late 1990s to describe the parenting ethos of the day—mandates: The best mothers always put their kids' needs before their own, the best mothers are the main caregivers, the best mothers make kids the center of their universe. That's the way Meredith Michaels and Susan Douglas describe the culmination of intensive mothering over a thirty-year period in 2004's *The Mommy Myth*.

In my own experience a decade later, it was no longer the best mothers who did those things but instead just the adequate ones. The best mothers saw those standards and raised them ten, as if the benefits of parental engagement knew no upper limit. In addition to contributing to their family's income, they attended inconveniently timed classroom parties, volunteered with the parents' association, devoted entire weekends to carpooling to far-flung sporting events, provided construction paper and ingredients for slime on demand, never missed a Fun Friday, carried snacks and water in their bags, sneaked vegetables into otherwise kid-friendly meals, made brownies for the bake sale, took part in the math-a-thon, left work early for school performances, and coaxed their kids into reading for thirty minutes a night just like the teacher said.

I was an adequate mother (see description of formerly "best mothers" above). I could not fathom ever devoting entire weekends to far-flung sporting events. I hoped I was not shortchanging my kids. I worried that I was. Here are your options in response to a mothering ideal that journalist Manohla Dargis has called "a noxious delusion, one that isn't suitable for real women": guilt for not trying to live up to impossible standards, or shame for trying to live up to impossible standards.

As Ohio State psychologist Sarah Schoppe-Sullivan says, "It's not okay to say mothers should prioritize family anymore. What comes out instead is that to be a good mom, you have to do all these things."

In 1996's *The Cultural Contradictions of Motherhood*, Hays defines intensive mothering as a gendered model of childrearing that is child-centered, expert-guided, emotionally absorbing, labor-intensive, and financially expensive. Hays describes the ideology as "neither natural or a given but . . . a socially constructed reality," charting its rise over two hundred years of steadily intensifying norms. Like others who contemplate modern motherhood, she notes that those norms paradoxically kicked into ever-higher gear as women entered the workforce in greater numbers. The most challenging part for mothers—the contradiction she refers to in her title—is that outsize expectations leave working women in what has been called "the crosshairs of two incompatible ideals: the unencumbered worker and the ever-present mother."

Erica in Portland looks at it this way: "I am so grateful that moms who work and work full-time are not as demonized as they once were, but I feel there is now the pressure to work AND be a super mom. The social events, soccer teams, play dates, birthday parties and presents, etcetera are definitely not necessary, but they have become the norm in my peer group. It seems to be a vicious cycle. We're all so busy and tired all of the time, but so much of this is self-imposed. I need to stop drinking the Kool-Aid and see what happens." Research out of Ohio State suggests that what happens is this: When parents both set and live up to their own benchmarks of parenting, as opposed to adhering to societal ones, they feel more satisfaction with family life.

In her interviews with women, Hays found that no mother is spared the Kool-Aid, no matter her age or race or class or ethnicity (except maybe the French, depending on whom you ask). While a working-class woman may not have the resources for so-called concerted cultivation—for karate or test prep or a

piano, never mind the lessons—she nonetheless "makes financial sacrifices on behalf of her children. She devotes a good deal
of time and attention to making sure that her children are well
fed, well dressed, and well behaved. She firmly believes that her
children's well-being is far more important than her own convenience."

Sociologist Cameron Macdonald expands on this: "Even
mothers who lack the financial resources, time, flexibility (or
sleep) to approximate the at-home mother will go to great
lengths to produce the image of the at-home mother. They
produce the image because in addition to being accountable to
others they are accountable to themselves and to the ideal of
motherhood they hold."

Carissa in Seattle told me, "Part of me feeds off of this cra-
ziness of being super mommy. I'm rushing home from court to
get the library book that my first-grader cried about forgetting
at home, and I'm picking up the class fish that she wants to take
home for the summer in the middle of my workday. I do every
well-child check. In February, you're going, 'What's the summer
plan?' Men are not thinking about that. The child care plan for
next fall, are the forms in, it's all crazy. A lot of other things fall
by the wayside."

We are both taken aback by and reluctantly impressed with
our own efforts. One recent morning I found myself taking a
picture of the weekday breakfast I had routinely been making
for my kids (from-scratch oatmeal-applesauce pancakes for
Tess; eggs over easy, a pan-fried potato, and cut strawberries
for Liv). I wasn't planning to show anyone. I just wanted doc-
umentation. The novelist Laura Lippman noted on Twitter in
2018, "When my biography is written (or my obit) (if either is

written) I would like it to begin with the morning that I got up at 6 and made mayo because I could not bear to give daughter a dry turkey sandwich for camp lunch."

In *Unequal Childhoods: Class, Race and Family Life*, Annette Lareau found that while class determined the specifics of what parents deemed best for their kids (and, of course, the material advantages they were able to offer them), still, across-categories mothers expressed a tangential awareness of and adherence to the basic tenets of intensive mothering. Sociologist Anita Garey interviewed working-class mothers, who, like all others, emphasized their awareness of the import of acting in accordance with the "dominant-culture conceptions of mother-appropriate activities."

Hays pins the tenacity and ubiquity of intensive mothering ideology on our cultural ambivalence about unencumbered self-interest in pursuit of financial gain, the flip side of that coin. It can be balanced only by a class of people who put their own interests last in every single possible regard. As French feminist philosopher Élisabeth Badinter has written, "The tyranny of maternal duty . . . has thus far produced neither a matriarchy nor sexual equality, but rather a regression in women's status. We have agreed to this regression in the name of moral superiority, the love we bear for our children, and some ideal notion of child rearing, all of which are proving far more effective than external constraints. . . . The best allies of men's dominance have been, quite unwittingly, innocent infants."

Historian Jodi Vandenberg-Daves says, "It's an ideology that exploits the sacrifices that women have shown themselves willing to make for their kids. Our neoliberal economy makes it so hard for parents, and we're exploiting those sacrifices in many different ways, in terms of what's expected of women in terms of holding it together while rent goes up and social programs get cut."

Quiz Alert: Are You an Intensive Mother?

Throughout the early years of the twenty-first century, the study of intensive mothering was largely anecdotal, based on interviews. Developmental psychologist Holly Schiffrin and her colleagues at the University of Mary Washington in Virginia wanted to parse the impact of the ideology on large swaths of women. "We were struggling with these issues ourselves. Why is there so much pressure on mothers? We wanted to quantify it," Schiffrin said. So they developed a fifty-six-question measure they called the Intensive Parenting Attitudes Questionnaire.

"We talk about parents, but when we say 'parent,' people think 'mother,'" she explained.

Each question addressed one of five dimensions, and I'll use those dimensions here to give you a bastardized version of the thing. Let's call it a quiz. On a scale from one to five, where one is "strongly disagree" and five is "strongly agree," rate the following statements:

1. Women are uniquely qualified to be primary parents.
2. There is no more pleasurable job than raising children.
3. A mother should constantly strive to optimize her child's brain development.
4. Motherhood is the most challenging job in the world.
5. Mothers should tailor their lives to revolve around their children.

Tally up your score. It will range from 5 to 25. The more Kool-Aid you have consumed, the higher your number will be.

Schiffrin and colleagues administered their questionnaire to 181 mothers of children five and under, along with a handful of measures of mental health. They found that intensive mothering beliefs and life satisfaction are inversely correlated—as one goes up, the other goes down. Women who agreed that mothers alone have a special talent for parenting felt less supported and more overwhelmed. These respondents also reported feeling generally dissatisfied and unable to cope. Women who strongly agreed that motherhood is extremely challenging also felt less satisfied, and more stressed and depressed. Finally, child-centeredness (mothers should tailor their lives to revolve around their children) predicted lower life satisfaction.

Schiffrin wondered, "If intensive mothering is related to so many negative mental health outcomes, why do women do it?" She told me, "I don't know who raised the bar, but once it gets raised, there's anxiety that if you don't go along, your child will be left behind. Other kids will have an advantage. My daughter had to do a diorama in first or second grade. When I went to her classroom for conferences, I saw dioramas I couldn't have done myself. I thought, Is she going to get an F? How can she compete? Her project wasn't as good as the others because hers was done by a seven-year-old. I try to find a balance, to resist. But it's hard not to buy in to it when everyone else is doing it."

With her example, Schiffrin demonstrates how the line blurs between intensive mothering and helicopter parenting. The much-maligned helicopter parent (and when I say "parent," I mean "mother") hovers over a child and, later, young adult to ensure that she never fails at anything—from crossing the monkey bars to writing a term paper. Intensive mothering can cover that ground, but its objective is a different matter. An intensive mother is not working primarily to assure her child's absolute success but to establish her own goodness as a mom—at what is, after all, the most important thing. A good mother, it has been said, is in the mother-appropriate place at the mother-appropriate time.

Schiffrin studies both helicopter parenting and intensive mothering. She's found that while the former is bad for kids, the latter is mostly bad for mothers, who then of course are shorter with their kids. Brigid Schulte, whose husband chose beer over helping with Thanksgiving meal prep, remembered staying up until two a.m. one February night, making cupcakes for her kids' Valentine's Day parties. "The next day, I was a complete bitch to my children because I was so tired. Who was I baking those cupcakes for? What was important there? I was doing it for the mommy police, as if they were watching me."

It's hard to fight the feeling that they are. Working mothers may be the most vulnerable to anxiety about those police—to imagining they must compensate for time not spent in service to their children. As a result, they sign up for what Nebraska comedians Kristin Hensley and Jen Smedley call "momming so hard" in order to make up for pursuing interests of their own. Christine in Illinois said, "When we first moved to the suburbs, it was a culture shock. There were not as many full-time working moms. I was self-conscious. I wanted my kids and us to be accepted. Moms sent home organic treats and homemade whatever, the best crafts I've ever seen. So when it came time to do Valentines, I thought we better really do them. I didn't feel like I could just buy the ninety-nine-cent Pokémon box. I had to make them by hand. Now I'm trying to see where I feel comfortable cutting corners."

A 2018 *Parents* magazine headline epitomized the rhetoric that mothers find themselves subject to: "Hilary Duff Doesn't Feel Guilty About 'Me Time' (And You Shouldn't Either!)." The assumption embroiled there does not need much unpacking. The article itself, like the many it resembles, makes clear that actress Duff's "me time" is laudable only in the context of her properly intensive mothering. Full-time working mothers traded in demonization for prostrating themselves before their children for all the world to see.

In an article that purports to be about self-care, the writer uses the bulk of her allotted word count to report that Duff teaches her son about philanthropy, takes him waterskiing, plays tag with him to the point of exhaustion, ventures out with him in the rain for the explicit purpose of jumping in puddles, plays with toys, makes cookies, and builds forts. Only once Duff's maternal bona fides have been established may we celebrate the fact that she doesn't feel guilty for reading "one chapter of a book while Luca plays Legos in the next room." In exchange for all those forts, there is your culturally sanctioned "me time." Party on.

Arizona State psychologist Suniya Luthar has done work similar to Holly Schiffrin's. Luthar has found that the presumed guilt *Parents* magazine is (not really) trying to absolve you of is linked to maternal distress. So is "role overload," the outgrowth of momming so hard. Luthar's research goes a step further, investigating resilience and the adjustment to these challenges. She found that the women who managed motherhood most adaptively had strong relationships with other adults. These women reported feeling unconditional acceptance, comfort from loved ones, authenticity in relationships, and partner and/or friendship satisfaction. Luthar wrote, "These findings are extremely encouraging in showing the strong protective potential of close, authentic relationships in buffering women through the myriad challenges of motherhood." Her conclusion reminded me of something an older male professor told my class during grad school: "It's the mother's job to take care of the baby, and father's job to take care of the mother." Before I had kids, this struck me as benignly sexist. Now it also feels incomplete. Because what is a father taking care of a mother if it is not also taking care of the child?

But here is where we lose them: Fathers do not swim in our water. In fact, as the traditional pressure on men to be primary breadwinners has lifted, the traditional pressure on women to be primary caretakers has not. George often sees my prioritization of our kids' needs as absurd. He's nice about it. "You're a very good mommy," he's taken to saying, and I am startled by how much I like to hear it.

On the other hand, his almost unflagging focus on his own needs feels equally outlandish to me, and my response is often testier. "I'm going to go get an espresso when we get home," he says in the car late one Sunday afternoon on the way back from our family lice recheck as I am planning dinner in my head. I pause before responding with language we learned in couples therapy: "I'd prefer it if you took the kids to the playground while I cook." He complies but with some irritation, because really, he feels no more compelled to meet my parenting standards than he does to give up carbohydrates to fit into his oldest jeans. If his pants get tight, he buys a bigger pair. If there's an hour before dinner, he plants the kids in front of the television. If he wants an espresso, he goes off and gets himself one.

"My ex can sleep through the kids saying 'Daddy, I'm hungry,'" Nancy, thirty-eight, who works in communications in Las Vegas, told me. "I can't."

Erica in Portland said, "I wonder if my husband and I just have different expectations. He'd be okay if they didn't go to birthday parties. I want them to have fun things to do. And I want to spend time with them. I don't want to sit on my phone with them while they watch TV. I don't know whether he has the same desire. If I lowered my expectations, perhaps I'd feel less resentful."

It's hard to relax into that if one is a woman, living in a culture that purports to celebrate motherhood while actually propagating ineffable standards. We are no longer demonized for working. In exchange, we prostrate ourselves before our children for all the world to see. We beckon our partners to join us. They have no interest in dadding so hard. Yana in California told me, "I think men tend to be more relaxed. They don't think well ahead or foresee problems. If a problem happens, they handle it, but so far as it hasn't happened, they're free to do something else until it does. Women are more proactive. We don't let kids eat too much sugar or watch too much TV. We're in hyperprevention mode. A lot of times guys look at us and go, 'You just make up all this unnecessary work for me.' And we feel like they are not caring enough or involved enough." Heather, thirty-nine, a lawyer and mother of a four-year-old in Las Vegas, was more blunt: "Men are lazy and have lower standards." I couldn't help but think: Might it not be nice to try that?

Boston College psychologist and psychoanalyst Usha Tummala-

Narra put it more gently: "I know it can be very frustrating. Mothers think, How come you don't feel this? And I think a lot of fathers wonder, Why do you have to do this so intensely? When one parent is attuned to the needs of the child and responds in that way, and the other parent holds the capacity for letting go, the two are in different psychological positions and need to learn from each other—how to nurture and how to let go. Both are necessary." Women might relax their standards, but only alongside partners who are working to raise theirs, who are stalwart in their own commitment to the role of being half in charge.

Controlling, Type-A Moms and Bumbling, Breadwinning Dads

With all the pressure on women to rejoice in puddle jumping in the rain, mothers might be forgiven for giving their male partners a hard time about half-hearted fathering. When a boy is carelessly dressed by his dad, it's the mother who gets a gently chiding text about the getup from the school. The conversation around women's supposed tendency to critique men's parenting work is often reduced to this: If your male partner doesn't do his share, it's probably for the best, because you are so controlling. That's what a mom friend of mine told me years ago when I lamented wanting more at home from George. "Oh, you wouldn't really allow that," she said in a just-between-us-girls whisper. "You wouldn't be satisfied with the way he did things, and you'd just end up arguing about it. It's better in the end the way it is." My friend was then a (recently laid-off) stay-at-home mother, living a life of separate spheres. When she was in the other room changing a diaper, her husband, whom I never saw change a diaper, liked to grumble to me that my friend had forgotten how exhausting it was to work. They had two kids under four at the time. He somehow imagined I'd be sympathetic to his experience. The interactions warmed me to neither of them.

My friend's wisdom was part of the water. Dads are incompetent, and moms are intolerant. It's the stuff of old commercials and lazy sitcoms. It's also got a name in academia, and that name is maternal gatekeeping. There is this gate around children, and mothers police it, keeping hapless fathers out. Or, rather, it is maternal characteristics that hinder paternal involvement. Per the literature, gatekeeping is "a collection of beliefs and behaviors that ultimately inhibit a collaborative effort between men and women in family work," and "a phenomena that either encourages or discourages fathers from acting on their paternal identity." If your baby daddy doesn't do that much, rest assured it is your fault.

Vidya in L.A., whose husband does all the cooking and cleaning while she cares for their son, has seen how this can work. Her husband gets tense when she tries to roast a chicken. She does not roast it the way he likes. "Women need to chill out. My husband and women need to chill out about things being done well. If you don't want to do everything, you can't say, 'This is exactly how you need to do this.' It has an impact. You're digging your own grave. Even if dinner is terrible. Women in my mothers' group take photos of bad dinners their husbands make and post them online. It's discouraging. It's understandable that you want to feel better in the moment. But it's such a self-fulfilling narrative."

The study of gatekeeping behavior has found that the way women feel about their partner's domestic role may impact men's involvement. A mother's beliefs and attitudes aren't the whole story, but they do have a moderating affect. One 2005 study out of the University of Illinois at Urbana–Champaign determined that a father's perception of himself as a highly committed parent manifested in high father accessibility only when his wife believed that he should play a significant role. On the other hand, a father's perception of his parenting commitment was not significantly related to his involvement when mothers reported more traditional beliefs.

Complicating the matter further is the chicken-or-the-egg question. Are fathers holding back because mothers convey that they should, or do mothers with partners who hold back arrive at the convenient conclusion that fathering is best done in moderation? A 2008 study out of Ohio State seemed to suggest the latter. It found that when fathers held egalitarian values, mothers were more likely to facilitate their participation.

An Israeli study in the same year determined that the typical female gatekeeper was characterized by low self-esteem, a strong feminine gender identification, and a salient maternal identity. A 2015 study by Ohio State's Sarah Schoppe-Sullivan and her colleagues likewise determined that maternal expectations and psychological functioning were better predictors of gatekeeping than gender attitudes. Mothers with perfectionistic standards, unstable romantic relationships, and poorer prenatal mental health were more likely to close the gate on their children's fathers. For their part, less confident fathers also seemed to invite more gate closing on the part of their partners.

To illustrate maternal gatekeeping, Ohio State sociologist

Claire Kamp Dush shows her undergraduates videos of couples interacting with their babies. "A grad student comes in and says, 'Here's a onesie. Someone undress the baby, someone dress her. You decide who does what.' Men will get the baby, put down the baby, take off the baby's clothes. Mom has a mortified look on her face. She tells him where the snaps are. She's telling him what to do. He's playing with the baby. She grabs the baby. Is she bossing him around because he isn't doing it right or because he never does it? Is he doing a bad job because he never does it because he's rejected this kind of caretaking, or is he doing a bad job because she's always standing over him telling him what to do? Society puts all of the pressure of having perfect children on women. We translate that into micromanaging men's parenting. It's not our fault, exactly. It's society's fault." Sociologist Sharon Hays writes that maternal behavior is ". . . neither a choice made by women nor a symbol of love and progress in society; rather, it is an indication of the power of men, whites, the upper classes, capitalists and state leaders to impose a particular form of family life on those less powerful than themselves."

UK author Rebecca Asher concurs. In *Shattered: Modern Motherhood and the Illusion of Equality*, she writes, "'Shell-shocked by the realization that the childrearing will be largely left to us, mothers become brittle and standoffish. The parenting efforts of men are routinely mocked and derided, with snarky comments about their ineptitude. . . . [T]his permitted and infectious caricaturing of men is a coping mechanism for women who have thrown in the towel on equality. . . . Gatekeeping is not the prime mover for pushing men out of the home: they were on the periphery or absent anyway. But it exacerbates a situation that already exists."

The women I spoke with acknowledged some micromanaging of their children's dads. Molly, the foster care worker in Tennessee, said, "I do sometimes wonder if we disempower our partners. I'm kind of a perfectionist. I want it done the right way. I take his power away. And so I wonder, as a strong female, if that doesn't play in to this. But I also watch more laid-back women, and I see the same situation."

Natalie, from the suburbs of Los Angeles, said, "My husband, unless he gets cues from me, he'll just be doing his own thing. This morning I'm rattling off what's happening after school, and he's like, 'Where is their practice?' And I'm like, 'I don't know, you have to look it up!' But then I know it's easier if I just take care of it, so I look it up. I enable him, but for my own sanity. For our own sanity, we take control."

Courtney, thirty-four, a teacher in Atlanta with a two-year-old, said, "I see women who want things done their way, so they just do it. I see my husband doing things different a lot, and I try to correct him only if it's necessary."

Others have felt similarly compelled to rein in the impulse to keep the gate. Laura, the business owner in New York City, told me, "Before my son was born, I went to this class, and they said, 'If your spouse is not harming the child, do not say a word.' If they are not changing the diaper the way you would do it, you shut up and let them help. I've adopted that."

The story of maternal gatekeeping is more complicated than the easy parable of the uptight, type A mom. As Kamp Dush acknowledged, it's hard to draw clear lines between a father's passive refusal and a mother's active constraint. Women who can't count on their partners to execute their duties in good faith may feel little choice but to keep the gate. Yana, the mother of three young boys in California, said, "I want us to be on time. I don't want the kids to be late for school. If a teacher complains that our kid was sleeping in class because he's not well rested, I care about that, and I want to fix it. I care about those things, so I have to be the one to be on top of them."

Laura in New York said, "I'll be out of town for work, and I'll call my husband at ten at night, and our son, who is four, is still up. And I'll say, 'Why is he awake?' And my husband answers, 'He told me he wasn't tired.' If I suggest to him that this isn't acceptable, am I nitpicking, or am I asking him to behave like a responsible adult? It's hard putting a kid to bed when he doesn't want to go. Accepting that our son is not tired is a good excuse. It's complete self-absorption. They prioritize themselves."

Ohio State's Schoppe-Sullivan is one of the leading researchers on maternal gatekeeping. I raise the issue of mother blaming when we talk. It's a concern she's heard before. "That's the criticism I experience in my work. But if you just say fathers need to do more, it doesn't recognize that we all exist within systems. Multiple people in families need to change in order for us to get unstuck and move toward greater equality. Including children. My daughter thinks only Mom can do certain things. It bugs me that she's gotten this message. In some circumstances, it may be true, but that's a fraction of the things that she comes to me with. And yes, fathers need to step up, to consider whether what they do is best for their child's development. But then what if a father gets more involved and a mother feels threatened? If she lets go, she can lose the only source of validation she's getting from the outside world." She is sympathetic to that conundrum. Schoppe-Sullivan believes that excessive criticism and controlling behavior can grow out of a mother's concern about losing maternal standing, the one thing a woman who's borne children might reliably feel valued for.

In *Opting In: Having a Child Without Losing Yourself*, Third Wave Fund co-founder Amy Richards writes, "Just saying 'parenting' rather than 'mothering' can threaten some women—and it can also be seen as disrespectful to those who see mothering as their primary identity. Some mothers have reclaimed 'mother' because using 'parent' felt dishonest—it was leading people to believing that the tasks and responsibilities were mutually handled, thus rendering their work less visible. . . . Not everyone believes that women are as smart or as strong as men, but a woman's maternal instincts are rarely questioned; therefore women hold on tight to that responsibility."

There is no socially recognized model of a mother who is a secondary caregiver. Danielle in Boston knows this because she is one. Her husband is around more, and he and their daughter have the tighter bond. Danielle says, "On one hand, I'm happy they're as close as they are. On the other hand, I don't really belong to the mom club. There's the feeling of being the odd one out. It brings up anxiety for me. Am I doing what I'm supposed to be doing? There are all these messages out there. In TV shows. In how people interact. Even after Jeff has taken Nora to play two or three times with someone, even if he's connected with the moms, they'll still email me and only me about birthday parties. The school calls me rather than him. I notice it a lot because our roles are reversed. All those things communicate that I'm the one who's supposed to be in charge."

Having stepped out of bounds, Danielle experiences unease. Sociologist Lisa Wade believes that men feel similarly on the other side. She says, "When push comes to shove, men want to be an equal part of children's lives, but not more than they want to be successful at work. Their identity as breadwinner is more important to them than their identity as an egalitarian parent. I think men still have a really difficult time imagining themselves as parents first and workers second. Women have seen themselves that way for a long time."

For her 2005 book, *Competing Devotions: Career and Family Among Women Executives*, Mary Blair-Loy looked at three cohorts of highly educated, high-achieving women forced to decide which role came first. Many of the successful older women she interviewed had eschewed children or spouses altogether, assuming they could not have both families and careers. In the younger generation, Loy watched women with kids struggle to choose between two options: that of devoted worker or that of devoted mother.

While parenthood and work satisfaction need not necessarily be in conflict, Loy notes, the intensive mothering and intensive working standards that dominate our culture often are. She writes, "If it were just a question of survival, families and companies would not demand so much of their members. The devotion to work and the devotion to family schemas are institutionalized: they create taken-for-granted rules of thought and behavior in everyday life." Loy's so-called devotion to work schema valorizes intense career commitment and dedication to one's job or earnings. The devotion to family schema demands that primary commitments remain with family and children. The stereotypes of the type A mother and the bumbling father are underscored by the gendered devotion to family and devotion to work ideals. Taken for granted in the social order, these roles acquire the air of the inevitable, with hardly an alternative to be found.

When actual lives diverge from the schemas, some research suggests that men and women feel the pull to declare fidelity to traditional postures. In the 1990s and 2000s, family researchers in the U.S. found that women who outearned their husbands were doing more housework or a greater share of housework than other women. The findings were understood to evidence so-called gender deviance neutralization, or the attempt to exaggerate gender-typical behaviors in order to offset atypical ones.

In 2004, a close look at families in the U.S. and Sweden found that men who earned as much as their wives did more housework than men who earned less than their wives. A 2012 study proposed that it was no longer a woman's greater income that predicted attempts to neutralize gender deviance but, rather, whether she worked in a predominantly male field. In 2015, University of Southern California sociologist Jennifer Hook compared time-use diaries to other kinds of self-reports about housework. From her comparison, she concluded that "gender deviants" were not actually spending any more or less time on housework; they were simply reporting their contributions in ways that hewed closer to gendered norms.

In 2013, a study of seven countries (Cameroon, Chad, Egypt, India, Kenya, Nigeria, and the UK) determined that women "ease the stress" their higher earning caused by doing more women's work at home. That study's authors conclude: "A woman's earning may seem like a burden rather than a gift to her husband. . . . In a society in which breadwinning is a social representation of manhood, wives whose husbands are not good providers often submit to their husbands' dominance because they feel guilty for contributing to [his] sense of failure."

While careful handling of the male ego might (or might not) go down smoothly in Cameroon, it's difficult on the coasts. The comedian Ali Wong answers "with a snap in her voice" when she is asked "with a note of concern" how her husband feels about her success: "He feels great. It's not hard to feel good about your spouse making money."

Laura, whose New York City business is the source of most of her family's income, tells me, "My husband is resentful of my professional success. When he lost his job, he finally agreed to come to one of my networking events, a cocktail hour with high-level people with big jobs. It just made him sad that he didn't have what I had. Instead of saying, 'I'm really proud of you,' he said that it made him sad." The two shy away from discussions about how much money Laura is making. "We don't talk about it," she says. "He knows how much I'm bringing home, but not how well the business is doing at all times. I told him at the end of the year last year that I'd had a good year, but I don't talk about it throughout the year. I'm protecting his self-esteem. I don't hide my success—I just talk about it in other places." Laura is not an outlier.

Psychologist Francine Deutsch's fieldwork with dual-earner couples led her to ask, "If men get praised for changing diapers, why don't women get praised for earning money? In the economy of gratitude, money doesn't do much for women. Women are as likely to have to apologize for their incomes as to be appreciated for them."

Clearly, it requires some mental gymnastics on the part of

women and men to restore an ephemeral rightful order to lives that are not quite traditional. Mothers control and fathers bumble. Fathers earn and mothers take care. Families agree to see a mother's employment as less essential than her parenting, even when she's an equal or greater earner. "It's nice that your mother makes money, but really, it's just extra," I remember my father, a lawyer in the public sector, saying to my sister and me when we were kids. It seemed a point of pride for him. And I heard it as the gender rule it was. I made careless financial choices in my twenties because of this message, which in truth came from everywhere. Why would a young woman bother to save when she'd someday have a man to do it for her? "It is so hard to give up the illusion that someone will always take care of us," Betty Friedan has said. Gender rules are rock, paper, and scissors to economically rational behavior. In Blair-Loy's study, it was always the woman who left the workforce to care for children regardless of which half of the couple was earning more.

Women and men also characterize their professional responsibilities through a gendered lens. In her study of 150 dual-income couples, Deutsch found that no matter a woman's profession, husbands and wives described her job as more flexible. In one pair she spent time with, the wife was a doctor, the husband a professor. In another, the genders of those occupations were reversed. Both couples independently explained that the wives' professions allowed them more leeway at work. Gretchen, forty, a mother of two and a reporter in Baltimore, is often on deadline but nevertheless told me, "My job is more flexible." Her husband works for an event planning company. When I asked her to say more about their relative flexibility, she went on, "I guess, you know, it's interesting. Women will be flexible when they need to be. And men hope that others are flexible. I work at an NPR news station. If I finish a story after the kids go to bed, my editor is understanding. But my husband has clients that are going bananas. I could say I'm not going to be flexible, or that I can't be, but it would make things very difficult."

Deutsch said, "I had somebody else in the post office telling me his job was so inflexible. Then it came out that a woman in his office had worked out her hours around her child care. Men are less willing to ask." As Deutsch writes in *Halving It All*, flexibility is in the eye of the beholder. And we see it in the glimmer of each mother's watchful gaze.

Can Women Father?

Contemporary mothering ideologies leave us with the idea that women must naturally and joyfully eviscerate all personhood for the sake of those they love so fiercely. This is what the poet Adrienne Rich refers to as "the invisible violence of the institution of motherhood." Intensive mothering is in the way—a thorny living thing between us and the nongendered parenting we'd like to live to see. It is the fantasy delivery system for what anthropologist Sarah Hrdy has called 24-hour lifelong shifts of unconditional love.

Intensive mothering directs mothers, and not fathers, to constantly strive to optimize every opportunity for their children, to tailor every move to meet their needs. We leave fathers in our dust, and they do not protest. I am not suggesting here that women be more like men. That is a model whose time has long since passed. But recall that fathers' time in child care has increased, and that mothers have failed to adjust with a correspondent downshift in what they themselves have taken on. Was this a missed opportunity? A chance to redistribute the 65 percent? The ideology makes that hard. Erica in Portland said, "I have a 'healthy' dose of mom guilt, the constant feeling that I'm not doing enough or doing it well enough. If I did less, I can only imagine I would have more of that."

Mothers in overdrive are an impediment to equity, but more so is the throbbing belief at the heart of the whole impossible system, the idea that women are better able to rear children. ("As if there were any other job on earth for which you'd argue that one half of the population as varied as it may be was uniquely qualified!" sociologist Kathleen Gerson said.) No evidence supports this, and some even contradicts it: In studies of single-parent families in the late 1990s, the sex of that parent was shown to be unrelated to the children's well-being. I'm not suggesting here that women be more like men. In our current state, few families would function well. I am suggesting, rather, that moms be more like dads. That mothers, like their partners, revere the fact that the child has another parent, and that their relationship is sacrosanct. Mothers—and here's Hrdy again—are an easily acquired taste. But they need not be the single, solo most important thing. Maybe that's an honor best shared by two.

Said Schoppe-Sullivan, "We can move toward equality and involved fathers, but not to the point where we can accept the fact that mothers and fathers are interchangeable for children. People don't really believe that. There's implicit bias, no matter what people say in surveys."

The widespread belief in mother knows best—the reigning philosophy among parents across class lines—must be over-written if gender equity in the family is ever to take hold. Its grip helps to explain why norms have shifted outside the family but remain powerful inside it. Parenting is both so private and so public. We hold ourselves accountable for its proper perfor-mance and risk condemnation if we go off script.

Those scripts are intimate and increasingly visible. In 2014, Pew Research found that 75 percent of parents in the U.S. use social media. Of those, 80 percent of mothers and 65 percent of fathers agree that they receive parenting support from their networks. Women bowing to the cultural prescriptions of the times also often appear to be using the medium to present evi-dence of their Herculean parenting efforts in beautiful pictorial displays or fifteen-second videos. Facebook and Instagram have become outlets for mothers who love to mother to share their love of mothering with the world. And they often have tens of thousands of followers (click here to shop the collection).

A 2014 survey of two thousand mothers by the website Baby-Centre found that Facebook was driving mothers in their thirties to "new levels of competitiveness." Publisher Mike Fogarty said, "The word 'competitive' came up time and time again when we asked millennial mums to sum up their experience of mother-hood. The pressure to be perceived to be an alpha mummy has rocketed since they all signed up to Facebook. Some said they felt [pressured] to go to baby swimming classes or baby sing-ing and music classes because they felt if they didn't they were looked upon as a bad parent." Social psychologist Lisa Lazard at the Open University in the UK interviewed mothers about their social media behavior and found that social demands placed on parents (and to be clear, when she says "parent," she means "mother") drive public expressions of pride in their children. She concluded, "Social media becomes one way parents can visually demonstrate how they are meeting these parenting demands." It can also be another task for mothers. In one survey, 87 percent of moms report that it is their job alone to share photos online for extended family to enjoy.

Schoppe-Sullivan, Kamp Dush, and colleagues at Ohio State also looked at the impact of Facebook but restricted their sample to new mothers. They surveyed 127 women from the Midwest with Facebook accounts to see how "New mothers, in particular, may use Facebook to practice behaviors that align with their mothering identity and meet broader societal expectations, or in other words, to do motherhood." They asked: Are individual differences in new mothers' psychological characteristics associated with their use and experiences of Facebook? And are these psychological characteristics associated with greater risk for depressive symptoms via their experiences on the site? Analysis of the data found that mothers concerned with external validation and those who believed that society holds them to excessively high standards were more active on Facebook; they also responded more strongly to the comments they received there. Mothers who were perfectionistic and prone to seeking external validation experienced increases in depressive symptoms the more time they spent online, where images of hard momming live on in perpetuity.

We're rewarded with likes and positive regard when we "do gender normatively." Even in Scandinavian countries, where work-family policies are engineered specifically to foster gender-equitable work-life balance, the ideology of intensive mothering encourages maternal sacrifice—and has shown inimitable resolve. In France, where women have largely refused to take up the ideology, they have the benefit of their unique history, of a long-standing recognition of their extramaternal identities. Most everywhere else, as Deutsch explained to me, "Someone might believe in a theoretical way that men and women should be equal but still believe that mothers hold a special place in a child's life that can't be duplicated by fathers. A number of things go along with that, like the belief that mothers have a special ability to nurture. And deep down, women believe it is their responsibility. They don't feel it's fundamentally a shared responsibility."

The position we are in is not our fault, exactly. As Kamp Dush says, it's society's fault. The psychoanalyst and podcaster Tracy Morgan has expanded on this idea. Describing a female patient's retelling of a difficult morning (her babysitter had canceled as she was supposed to leave for the dentist), Morgan recounted: "[She said,] 'I never think to even ask my husband if he would come home from work and watch our child so I can make it to the dentist. What's wrong with me that I don't think to ask him? It's so stupid of me.' Her attack on herself was very difficult to sit with but also very common—this turning a situation that we could understand as institutionally arranged, as politically arranged, and personalizing it, and saying, 'This is just me. What's wrong with me?'"

The particularly American ideal of nuclear-family self-sufficiency (as opposed to the one where it takes a village) requires an intensive parent, and then all that can follow are the gender inequities inherent in that setup. Women who stay in their rightful place can take pleasure in the stereotype of the strong woman—selfless, nurturing, supportive—the one who undergirds her family's success. Men don't make this easy to set askew. Erica says, "My son comes home from school every day with a folder with a homework sheet and notes from the teacher. I look at it every night. I went out of town for work. I asked my husband to make sure he did his homework and put it in his backpack. My husband didn't do it. He tells me, 'I don't think of things, you have to remind me.' But I lay things out for him, and they still do not happen." And women, despite their resentment, can't always envision giving up the honor. They hesitate to do what fathers have long been able to do: revere the fact that the child has another parent, and that the relationship is sacrosanct.

Nicole in Portland said, "I'm not sure I would ever give up being the primary parent. The unconditional love is very, very addictive. I like the idea of being irreplaceable. I can be replaced in my job and even in my marriage. No one can replace a loving mother."

Christine in Illinois said, "I feel a sense of accomplishment and pride in being the primary parent and being a supermom. I never anticipated that, but since the responsibility arose, I've given a hundred percent, and now I just own it. When I was pregnant with my first, I was actually really reluctant about any identity change with regard to being a mom. If my husband had stepped into the role, I may very well have welcomed that. However, since he didn't, I went full in. Now, seven years later, I find so much self-worth in my role as a mom, even though it can still feel like too much or unfair, even though there is still resentment."

Like all labor, the job of most important is divided with some difficulty. To give up one's primacy is not effortless, no matter if it's a privilege fraught with strain. It's hard to admit, though I know it to be true, that I relish being my daughters' best parent (they adore George, but adoration is no substitute for need). If George had stepped into the role, I may very well have welcomed that, but when he did not I ceded sleep, leisure time, and a feeling of fairness in my home for the fantasy that my daughters would choose me first, love me most. Too often my husband absents himself, and then I've also responded by closing him out—not with criticism but with omnipresence. With chocolate chip pancakes and ponytails and dance parties and *Friends* binges. The data supports this contention of scholars, that we must challenge the perception that women are inherently better at parenting in order for things to change. But what will we be giving up when we do?

Men, for their part, don't seem to get quite what they are missing. April, the New Yorker raising two children with her wife, was the secondary parent when her kids were first born, and remembers the experience like this: "When Jill was primary-parenting, I felt so restricted. I felt like the sidekick, the fifth wheel. They were moving in a groove together, and I was left flailing behind."

Mothers and fathers may both have something to lose when men become co–primary parents. But likewise, there is so much that they'll gain.

CHAPTER 6

Successful Male Resistance

Gaslight

☑ Social scientists suggest that the last decades' slow change in child care participation by men should not be mistaken for egalitarian achievement but, rather, understood as "a largely successful male resistance." Do not ask why change is so slow; instead, ask why men are resisting. "The short answer is that it is in men's interest to do so," sociologist Scott Coltrane has written. That resistance "reinforces a separation of spheres that underpins masculine ideals and perpetuates a gender order privileging men over women." The vigil of the privileged to maintain a crumbling contract—the sordid, steely mission of our times. In marriage, this requires a stalwart commitment to denial of the obvious: that men simply feel entitled to our labor.

The glow of this entitlement shines so bright. Christine in Illinois told me, "My husband is a participatory and willing partner. He's not traditional in terms of 'I don't change diapers.' But his attention is limited. I remember this profound moment where I had asked him to put the car seat back in my car after it had been in the shop, and he was like, 'I promise I'll do it.' I moved on to other things I had to do. When I went to take my son to school in the morning, the car seat wasn't there. I said to [my husband], 'It's great if you want to help, but I'm juggling balls, and if I throw you one and you drop it, I might as well be doing everything myself.' We'd have these discussions: 'Can you take the balls and keep the balls? It's draining me.' I can't trust him to do anything, to actually remember."

Sometimes a cigar is not just a cigar, and forgetting is not just forgetting. To employ "limited attention" is to announce that one cannot be bothered, and when the task must ultimately be completed by someone, the forgetter is asserting his right to fail to attend. Who has the leeway to forget in parenthood? Who bears the ultimate strain of that thoughtlessness?

As my kids got older, it was male forgetting that irked me most in my own relationship. Last summer, after spending chunks of the year taking charge of all that was required to get both girls signed up for camp, I realized I was missing Liv's medical form. With two months to go, I asked George to take care of it. He agreed he would. One month later, I checked in. He hadn't gotten around to it yet. The week before the deadline for medical forms, I asked again. "I've been thinking about doing that," George offered. "I'll walk over to the office this weekend." That is not how getting forms from the doctor's office works. The very fact that he did not know this as he approached his second decade of fatherhood was in itself endemic of the problem. As had so often been the case, enlisting his participation had turned into more trouble than it was worth. I called the office and requested the form. They told me it would be ready in five to seven days. Seven days later, I hiked over and retrieved it. "I got Liv's medical form," I texted George, not that he'd seemed concerned. Indeed, had I never mentioned it again, the very notion of that form would have vanished in the murk. I texted wanting an acknowledgment of his forgetting, a commitment to doing better next time. An apology would also have been nice. Instead, he wrote back, "Oh great, thanks." Déjà vu all over again.

The kids' needs have changed since Tess was a baby and this all first became a big issue; the girls have gotten easier to manage, at least for this mercifully restful period between complete dependency and adolescence. ("The glory years are when they're both in elementary school," said Nicole in Portland with two high school students. "Then middle school hits, and it's horrible, pre-warning.") The dynamic with my husband barely shifts. Without intention, he continues to perpetuate a gender order that privileges men over women, him over me—and continues to deny that this is so. What changes if you write about this subject is that when you wearily address your frustration with your husband, he will occasionally retort, "Put it in your book!" (Maybe he's just being generous, giving me material.) These days, George also considers what I've said once he's had a little space. Later, after the fight we went on to have about the form, he came home with flowers. He trimmed the stems and put them in a vase on my desk.

"Did it ever enter into the mind of man that woman too had an inalienable right to life, liberty, and the pursuit of her individual happiness?" Elizabeth Cady Stanton asked a male cousin in a letter in 1855.

Are you being unfair to your wife?

It's a question I posed to many fathers—the husbands of

the women I'd spoken with as well as other motley volunteers. Some of them answered in the negative, even those whose wives saw it otherwise. One mother had a lot to say about struggling for her husband's investment. Her husband later told me, "We both worked less when our children were little. That was really good for us. She felt like we were in it together. We were both sacrificing to make that happen. What was negative about that, we were both really stressed out. But I think it paid off. We both know either one of us is willing to sacrifice for the greater good of the family."

It might not surprise you to learn that interviewing men about their division of labor at home proved difficult. While they were generous with their time, it was not an idea that most of the fathers had given much thought, and even under direction, it failed to spark interest. Other women had come up against the same insouciance. Laura in New York City has been unhappy with the division of labor in her marriage since her four-year-old was a newborn. She said, "I've worked hard on identifying how I played a part and tried to fix it. My husband has not put any thought or energy into it even when I said, 'This is kind of a deal breaker for me now.' He got upset and cried and said, 'Oh my God,' but I haven't seen personal work there. He always goes back to this lack of self-awareness." For fathers, it seemed, the issue has never risen to the level of recurrent concern. The gender order works for them. It's nothing to get hot under the collar about. They can resist without doing a thing. They quite literally resist by not doing a thing.

"Nobody gives up privilege voluntarily," neuroscientist Lise Eliot said. "You really have to be very enlightened to do that."

In San Diego, Gabe, thirty-eight, husband of Deanna, who at

the outset of her marriage aspired to a 1950s television fantasy of married life, spoke with slight irritation about what he sees mostly as his wife's uptight nature. "If I'm busy, I use lists, too, but when it comes to my life outside of work, I don't. I carry what our plans are in my head; she writes everything down. She'll wake up anxious on a Saturday morning, which is frustrating to me. I might carry the same ideas about what we need to do, but I'm not going to get myself worked up over it." Fathers balk at mothers' efforts but then also at a lack thereof. Sociologist Annette Lareau recalls observing parents for her book on race, class, and family life, "I found that some fathers were angry that moms signed kids up for so much. 'Why can't we just hang around?' They'd get mad about it. But they'd also get mad if the mom goofed up and the kid missed a deadline for soccer or baseball. Everyone proclaimed it to be Mom's fault."

Jeremy, thirty-seven, in suburban Illinois, had been out with his guy friends the night before our scheduled conversation, and he brought up the topic with the group. He told me that it fell pretty flat. "It didn't become a huge topic of conversation," Jeremy said diplomatically, though one friend did offer that "if it were up to him, his family would just sit around the house. That's his personality. He's never planned anything. Even in high school and college." He resists without doing a thing.

After months of putting it off, I finally sat down to interview George. "We have to do that interview," I kept saying at inopportune moments. If the genesis for this project was a bleak period between us, things had really been much lighter for some time. (See above re: the kids' needs becoming easier to manage. Remember, the research demonstrates that mothers of children under four report the greatest sense of injustice. I began thinking about this project when Tess was three. She was a month shy of six by the time I finished.) I was reluctant to dive back into that old darkness with him, even for the sake of a brief and theoretically academic discussion.

Having myself given our patterns a lot of thought—"Writing toward answers," as feminist author Roxane Gay has called it—I asked George, for the record, what he made of them. "For me, I know I often have a lot on my mind. I work five days a week. We've had other things going on. We had two new people to contend with and think about. I went from having to think about me and you to having to think about a number of people."

He sounded defensive as he spoke, and as was not atypical for me, some trace hostility in his voice shut me down. Nothing he was saying was untrue. But his dilemmas applied equally to me, and I hadn't responded by keeping my head down. Another woman might have had the stamina to remark on this. Characteristically, I did not—I knew it would lead to a fight I didn't want to have. Such inability to pursue my co-parenting goals unabated had certainly gotten in my way over the years. This takes a lot of effort, and the fortitude required for it was apparently more than I'd had.

George went on, "Did I take it for granted that you were doing things? Yes, I suppose I did. But I didn't like the fact that you were doing them and then criticizing me for not doing them. I'd have preferred you just not do it and tell me to do something." I reminded him that he often forgot the things I asked him to take care of, and that having to ask in the first place was just another form of responsibility. "There's probably something about men taking women for granted. Maybe men are much more responsible for that than they would care to think. There's a truth to it," he ultimately allowed.

Here is what I would have preferred to hear from my husband—unequivocally and without shame: "I am sexist." That was the headline of a *New York Times* opinion piece by Emory University philosophy professor George Yancy, who took it upon himself, late in 2018, to implore men to join him "with due diligence and civic duty, and publicly claim: I am sexist," to take responsibility for misogyny and patriarchy. Yancy's sexism "raises its ugly head" in his own marriage. He writes, "I should be thanked when I clean the house, cook, sacrifice my time. These are the deep and troubling expectations that are shaped by male privilege. . . ." I nearly wept in gratitude for his admission. When men deny their sexism, they gaslight their partners, compounding an already painful problem by insisting that its clear and obvious precursors are the imaginings of a hysterical mind.

While Yancy made the unabashed admission of male privilege look easy, not every man can pull that off. One mother I'd interviewed got back in touch to tell me she'd shown Yancy's piece to her husband. "I was really hoping this writer's introspection might get through to him about this thing in our relationship that's been a big problem for me," she explained. Instead she was met with outrage. Her husband proclaimed that they lived as equals, and that patriarchy had no influence on their division of labor with their two young children. "We ended up in the biggest fight we'd ever had," she told me.

I tugged at the sexism thread with the fathers I spoke to. Lowell, thirty-four, in Vermont, married to Miranda, was the only to allow: "The expectation among my male friends is still that they will have the life they had before having kids. I have some degree of that, too. My mom was a professional. She ran her own preschool. To this day, she cooks for my dad. He's barely ever made a meal. I think I've strayed from that. But subconsciously, the thing that makes you motivationally step up and do something when you're not being asked . . . I have justifications. It's a copout."

Copping Out

Because of the inimical success of male resistance, copping out of drudge work remains a viable option if one is a man. This is true not only at home, in relationships based on love, but also at work, where little love is lost. In 2018, a headline in the *Harvard Business Review* teased, "Why Women Volunteer for Tasks That Don't Lead to Promotion." Here's the answer per the research: because someone has to do them, and all the men tend not to, at least not if there are women at the fore. In a series of lab studies, economists Linda Babcock, Maria Recalde, and Lise Vesterlund, along with organizational behaviorist Laurie Weingart, found that women are 50 percent more likely than men to volunteer to take on work that no one else wants to do. Women are also more likely to be asked to perform this work (no matter the sex of the requester), and then to say yes when asked.

In an interview with NPR, Versterlund explained, "The belief or expectation that women will step up to the plate is a pretty important factor in all of this. . . . The reason why [the women are] doing it, at least in our study, appears to be because they're expected to. The men come into the room, they see the women, they know how we play these games. They know that the women are going to volunteer. And the women look around and they see the men and they also know how we play these games. We know that the women are going to be the ones who will raise their hands." In the all-male groups in the study, men volunteered as readily as women. It was only in the mixed-sex groups that men deferred responsibility. Many of the mothers I interviewed emphasized that their husbands capably take over when they themselves are out of the house. The assignment of thankless tasks to women over men appears not situational but universal.

Marla, a social worker in Chicago, told me, "When I moved in to Brian's apartment, the moment my stuff got unpacked, I became the one responsible for everything. 'Marla, where do we keep the blah-blah-blah?' One day I was in the kitchen and he asked me, 'Where's the peanut butter?' It's exactly where you've been keeping it for the last four years! A switch goes on in a man's brain once there's a woman. 'I'm not responsible for anything anymore.'"

We know this without knowing it. In the summer of 2018, on the heels of two tie-dye parties (one at the end of school and one in the middle of camp), I laughed out loud at the following on Twitter: "It is 3 pm on wednesday and camp just emailed to say that tomorrow every camper has to bring in a white tee shirt to tie dye and then I jumped out of a window to my death." When I stopped laughing and looked closer at the writer's profile picture, I saw that the tweet had been composed by a man. This threw me. Sure, George had been the one to stop by Kmart for the six-pack of extra-small children's white T-shirts after I asked him to, but the idea that a father would 1) read that email, 2) feel compelled on his own to be concerned about that email, and 3) have clearly had enough prior experience with such emails as to understand their tragicomedic appeal? Well, it didn't make sense. I Googled the man to see if he was a single father—since he was a public figure of sorts, it was easy to learn that he was. Without a woman to take care of all that for him, he'd been the one to step up to the task.

Gender dynamics write the rules for what Vesterlund calls these games. Inasmuch, the concept of fairness comes to dominate the minds of mothers but not dads, who are willfully blind to their own copping out. The anthropologist Sarah Hrdy explains, "Long socialized for subordinate roles, women may be more inclined to look at the world from more than one perspective, male as well as female, dominant as well as subordinate. For those accustomed to the perquisites of patriarchy, however, it would less often be useful to see the world from the point of view of those female subordinates. . . . And few men—without guidance and extra effort—seem eager to do so."

Research in economics moves in parallel. There are "substantiated gender effects" in how men and women perform in the popular lab experiment known as the "dictator game." The game involves a participant dubbed "the dictator" distributing a good, often a cash prize, between him- or herself and another unseen player with little to no decision-making authority. Women worldwide distribute the money more fairly than men, keeping the experience of the other (less powerful) player in mind. From East Asia to the United States, women are more likely to equalize payoffs, while men keep more for themselves.

Men do not pause to consider the experience of the other, or at the very least, they appear unmoved by it.

Thinking about the experience of another is called empathy. You've likely heard that women are innate empathizers and that men are not so much. You've heard that because old research in psychology seemed to attest to it, and when research findings match sexist stereotypes, they get a lot of press and then stay locked forever in our minds. Indeed, in multiple experiments, when men and women are told explicitly that they are participating in tasks measuring empathy, the men perform worse than the women. Except. Do the same experiment and change the conditions—do not say you are measuring empathy (a known female trait); call it something else. Suddenly, the men perform equally well. Or continue to call it empathy, but attach a monetary prize to stellar performance. Again men's scores rise to match women's. So much for the story about hardwiring and women and being born to consider others all the time.

Related to women's greater willingness to engage empathy, gender studies find that women consistently handle conflict differently than men. Women are more likely to use cooperation and collaboration to resolve discord. Men take a competitive stance. Writing in 2014's *The Silent Sex: Gender Deliberations and Institutions*, their book about sex-typical behavior in the workplace, political scientists Christopher Karpowitz and Tali Mendelberg explain that this difference, too, is driven by cultural norms. Anthropologists have compared competition in Masai and Khasi culture, two hunter-gatherer societies that differ in women's status and role expectations. Like most of the world, Masai culture is patrilineal; Khasi is matrilineal. In the female-dominated society, women are the more competitive sex. They are literally more likely to enter competitions. Of male-dominated societies, Karpowitz and Mendelberg write, "women are socialized to be more cooperative and interdependent with others, then . . . may dislike situations where there is conflict or competition, or even merely a lack of cooperation. When they are in such situations, women may tend to withdraw from the interaction in order to distance themselves from the conflict. The common denominator for these preferences may be the aversion to situations where the social ties of the participants are frayed." If women in patriarchal societies are oriented toward maintaining social bonds, and men in patriarchal societies are oriented toward winning, the two will never even cross paths. The women will try to collaborate, and the men will leave the field without a fight. Successful male resistance rules the world.

Progressive Behavior and Retrogressive Ideals

bell hooks has written, "Certainly many women in relationships with males often found that having a newborn baby plummeted their relationships back into more sexist-defined roles. However, when couples work hard to maintain equity in all spheres, especially child care, it can be the reality; the key issue, though, is working hard. And most men have not chosen to work hard at child care."

When men choose to work hard at child care, it can be disorienting even for them. "Why are no other dads in this text chain!?!" I overheard Pete, whose kindergartener plays soccer with Tess, asking the mothers sitting near him at practice one crisp fall Saturday as he shook his phone in the air for emphasis. He was referring to a two-years-running text chain among some local parents (and by "parents," I mean "mothers") that covered school activities, group get-togethers, and other life concerns. About fifteen families from his daughter's former preschool were involved.

None of the mothers answered Pete. I wasn't part of the chain in question, but I asked him what he thought. He said, "At least in this neighborhood, the moms do the planning, and the dads will show up if it's a dad thing. Dads will ultimately participate, but the moms take the lead, do the logistics, make sure everyone is on board."

This wasn't satisfying to Pete—an accountant with one child—who'd long been agitating for greater involvement among other fathers. "I've mentioned the text chain in front of them a few times intentionally, usually using humor to see how they take it. And they just don't have any interest in being part of it."

Pete describes an intrinsic motivation to take part in his daughter's activities. What he and his wife seem to have in common with some other equally sharing couples I spoke with or read about is that they didn't divide and conquer—they just preferred not to. Pete said, "Our goal is always to do things together. School registration, her doctor visits. There are some areas where we like to divide things—it lessens the load. But when it comes to experience things like planning a birthday party, or joining soccer, the idea of fifty/fifty saddens me. Then one person misses half of the events. For us, on those things, full engagement from both sides is better. Somebody might take the lead, say, on planning a party, but the other will remain involved.

"There will be times when our schedules mean different responsibilities. In preschool, Sherry did all the drop-off and I did all the pickup. I didn't master the morning routine. But now this year, with elementary school, I'm doing drop-off. So I've gotten better at hair care, dressing, breakfast. I used to be completely helpless with all that, but it was a learned deference. Once you get into a new routine and learn a new set of skills, there's no such thing as default care."

Matthew, a father from suburban Detroit with two teenagers, decided to work harder at child care after the birth of his second baby. When his wife's maternity leave ended, he took the twelve weeks of unpaid family leave guaranteed by the Family and Medical Leave Act. The time off made him rethink his role as the secondary caretaker, and upon returning to work, he asked to cut back his hours. Matthew said, "I had all this time with Isaac, and it was so nice, and while I was doing that, I was thinking, I don't think I can go back to work in the same way." His company allowed him to cut back, but Matthew remembers being greeted with suspicion. "Even now, more than ten years later and with my company being better about paternity leave and things like that, nobody does that. No father does. As soon as I said, 'I'm not full-time,' I had an asterisk by my name, almost literally. I was flagged as the guy who's not here every day, who's not fully on the corporate train. I was passed over for promotions and marginalized from that point on. But I kind of didn't, and don't, care."

Matthew and his wife had lived more traditionally when their older child was born, but were co–primary parents from Isaac's babyhood on. In my research, I found that equal co-parenting tended to happen under only three, often overlapping, conditions: when there was an explicitly steadfast commitment on the part of both partners to staying on top of parity; when men really enjoyed the type of regular and intimate contact that only mothers more typically have with their kids; and after fathers had taken substantial paternity leave. Research has found that men living with children in countries where they are eligible to take paid parental leave continue to perform 2.2 more hours of domestic work per week than men living with children in countries not offering that time long after their children are older and they are back at work.

Matthew set aside his professional ambition for the sake of enjoying his family, and placidly, if not without some envy, watched his wife's career take off. He may be the exception, not the rule. Anecdotal evidence and empirical work suggest that men have long been threatened by more successful wives. Research has found that for couples married in the 1960s and 1970s, a high-earning wife meant higher risk of divorce, and this was thought to evidence male discomfort with being outpaced. This correlation disappeared in the 1990s, but outsize female success remains a deal breaker for some men.

Studying the marriage and co-habitation histories of best actress and best actor nominees and winners from 1936 to 2010, researchers at the Johns Hopkins and University of Toronto business schools determined that after the award ceremony, best actress winners remained coupled for half the amount of time as those who were nominated but didn't win—4.3 years as opposed to 9.5 years. Best actor winners, in contrast, stayed in their relationships for an average of 12 years, the same as the actors who'd been nominated and lost. The study's authors write, "[T]he social norm for marital relationships is that a husband's income and occupational status exceed his wife's. Consistent with this norm, men may eschew partners whose intelligence and ambition exceed their own. . . . Violating this norm can cause discomfort in both partners and strain their marriage."

A woman who wins a political race finds herself in a similar position. Research in Sweden has found that for female candidates, winning a race for government office doubles the baseline risk of subsequent divorce; campaigning and then losing does not. Whether a male candidate wins or loses an election has no direct bearing on his marital future. The same Swedish study found that married women who become CEOs are twice as likely to divorce within three years of this achievement than men who accomplish the same.

While conducting interviews for their 2003 book *Women Don't Ask*, economist Lisa Babcock (see women and menial tasks research above) and journalist Sara Laschever repeatedly heard the same thing from successful women: It was important to behave deferentially and unassumingly. It is hardly deferential to win an Oscar or an election or a high-profile leadership role. Some markers of success are harder than others to disown. An experiment conducted in the early aughts at Columbia University reinforced the notion that men who date women prefer less successful mates—or, more to the point, that they feel compelled to occupy the traditional place in the social order of romantic love. Behavioral economists recruited grad students to take part in a speed-dating event, quickie conversations with a dozen or so potential partners. After a series of four-minute interactions, daters were asked to rate both their own intelligence and ambition (among other qualities), and that of the people they'd met on a scale from one to ten. Next, participants had to decide whether they wanted a proper date with that person in the future. For every additional intelligence point they gave their male date, women were 4.6 percent more likely to hope to see him again. In contrast, for every intelligence point that men gave women, they were only 2.3 percent more likely to want to see her again. Men's response to female ambition skewed similarly. The men didn't mind ambitious women, but only insofar as her score was not higher than his. The researchers concluded, "[O]n average men do not value women's intelligence or ambition when it exceeds their own; moreover, a man is less likely to select a woman whom he perceives to be more ambitious than he is."

In the real dating world, men, like women, sometimes find themselves involved with people a little more intelligent or a little more ambitious than they are. Ambition, at the very least, is likely to ebb and flow over the course of a life. A woman's extrafamilial aspirations may be interrupted during the period when she finds herself largely responsible for her children. It would be overly cynical to propose that men intentionally keep women in their place by eschewing family (and office) busy work, but doing so certainly supports their own position at the top of the status hierarchy. Sociologist Claire Kamp Dush told me a story about an ambitious friend of hers: "My friend is a firefighter, and she was thinking about going for a promotion. The [male] firefighters were telling her she should really just be home with her kids. She was feeling guilty. I told her, 'They want that promotion! They are not your friends!' They were using maternal guilt to try to get her not to achieve." Or, as Sharon Hays writes, "[T]he ideology of intensive mothering serves men in that women's commitment to this socially devalued task helps to maintain their subordinate position in society as a whole."

The Pygmalion Effect

Back in the 1960s, psychologist Robert Rosenthal and school principal Lenore Jacobson set out to test "the experimenter effect" in classrooms of elementary school kids. The experimenter effect suggests that the expectations held by an experimenter can impact the results of the experiment. As a young professor, Rosenthal had demonstrated the experimenter effect with rats. He deceived a group of lab workers, telling them that some rats in their care had been bred to be exceptionally good maze runners, and that others had been bred to be exceptionally bad. The rats' cages were labeled accordingly. After the duped experimenters trained the rats to run the maze, the rats in the group labeled "maze bright" performed with more speed and accuracy than the rats in the set labeled "maze dull." The researchers' beliefs about the rats' potential impacted the rodents' success.

Rosenthal imagined that if rats were vulnerable to human expectation, the same might be true for children. At the beginning of an academic year at a California public school, tests of general ability were administered to students in grades one through six. Twenty percent of the students in each class were then randomly selected to be part of the experimental group—their teachers were told that these were the kids "most likely to bloom" over the course of the year. At the end of the school year, all children were retested, and the kids in the experimental group had indeed made remarkably more progress than the others for whom expectations were less high. Over the years, what became known as the Pygmalion effect (named for the Greek myth about the sculptor Pygmalion, whose desire for his beautiful female statue brings her to life) was found to have an impact everywhere from homes to military training centers to corporations. Wherever social or relational expectations exert influence, their preconceived notions become powerful. People perform better when a lot is expected of them and worse when it is not.

I initially imagined that George would get Liv's medical form. But I also knew I'd have to remind him to do it. Am I contributing to his lackluster performance with the soft bigotry of my low expectations? Is the world? In New Zealand, educational researchers have filmed teachers interacting with students as part of a study they called the Teacher Expectation Project. In watching themselves on video, teacher after teacher commented that they'd had no idea how much they were communicating with nonverbal cues: a raised eyebrow, a bored expression, a wandering gaze. A similar project at the University of Virginia trains teachers to be aware of their body language in order to help them establish more productive relationships with their students, and the students they've taught have shown improved performance on standardized tests. I often feel trepidation when asking George to take something on. I don't trust him to remember. I communicate my hesitation.

The norms of parenting are so sticky because what supports them is completely circular. When we begin with an overarching presumption of inferior male capacity, the men fail to master the maze. The self-fulfilling prophecy plays out and then again. Believe it and it will be so. Gabe, Deanna's husband, experiences his wife like this: "I think there's a belief that if she's not going to do it, then it won't get done." Deanna confirms this but emphasizes that her belief is based on past experience. "We fell into this easy pattern where he learned to be oblivious, and I learned to resent him," she says.

The theory of "stereotype threat" is not unlike the Pygmalion effect, with stereotypes substituting for the role of experimenter, contributing to the outcome of a task. Stereotype threat is fear of "being judged and treated poorly in settings where a negative stereotype about one's group applies." As performance anxiety is triggered, the fear often manifests in stereotypes being borne out by reality. The research suggests that awareness of a negative stereotype about one's group can interfere with the performance of the members of that group whenever the stereotype is invoked. For example, distribute a math test to a roomful of male and female students of similar ability levels, and they will perform similarly. Give the same test but introduce it with "This test has been designed to determine why some people are better at math than others," and the women's scores will plummet. The well-trod notion that women are bad at math is activated by the introduction, priming a sense of uncertainty for women about their own ability. In similar experiments, Caucasian men perform worse when told they will be compared to Asian men.

One group of researchers hypothesizes that the effect of the stereotype is "to make sure that any sign that they might be confirming the stereotype is identified and suppressed. Ironically, this increased vigilance and control hijacks the same central executive processor (i.e., working memory) needed to excel on complex cognitive tasks, producing the very result—poorer performance—that they are trying to avoid." Stereotype threat research has been carried out over multiple domains, from academic to athletic to affective. The expectations laid out by stereotypes influence results. Research has also found that people engage in self-handicapping to reduce the applicability of a negative stereotype to their performance. That is, they will not try as hard—say by failing to practice a skill—in order to avoid hits to their self-esteem. When they fail, they can attribute their failure to lack of personal effort rather than natural inadequacy.

Stereotype threat research warns that members of marginalized ability groups—in this case, let's call them fathers—are stymied by their own knowledge of how they're popularly perceived. The threat doesn't even have to be explicit. Women who are especially good at math do more poorly on math tests when the ratio of men to women in the room is high. The more men relative to women taking the test, the more intense a woman's concerns about whether she belongs among the group. The combination of familiarity with a stereotype and membership in a stigmatized group impairs performance. Even the gender of an experimenter can cue the stereotype threat, heightening anxiety and depleting cognitive resources. Imagine yourself a father in a mommy-and-me class. Imagine that class as a metaphor for the fathering life.

University of British Columbia social psychologist Toni Schmader studies stereotype threat. I asked if she thought stereotypes about fathers might get in the way of men becoming the most effective and involved parents they might be. "It's a sensible hypothesis," she said, before adding more dubiously, "I think we all have our areas of feigned ignorance that can help get us off the hook for certain things we don't really want to do."

The 1971 Stanford Prison Experiment is one of the best known in the history of social psychology. Twenty-one volunteers solicited from a California newspaper agreed to participate in a mock jail exercise in which half of them would be assigned to act as prisoners and the other half as guards. The guards underwent a job training session, while the prisoners were arrested at their homes and booked into rooms that looked like cells. Though the study was supposed to last two weeks, it was halted prematurely after only six days, as the guards became abusive and the prisoners broke down.

The study was thought to demonstrate the banality of evil, the idea that institutional power might make any man exploitative and inhumane. In the time since the prison experiment, though, the conclusions drawn from it have been reexamined. It seems it is not evil that is so banal but, rather, our desire to meet the expectations of our social environment. The so-called demand characteristics of the prison experiment influenced the behavior of the participants. The guards and prisoners inferred the expected outcome of the study and carried on accordingly, as cooperative people do.

Expectations, stereotypes, and demand characteristics hang in the air as we calibrate to family life. But forewarned is forearmed. Writing about the potential undoing of stereotype threat, Toni Schmader has noted, "[T]hese differences can be reduced if not erased by changing the nature of these performance environments to encourage more positive views of one's group or one's own abilities, or through greater transparency of the pernicious effects that stereotyping can have. By deconstructing stereotype threat, we can diffuse the damage it can do." What Schmader means is that the power of stereotype threat lies in its invisibility. We can counter it in one of two (not unrelated) ways: by putting a stop to the ways in which we marginalize fathers, or by shining a light on the fallacy of the stereotypes.

Lise Vesterlund, of the women and menial tasks research, suggests a third way: "We've spent time thinking at the top end of the spectrum, how do we break the glass ceiling, how do we lean in? We've spent much less time thinking at this end of the spectrum. Anyone can do these tasks. Rather than ask for volunteers, we should just take turns. It's an easy way. It's not even that I need to debias anyone. We just need to become aware that we have a systematic problem . . . and then take charge." Here Vesterlund echoes Elizabeth, the mother in Northern California who spent her twenties carefully considering division of labor. Forearmed with knowledge about the systematic problem, she and her husband resolved to stay on top of their biases. They didn't have to debias anyone. Instead they made an Excel document. They took logistical charge.

Immunity to Change

Implicit biases, stereotypes, and demand characteristics are socially acquired impediments to progress. Lisa Lahey is a faculty member of the Harvard Graduate School of Education and cofounder of Minds at Work, a consulting group that specializes in facilitating organizational change. In *Immunity to Change: How to Overcome It and Unlock the Potential in Yourself and Your Organization*, she and co-author Robert Kegan propose that more idiosyncratic and personal unconscious motivations often also impede transformation. Lahey and Kegan use the body's immune system as a metaphor for our psyche's automatic attempt to fight change, that perceived threat. For example, a manager who explicitly expresses that he wants to be more receptive to the ideas of others might alienate employees with curt feedback because of an underlying and unconscious commitment to getting his own way. Without knowing it, the change he wants becomes the very virus he's working to ward off. Conflicted, he undermines his best intentions with counterproductive behavior that maintains a dysfunctional but familiar system.

Lahey's work builds off of concepts in my own field about conscious objectives versus unknown and forbidden wishes. I spoke to her when I was stewing about Liv's medical form and asked her to weigh in. "It's a good example of a system that is being reinforced by your holding the responsibility and delegating in ways that are not effective," she said. "And what's happening is you continue to micromanage, and he continues to know he can count on you. He is not where the buck stops. Change really requires everybody to do a better job of being much more explicit about what makes this unsuccessful."

Lahey suggested that I express the following: "If this doesn't come through, it's your responsibility." She asked me, "What are the potential consequences? It would be great to bring him along there." Had I let the situation with the form play out, Liv would not have been able to start camp on its all-important first morning. George would have had to stay home with her, upsetting both of our kids, reneging on his professional commitments, and losing a day's worth of income.

I might have laid that out when I initially asked him to get the form. George agreed it would have helped him to remember, but he also deemed that way of speaking to him "pissy and confrontational"—though wasn't I entitled to be both of those things? Our societal orientation to female anger complicates the predicament further. Without a greater comfort with our own human ire, we are left only to seek lukewarm solace from our friends.

Lahey asked, "What are the complexities for each of you that need to be seen and not swept under the rug?" It was a subject I'd certainly considered: our respective immunities to change. To be reductive, George grew up resenting the complaints of his overtaxed single mother; I grew up with the sense that my concerns fell on deaf ears. The personal narratives we weave around the parenting dynamic we've established coalesce in old familiar ways. He resents my complaining, and I feel perpetually unheard.

Our situation was overdetermined, though also and not least by our genders. This very scenario—fueled by any number of idiosyncratic life histories—plays out too reliably in one direction. Had I been raised in George's home and he in mine, our respective positions in the adult family we'd built would hardly have been reversed. These gendered sticking points are all but never reversed. This is because the immune system that Lahey invokes kicks in not only in response to personal history but also in response to the social world at large. She acknowledged as much: "There are different levels of analysis. Men feel they need a wife who's in charge at home. Women don't feel they have the right to ask for more and then don't ask wholeheartedly." Like the boss who unwittingly discourages feedback, the men who say they want to be equal parents have other, less conscious motivations. They fail to seize what Lowell called "the thing that makes you motivationally step up and do something when you're not being asked." They fear, as George Yancy says, "the 'loss' of [their] own 'entitlement' as a male." Their immune systems work to maintain their patriarchal privilege without ever forcing them to reckon with the fact that they have it in the first place.

In *Couples, Gender and Power,* Carmen Knudson-Martin and Anne Rankin Mahoney state plainly, "[G]endered behavior is kept in place in part by the latent and invisible power that accrues to men in a society based on a gender hierarchy. This is hard to identify and address."

A New Masculine Paradigm

We're living in a time of embattled masculinity, and we have seen that it exacts a rancid toll. Stereotypes of men are rigid and slow to change. They confer status and power but have a dark underbelly. Manhood once anointed must also be defended. The dominant need someone to submit. To live differently can be isolating. Derek, twenty-nine, a stay-at-home father in North Carolina, has felt shamed for his choice to be his young children's primary parent. "When I first said I was staying home, my dad would say, 'Oh, I'm so glad you're able to do that,' but I know he'd go back to his wife and they would talk. My brother is four years younger than me. He had a kid a year ago. He believes that the breadwinner just breadwins and comes home and should not do anything else. He thinks that I'm lessening myself by staying home with the kids. He said to me, 'At least I can take care of my family.' It's affected our relationship. We don't speak. My wife and I recently moved, and I don't feel the need to go make friends. It's not embarrassing, but I always kind of feel that other people are judging. That's the thing. I don't want to be judged, even by another stay-at-home dad."

It has been said that the work of feminism remains incomplete in part for paying little mind to advancing a more egalitarian masculinity. One solution to that might lie in encouraging men to fully embrace the identity of dad. In their research, University of Colorado Boulder social psychologist Bernadette Park and her colleagues have found that the cynical attitudes that rain down on men as a category do not extend to fathers. When asked to associate adjectives to the two groups, participants characterized "men" negatively but "fathers" favorably—as favorably as "women," who in turn are viewed as favorably as "moms."

Park suggests that the social role of dad could be leveraged to change gender stereotypes of men. She writes, "A less constrained definition of manhood and masculinity would likely afford greater flexibility in how to 'be a man,' an outcome desirable not only for men, but as a means for decreasing rigid demarcations between the genders more broadly." In Sweden, where ninety days of paid parental leave are specifically apportioned to fathers—who must use it or lose it— latté pappas, also known by the acronym DILFs, are lauded for their sexy, masculine swagger-with-a-stroller. Since 1995, when fathers were first encouraged by government policy to take parental leave, divorce and separation rates have also been falling in that country—in a time when they have largely risen elsewhere.

Park told me, "There's been a fairly recent uptick in conversations around men in this country, the notion that white men in particular are feeling disenfranchised and don't see a role for themselves. They don't have the old traditional role of being a sole provider, the head of family. The idea is, all these problems we're seeing now with men—health issues, lower graduation rates, higher levels of drug abuse and incarceration—they've lost their sense of identity and, in some ways, are trying to find a place in the world." Park proposes fighting so-called toxic masculinity by granting men greater and deeper access to fatherhood. "In implicit association tests, dads are more closely linked with the professional world than the parenting world, which is crazy, given that a dad is also a parent, but it's a holdover from the 1950s prototype of what a dad is and does." Some evidence suggests that the implicit associations like the ones Park mentions aren't as slow to change as one might guess. A study of undergraduates at an all-women's college found that entering students were slow to pair the word "female" with leadership terms. That changed after just one year at their single-sex school.

Park says, "There have been shifts both behaviorally and in terms of stereotypes about dads and involvement, but there hasn't been as strong a shift in making that connection to men in general. There is this group called *dads*, and they do this thing, but *men* as a group remain less tightly connected in people's minds, from a social-perception perspective, to fatherhood. When manhood is threatened, aggression tends to be the response. But if you could answer a threat to manhood by invoking the social role of fatherhood, that could repair the threat and ameliorate the aggressive response. Fatherhood can be an important part of your identity. It lets you feel a sense of fulfillment and purpose, allowing you to think of generative and positive ways you can affect the world."

Sam, thirty-two, is a stay-at-home father in New York City. He left his job a year ago to take care of his toddler daughters after their nanny quit and he and his wife realized they could get by on her salary alone. He said, "I was raised by women, my grandmother and my mom. I'm very grateful for that. They were dad and mom to me. If I'd had a macho dad, I don't think I'd have this attitude toward being home at all. I would feel like I wasn't a man. I have a more rounded view of things because of female influence. For me, personally, that's the biggest thing in allowing me to do this." Without a man in his childhood home to steer him subtly away from his own feminine-typed traits, Sam never experienced shame around his impulse to take care of others, impulses that his imagined macho father might have derided.

Michael Kimmel, director of the Center for the Study of Men and Masculinities at Stony Brook University in New York, endorses helping men embrace their feminine impulses, shifting their focus from being "real men" to being "good" ones. Lecturing in 2017 at West Point about sexual assault, he asked the cadets to define each. Real men, they told him, were tough, strong, "never show weakness, win at all costs, suck it up, play through pain, be competitive, get rich, get laid." A good man, in contrast, was defined by sacrifice. "Honor, duty, integrity, do the right thing, stand up for the little guy, be a provider, be a protector." Kimmel later said, "I was not there to tell them that their behaviors were toxic. I was there to tell them that they are already experiencing a conflict, inside them, between their own values and this homosocial performance. So my job then shifted. . . . I [also] work a lot trying to engage men to support gender equality in corporations. . . . So my job has been to find what are the entry points for men into this conversation about gender equality? One of them turns out to be involved fatherhood."

Kimmel, the author of books on masculinity, is a popular speaker precisely because the unflinching demands of masculine performance are hard to cast aside. Patrick Coleman is an editor at *Fatherly*, a Web portal for dads. In his early forties, he's also the father to two young kids. He told me, "I don't think that men are just blithely traipsing through their days in the family not understanding there's an unequal division of labor. A lot of them do recognize it. I consider myself a progressive guy, but even when my wife was still working full-time, there was an unequal division of labor at home. It's so stuck. I'm not trying to say that men are victims—obviously, they have agency; if we were more mindful, we'd be able to snap out of it—but a lot of men continue to internalize this idea of masculinity. It's so in our face every day. We're supposed to be this strong pillar of authority, but what happens if I'm washing dishes and I'm cooking? I don't have this authority anymore in my household. I think that can feel very crippling to men. That strong, independent, quiet authoritative character has been so internalized, even if a guy wants to be progressive and wants to do this stuff, there's a fear there that just kind of locks us down."

In 1970, the lawyer, priest, and civil rights activist Pauli Murray said, "Men have become enslaved by their dependency as well as their dominance. They pay a heavy price in shortened lives, military casualties, broken homes and the heartbreak of parents whose children are alienated from them. Many men find themselves unable to live up to the expectations of masculinity which men have defined for themselves, and many are now chagrined to find that women are no longer willing to accept the role of femininity which men have defined for women."

And we won't be moving backward. Women, Kimmel said in an interview with the feminist journal *Signs*, are "not going to have an Ann Coulter moment where they go, 'Oh, you know what, they're right. Let's stop voting, let's stop serving on juries, let's stop working, let's stop driving cars, let's stop having orgasms.' I mean, that's not going to happen. The fix is in. Men's choice is, are we going to be dragged kicking and screaming into that future, or are we going to say, 'All right, that's the deal, let's check it out, it might not be bad for us also'? And I don't think that's a bad thing to say."

The rewards of living outside of cultural scripts are not negligible. Despite his insecurities, Derek finds fulfillment in the time he has with his children. Matthew, who took his FMLA leave and then cut his hours, said, "When our older child was born and I was still working full-time, my wife was on maternity leave and would go to all these mommy groups. She got all this time with Leah and was introduced to a whole new social scene that she loved. These women are still her best friends to this day. Not that I wanted to hang out at the coffeehouse with a bunch of mommies, but she was in this other world that I was not a part of. It didn't feel great. I didn't want to hear about it after a while. I was jealous, especially with the first kid. I just wanted to play with her all day, and instead I'd come home at seven and get to see her for forty-five minutes before she was asleep. After Isaac was born, I cut back on work and it was ultimately fatal to my career, but during those years, I had Fridays in the park with my son, and when he was in elementary school, I got to pick him up three days a week."

As long as cultural scripts remain largely intact, evidence suggests that even the modern, involved father will remain less likely than his female partner to see his transition into parenting as a major life development. Anthropologist Sarah Hrdy reports that in industrialized countries, almost half of all children lose touch with their fathers not long after their parents divorce (within ten years, that number shoots up to two thirds).

The relative failure to see fatherhood as that major life development underscores all sorts of misfortune. Education may offer a solution. The 1960s gave rise to childbirth education classes, which set out to teach women and their partners how to manage labor and delivery with minimal medical intervention. Hospitals and obstetricians rallied around the classes. By the year 2000, according to the nonprofit Childbirth Connection, 70 percent of first-time mothers who gave birth in hospitals had participated in a birthing class, most commonly alongside their partners. What to do once delivery is over, though, has been left for parents to untangle on their own.

Sociologist Anne Rankin Mahoney and psychologist Carmen Knudson-Martin have proposed that formal parenting education might help couples achieve greater parity. Their proposed curriculum includes emphasizing the fact that parenting is a gender-neutral talent, reinforcing the need for couples to talk about their plans to share responsibilities, and helping them develop ways to maintain collaboration.

The research of husband-and-wife psychologists Carolyn and Philip Cowan suggests the potential benefits of such an intervention. In a series of studies culminating in the Supporting Father Involvement Project, the Cowans have shown that couples who attended four months of weekly groups on the potential challenges of family life showed significant increases in both father involvement and relationship satisfaction. Among at-risk families referred by the child welfare system, attendance at these groups also reduced alcohol use, couple conflict and violence, and older siblings' problem behaviors.

The Gottman Institute in Seattle offers the Bringing Baby Home workshop, which has likewise shown promising results. It offers a gender-neutral take on prenatal family education. This remains rare. Popular parenting books continue to emphasize the special and exclusive role of the mother. The workshop—usually given, like childbirth classes, in two-day-seminar format—prepares parents-to-be for relationship strain, offers primers on infant development and interaction skills, and stresses the equal importance of father involvement in family life. By 2018, the Gottmans had trained more than two thousand educators worldwide to teach Bringing Baby Home. In follow-up research with new parents, compared to families with no child care education, fathers who'd attended Bringing Baby Home were rated more positively in infant-father attachment, reported greater satisfaction with their domestic arrangements, demonstrated better co-parenting in a play study, showed greater responsiveness to their baby's signals, were less likely to exhibit signs of depression and anxiety, reported more stable relationship quality, and had babies who responded more positively to their soothing. (Benefits accrued to mothers in the study as well.) The men who took part in these classes—exposed to alternatives to patriarchal privilege—saw the fruits of a reimagined fatherhood.

Michael Kimmel says, "I want to sell feminism to men. Because greater gender equality—embracing a fuller palette of traits, attitudes, and behaviors—cannot help but be good for men as well as for women. Women have shown us over the past fifty years, 'This is really good, this works really well, see, aren't we awesome? Aren't we more interesting now?' So now men need to be whole human beings. You've asked me, what can we offer? How can we sell this? We sell this by saying, 'You've cut yourself off from half the human experience by embracing this traditional notion of masculinity, the thing that we call *toxic*. You'll have a better life if you could actually be a person.'"

Are You Being Unfair to Your Wife?

A 2014 study out of George Washington University found that men talking to women interrupt 33 percent more often than when they are speaking to other men. That same year, linguist and tech industry CEO Kieran Snyder began cataloging the interrupting she often found herself witness to in mixed-sex meetings. In fifteen hours of conversation over four weeks, she found that men interrupted more than women overall, and that they were also almost three times more likely to cut off women than other men. When women do interrupt, they are similarly much more likely to be interrupting women. Eighty-seven percent of female interruptions were made when another woman was speaking. The lower relative status of women is preternaturally reinforced. It almost looks like equality. It was not until his daughters were practically grown that Barack Obama said, "I can look back now and see that, while I helped out, it was usually on my schedule and on my terms. The burden disproportionately and unfairly fell on Michelle."

Because how on earth would a man embroiled in it know? If a tree falls in the forest and that's just what trees do, who cares if it even makes a sound? Men use what has been called hidden power to resist. Hidden power is not overt power—telling the little woman what to do. Neither is it covert power—purposely ignoring something that makes your wife unhappy in order to maintain your comfortable position. Rather, hidden power exists beneath a surface, baked into ideologies that give one person advantage over another—say, the right to interrupt or to sleep late all weekend long. Ethan, a father of two in Brooklyn, told me, "Let's say we both have to be at work, and the kids get sick. I'm sorry, I'm going to say this: I don't give it a second thought that my work comes first. That's an entitlement that I feel." He and his wife have no discussion. Hidden power at his back, Ethan gets dressed and heads on out the door.

Back in the early aughts, San Francisco–based clinical psychologist Joshua Coleman was the father of three young children and a contributing editor at a magazine for the parents of multiples. In the latter capacity, he got a lot of mail from women complaining about their husbands' resistance to family work. Hearing similar grievances from his own wife and the couples he saw in marital therapy, he decided to write a book he eventually called *The Lazy Husband: How to Get Men to Do More Parenting and Housework*. In *The Lazy Husband*, published in 2005, Coleman suggests strategies that women can adopt in order to mitigate their husbands' lethargy. I asked him, based on his personal and clinical experience, what makes it easy for men to be so lazy. He said, "I, like everyman, would never call myself lazy. I think that's how women think of us. We don't think of ourselves as lazy.

"When I was raising my kids, I earned more money. I had the arrogance that comes from men who earn more money. I can buy my way out of those activities. That kind of thing. I also think that I, like many men, have less guilt about being more self-centered. I have a greater feeling of entitlement to taking care of myself. Women have a more collaborative identity, and so they're easier to manipulate in that way, to take advantage of.

"Women also have more sensitivity to feelings, to the internal world of the child, than men, myself included, even though I'm a very involved father. I'm not tracking stuff, but it isn't because I don't see it. I don't think these things are worth attending to. A certain percentage of parental involvement that my wife did, I would see as valuable but unnecessary. There were many times when if I could choose that level of involvement versus something more selfish, I would probably have chosen to do the more selfish thing."

I called Coleman because I knew he'd given co-parenting a book's worth of thought, and I hoped that he'd be willing to speak freely. He was. Men's resistance would be an abject failure if there were more men who spoke like he did (to be clear, he was not condoning his own behavior). Imagine if your children's father said these things to you, directly and out loud: Women are easy to take advantage of, your efforts are ultimately unnecessary, the needs of our family are not worth my attention, and I'll choose the more selfish thing. Fathers are implying every last bit of this with their resistance all the time. You are easy to manipulate. These things aren't worth my attention. I'll choose the more selfish thing.

In *Love's Executioner*, his 1989 book of essays about his clinical work, the psychologist Irvin Yalom includes a piece about a couple's treatment that has long stayed in my mind. A man named Marvin comes for marital therapy alone because his wife, Phyllis, has developed agoraphobia and rarely leaves their house. After many sessions, Yalom intuits that Marvin's unexpressed dependency on his wife is serving to virtually imprison her. The agoraphobia—her symptom—is not hers alone but theirs. Yalom instructs Marvin to spend the next weeks repeating the following to his wife every two hours: "Phyllis, please don't leave the house. I need to know you are there at all times to take care of me. . . ." Only once Marvin's long-implicit demand on her is clearly and regularly articulated is Phyllis freed to be indignant and uncooperative. Her agoraphobia is cured.

Successful male resistance has necessarily required reasonable men to obfuscate unreasonable demands. Their entitlement hangs in the air, omnipresent and indiscernible. In response, women become like the agoraphobic wife acquiescing to gratuitous requests, directives at once clearly made and never quite delivered.

CHAPTER 7

What Are We Trying to Achieve?

The Case for Female Power

☑ Like pretty much every endeavor but childrearing throughout the whole of human history, the sciences have been dominated by men. Gender essentialist biases are reflected in their work. Evolutionary science is not without those biases, and so the field has historically identified an evolutionary advantage (read: innate predisposition) for male, but not female, promiscuity. Males across species, men theorize, evolved an indiscriminate sexuality because it conferred a reproductive advantage. The more females you inseminate with your endless supply of sperm, the more children you might father, your evolutionary purpose realized. Ask anyone.

Males of most species were presumed promiscuous, while females, whose reproductive success was limited by the finite number of eggs they could produce or offspring they could gestate, were presumed to be invariably standoffish. The dogma around choosy females and opportunistic males was rarely challenged, even when evidence in nature contradicted it. It came to undergird (as it simultaneously grew out of) the sexual double standard and its expectation of the exercise of male prerogatives.

In the late 1940s, an experiment by the English geneticist Angus John Bateman lent support to gender essentialist conclusions. He observed fruit flies in captivity and counted their mates and their offspring. He concluded that the greater the variance in number of partners the males (but not females) had, the greater their variance in reproductive success, and he counted it proof of the evolutionary imperative for male voracity. His experiment was lauded, becoming the basis for later work that posited that the sex bearing the brunt of the costs of reproduction (and in all mammals, that is females) would be the object of competition and the greater-investing sex, or the one that did all the work. Males are hedonistic and competitive. Females are choosy and coy.

In the 1990s, Bateman's hypotheses became Bateman's Principles, propping up the idea, as UCLA distinguished professor of biology Patricia Gowaty later wrote, "that there are no fitness benefits for females of mating with more than one male." Female primatologists saw evidence to the contrary in the field (evidence that their male colleagues were blind to), but for decades, work that put the female organism in the sexual selection spotlight was widely disregarded and dismissed. It was as if sexual selection, or within-gender variation that grows out of intrasex competition, might take place only among males. Gowaty writes, "I suspect that typical gender schemas have obscured the visionary works of skeptics in anthropology and evolutionary biology about female enthusiasm for mating and multiple mating. In addition, the implications of female multiple mating are often overlooked and the imperative is ignored to study a range of potential fitness benefits, not just costs, for females who mate multiply."

Typical gender schemas have the power to obscure quite a lot. When it came to Bateman's seminal experiment, it turned out his work was plain wrong. Gowaty explains that third-grade-math proficiency was all that was required to understand that his calculations were incorrect. He'd overcounted the number of offspring for fathers, among other more complex errors. The experiment could not be replicated. It was so-called theory tenacity—the persistent belief in a theory despite all evidence to the contrary—that assured the Bateman's Principles their longevity. His conclusions made such intuitive sense to so many male scientists that few bothered to look closely at the data. One is reminded of the doggedness around maternal primacy and paternal irrelevance—and oh, that theory's tenacity.

In actuality, depending on external conditions, females may be indiscriminate, and males may be choosy and coy. Perhaps you yourself have been both. Male scientists tried to explain their own lived experience with biology, and their theories weren't always disturbed by unfamiliar facts. "I'm glad I'm not a woman," George has said to me more than once, in an attempt to be sympathetic about one thing or another (I believe he said it when I was pregnant, despite the fact that I loved being pregnant). Imagine if George were the only scientist. For all intents and purposes, he has been.

Aristotle deemed female nature afflicted with a natural defectiveness, while Darwin hypothesized that women were intellectually inferior, and Freud that they wanted nothing more than phalluses of their own. Along the same lines, a traditionally male-biased perspective on reproduction frames bearing children only as a cost and not also as a benefit. If the whole of our purpose as animals is to procreate, propelling our genes into the next generation, internal gestation is also an evolutionary advantage bestowed upon women. We control the means of production.

Gowaty offers me this take on reproductive expenditures: "If we jiggle the 'wisdom' around a bit, it is easy to see that gestation and lactation are not only huge reproductive 'costs' but, at the same time, put mothers in control—physiological and epigenetic—of offspring, which may have major, major benefits for one sex of parent, mothers, compared to fathers. Looking at mammalian patterns of parental care suggests that there has been extremely strong selection among females to control many reproductive outcomes, including the quality of their children via gestation length—which does vary, it turns out—and also in terms of lactational feeding, not to mention probably other aspects of care. I am thoroughly fed up with typical evolutionary scenarios of 'differential costs of reproduction' without any characterization of the 'differential benefits of reproduction' for the sexes. Mothers have far more power and influence than fathers because mothers gestate, lactate, and do most of the teaching of their children."

She stipulates that she feels like a traitor to the feminist cause when she adds, "How do I look at the distribution of child care in modern families? Mothers are still winning! Yes, they are also working very, very hard to do it all. If we had different metaphors for discussing the different investment times of fathers and mothers, would we see these typical distributions of child care between parents as something we all want to even out? In other words, what are we really fighting about, and who wins and who loses with different distributions?"

Cultural critic Jacqueline Rose believes that it is the very fact that men can't tolerate truly knowing about the visceral mess of mothering and the emotional complexity it requires—what transpires as mothers are winning—that keeps them asserting their scanty privilege in the slippery ways they do. Citing Adrienne Rich's *Of Woman Born*, Rose emphasizes that men's fear of dependency—of acknowledging their own human vulnerability—contributes to their failure to work to ease mothers' burdens. Rose says, "Men cannot get over the fact that they were of woman born. There is something about that irreducible fact . . . there is something about that irreducible bodily provenance . . . that is for man impossible to countenance. And I think that plays a large part in women's failure, over and over again, to get the problems of mothering recognized as socially and in- stitutionally organized in ways that could therefore be simply addressed and reorganized for the better." In public and private life, men refuse to fully appreciate, and then to work to alleviate, the entrenched complexities of motherhood.

Is this why lesbian couples struggle less? Research has found that biological mothers in lesbian couples, women whose part- ners are likewise able to bear children, may stake out their power in the relationship by taking charge of the household work—not by deferring it. Conventional power dynamics abated, women in love carve out their roles on a relatively blank slate.

Barnard College sociologist Mignon Moore has studied working-class black lesbian stepfamilies. In contrast to the higher-income lesbians who are the focus of most same-sex fam- ily research, Moore found that her subjects placed less emphasis

on setting egalitarian caretaking goals (an act that is itself a reaction to the typical patriarchal frame) and greater emphasis on
both partners' breadwinning. And ultimately, decision-making
power was often assigned to the partner who took on more in
the domestic sphere. Moore tells me, "One thing I would like
heterosexual couples to consider is that power in a marital relationship can be found outside of economic assets, or who brings
in the greater income. In the absence of sex differences telling
us how to value various aspects of relationships, we can see how
the division of labor might be explored in alternative ways. The
ability to have the final say over certain household decisions is a
type of power that may be overlooked under different circumstances."

While the subjects in Moore's study typically shared the
earner role, the biological mothers took on significantly more
household chores. This was not, however, viewed solely as a
cost. Rather, chore responsibility was used as a trade-off for
greater authority over the home at large. Moore observes, "Unlike in married heterosexual households, where husbands dele-
gate family decision making to their wives, biological mothers in
lesbian relationships *want* to take control of this activity—their
partners do not assign it to them." Further, while research has
shown that men in dual-earner heterosexual couples underestimate the number of hours their wives spend taking care of their
families, the overbenefiting lesbian partners who participated
in Moore's research overestimated the same. Moore speculates
that appreciating her partner's caretaking effort—in contrast to
feeling entitled to it—supports this overestimation.

Gowaty and Moore tell us that the paradigm can turn on
its head. Gowaty's work highlights the biological advantages of

motherhood, a role decreed by sex but defined by patriarchy. So we frame talk of reproduction as if it were only a cost. "I'm glad I'm not a woman," then all the men can say. For those of us whose romantic lives are also outlined by patriarchy, it only makes sense that what proceeds would be viewed in those sepia tones. Moore's starting line is a choice point. With gendered power (or powerlessness) off the table, one becomes a primary parent not by default but by design. The role is, then, more clearly also a benefit. For this currently overdetermined outcome to become a choice, it must truly be free from the influence of gender—a preference either partner is as likely to embrace.

Internalized Sexual Racism

Political philosopher Harry Brighouse and sociologist Erik Olin Wright have written about what they see as the dim prospects for the future of egalitarian caregiving. They offer that inadequate social support for caretakers alongside gender biases at work lead to income inequality between men and women, and then income inequality reinforces social norms. Norms reinforce stereotypes, which in turn reinforce norms. And we wind up at this impasse where "Women are more likely, in the 'game of chicken' over the distribution of family responsibilities, to give in."

Gretchen in Baltimore plays the game of chicken like this: "One night I did what my husband often does to me. I told him I wouldn't be there in the morning, and he'd have to get the kids ready, then drive them to different schools, including our daughter's preschool, which doesn't open until nine, thus making him late, like I am every day. He looked at me like I was crazy. Exhaled loudly. Said nothing. Of course, I felt guilty. I got on the phone and found a friend's house where he could drop our preschooler off."

I didn't bother with a follow-up question. I, too, am a woman living with a man. What more is there to say? Gretchen imagined the strain her husband was facing and acted to spare him the inconvenience, one that she manages regularly. This game of chicken resolves in one direction. I play it all the time, in the end always going out of my way to relieve my husband of some mundane hassle that parents (and by "parents," I mean "mothers") routinely face. I've reinforced repeatedly with my behavior: This is something only I should have to manage in the end. Acting out male privilege is hardly an exclusively male endeavor.

Cornell philosopher Kate Manne refers to this game of chicken as "himpathy," the excessive or inappropriate sympathy extended to a male person over a female one. In her book *Down Girl: The Logic of Misogyny*, she invokes the canine command (down), emphasizing that it not only controls but also soothes a dog. In 2018 Manne told *Jezebel*, "Misogyny can have so many different ways of putting women in their place or punishing or threatening them for subverting or violating patriarchal norms and expectations. But the playful, secondary meaning of 'down girl' points to how hard it is to let go of the internalized 'down girl' moves that we either do automatically or we take those social cues and kind of lay down on all fours. Even for a very strong-willed or feisty dog—in my case, a Corgi very much enjoying her life—sometimes the anxiety of pure freedom means that it's actually very nice to have a command to obey. If she's anxious, asking her to touch your hand with her nose or lay down is something that alleviates anxiety. I wanted to gesture at the way that for women to give up some of those forms of patriarchal obedience can be terrifying. It can leave us feeling devoid of meaning and requires being creative about how to fill a gap that's often filled with 'good behavior.'" How might Gretchen and I be spending our time were we not organizing it around our husband's and children's needs?

When I was growing up, holiday dinners were prepared and served by women. My great-aunt did the cooking, and set the table, too. The men would sit expectantly, cloth napkins on their laps, while Aunt Margaret, my grandmother, and my mother emerged as if in a dance line from the kitchen with bowls of chicken soup. At meal's end, but before dessert, the women rose to clear. I was expected to participate in this good behavior, though I was never sure if it was because I was a lowly girl or because I was a lowly child. My gender or my age? Without a brother or a local male cousin, I could wonder but never know.

Still, I saw what adulthood conferred upon women and understood it as the one-down position. The men would sit expectantly, cloth napkins on their laps, their food placed before them as if they were the king. The women were himpathetic; men should be spared this inconvenience. My mother likes to say that Judaism is a feminist religion because women are revered for their special place in the family. One is honored to be bringer of the soup. But the morning prayer for Jewish men reads: "Blessed art Thou, oh Lord our God, King of the Universe, that I was not born a woman." (The Koran and the New Testament express similar sentiment.)

Is female gender a cost or an advantage? If women are so revered, why are men implored to give thanks every morning that they were not born among those ranks? And do they let their daughters hear them at their prayers?

In *An Unconventional Family*, the late psychologist Sandra Bem shares a sermon she and her husband, Daryl, began delivering in the late 1960s, trying to spread the word about what they called sexual racism (the term "sexism" had not yet been coined). In 1998, Bem wrote, "Many people today jump to the conclusion that the ideology expressed in [religious] passages is a relic of the past. Not so. It has simply been obscured by an egalitarian veneer, and the same ideology has now become unconscious."

Egalitarian attitudes remain common, but the unconscious is the powerhouse. To measure it, psychologists use implicit association tests. These computerized tests ask participants to quickly categorize words or images into groups. The relative speed with which they perform the tasks suggests whether their associations are automatic or labored. In 2010 University of Colorado Boulder social psychologist Bernadette Park and colleagues used implicit association tasks to measure whether mothers as compared to fathers are more easily associated with lunch boxes and strollers than briefcases and laptops. You might have guessed they are. The stronger these unconscious associations between moms and caretaking versus dads and breadwinning, the more likely participants were to say that mothers should resolve work-family conflict on the side of the family and that fathers should do just the opposite. Park and her colleagues write, "[The] differential outcomes for the genders in both work and family domains may be driven in part by well-learned cultural associations pairing women with child care and men with the work world. Although explicitly societal norms may espouse the importance of equality between the genders, messages learned through media depictions as well as through direct observations subtly convey that the 'natural' division of labor is along gender stereotypic lines. The concepts of mom and parent are more easily kept simultaneously in mind than mom and professional, whereas the exact opposite is true for dad."

When Laura, the New York City business owner who often feels like a single parent, met the family of the man she would eventually marry, she remembers, "I saw his parents interacting, and I had concerns. He's from a one hundred percent Italian family where you serve the man at all times, physically, emotionally. Every meal is what they want. Once I saw that, I flat-out said, 'Just so you know, I will not be serving you.' He got very defensive. He said, 'My father's a good man.' He took it as a criticism of his dad."

In my great-aunt's home, filled with carpeting and trinkets, other relics of the past, it would have been a clear violation of unspoken rules if I had remained in my spot after dinner. It would have served to criticize the men. I wish I'd been a girl who thought to do that. Didn't my grandfather and my great-uncle— Laura's soon-to-be-father-in-law—deserve a little flak?

I appreciate Gowaty's perspective as well as Moore's. Clearly, there are other ways to see this. There is a modicum of power in all control, even in the kind we have not sought. But there is also the twentieth-century French philosopher Simone de Beauvoir, whose thoughts resonate with how I understood as a girl what it meant to be female. Women are the second sex. As Jennifer Hockenbery Dragseth writes in *Thinking Woman*,

"Men are considered the normal human observer, the typical subject. In contrast, women are taught from a young age that they are divergent, atypical. They are not human; they are women. Women are, thus, used to considering themselves as that which is *Other* than the man." The strange part of this scenario, de Beauvoir says, is not that men objectify women in this way. It's that women participate, too.

Tess was four when her preschool teacher began incorporating money into the math curriculum, and Tess began stockpiling the change George left on his desk at the end of the day. Short stacks of pennies, nickels, dimes, and quarters lined up before her, she asked, "Mommy, who is that?" Abraham Lincoln, I told her, Thomas Jefferson, Franklin Roosevelt, George Washington. How many holiday meals does a daughter have to attend, how many coins does a girl need to drop into her piggy bank, before she understands her lower position in the world?

On Twitter in 2018, a man I didn't know posted a conversation with his young daughter. They were somewhere with statues, and she asked what they were for. "To recognize people who did important things," he replied. "Well, girls must not do important things," she said with some conviction. Because, of course, all those statues were of men. The Smithsonian reports that of the estimated 5,193 public statues of historical figures in the United States, 394, or less than 8 percent, are of women. In New York City, it's 3 percent, or 5 out of 150. And in Central Park, the most visited urban park in the U.S., there are 23 historical statues of men, while the only female representation shows up in the form of angels, Alice in Wonderland, and Mother Goose. Women, as sociologist Gaye Tuchman has noted, are also being "symbolically annihilated" in the media, where analyses of news stories have found that men are quoted three times as often as women—and no matter the gender of the journalist doing the reporting.

More Agentic Women, More Agentic Men

Sociologists track changes in gender stereotypes across the decades. In the last thirty years, the way women describe themselves has become less stereotypical. Women have become likely to report feeling agentic. Agency is a conventionally male trait that encompasses competence, assertiveness, and independence. What has not changed for women is their reporting of their own communality. Communion is a conventionally female trait defined by expressivity, warmth, and concern for the welfare of others. Women today feel more agentic but no less communal than their sisters in the 1970s. Similarly, contemporary men report an increased sense of agency (though on a less dramatic slope than women's) than they did in the past, with no change in communality, which they never took much stock in from the get-go.

As we see reflected both at work and at home, women have become more like men, men have become more like men, men have not become more like women, and women have not become less like women. "Of course, I felt guilty," Gretchen told me, concerned for the welfare of others, a concern her husband does not, at the very least, act on in the same way, "one night I did what my husband often does to me."

As women adopt agency, what has stopped men from embracing more communal traits—from becoming, in short, more like women? Few have shown much interest in solving for that x. In a 2015 paper, University of British Columbia social psychologist Toni Schmader and colleagues point out that while plenty of research has been devoted to understanding and mitigating "the psychological barriers that block women's interest, performance, and advancement in male-dominated, agentic roles (e.g., science, technology, engineering, and math) . . . Research has not . . . correspondingly examined men's under-representation in communal roles (e.g., careers in health care, early childhood education, and domestic roles including child care)." Such are the biases of science: Women should be encouraged to become more like men.

The thought is not without some logic. Agency is associated with healthier self-esteem. Or, rather, self-esteem tends to be higher in people who report feeling strong, independent, and confident. Communality, on the other hand, is associated with lower self-esteem—or, rather, self-esteem tends to be lower in people who report feeling warm, expressive, and submissive.

The self-esteem esteem of males is marginally higher at all stages of life than that of females, a difference that peaks during high school and decreases thereafter but never completely disappears. It is not necessarily "realistic self-esteem," as we say in my field, either. Female undergrads at Princeton, for example, have a higher chance of graduating with honors, but their male peers rate their own "intellectual self-confidence as compared to the average person your age" as higher than the young women do theirs. This can't be divorced from the value we assign to agency and communality, traits that do not inherently need to be so completely at odds.

There can be compassion in agency and power in communality—

witness the successes of Mothers Against Drunk Driving or Moms Demand Action Against Gun Violence, just to name a couple. Recall the nineteenth-century spirit of Mother's Day, which honored the transformative political activity of mothers outside of the home, women's work as community organizers. In 1914 Congress made the holiday "official," and reduced its communal acknowledgment of the importance of mothers' social action into a myopic celebration of their family devotion.

As Stanford sociologists Cecilia Ridgeway and Shelley Correll have observed, "What is interesting about the age-old gender system in western society is not that it never changes but that it sustains itself by continually redefining who men and women are and what they do while preserving the fundamental assumption that whatever the differences are, on balance, they imply that men are rightly more powerful." As women surpass men in many traditional measures of success like education, employment, and earnings, motherhood may be the final frontier in that power struggle. Women will never be as powerful as men as long as their strivings and comforts are more encumbered than men's in the home.

In 2018, the gender pay gap at British universities averaged 15 percent. With the female student population in Great Britain hovering around 56 percent and their female academic staff at 40 percent, less than a quarter of full professors were women. Writing for Wonkhe, a website focused on higher education policy, University of Bristol education professor Bruce Macfarlane attributed this "serious leak in the pipeline" to the responsibilities that female academics tend to take on at much higher rates than their male counterparts. He notes that women are overrepresented in the arena of "academic housework." Advising, mentoring, and committee work keep university communities thriving, but those communal activities are not what lead to promotion. Empirical work has shown that women are slower to become senior lecturers and associate professors as a result. In contrast, men devote their time to the research and writing that furthers their own careers.

Women contribute more to the university community but at some cost to greater power and influence. Macfarlane suggests that women alone can solve the full-professor problem by resisting pressure to become so involved with academic citizenship work—you know, they need to be more assertive. He does not acknowledge that whatever work women choose tends to become marginalized, or that women are often penalized in professional settings for withholding altruistic behaviors. Nor does he try to persuade men to up their efforts in the communal roles they typically eschew. Such are the biases of the professions: Women should be encouraged to become more like men.

Toni Schmader has another thought: Get men to become more like women. With her work, she provides a way to understand and combat men's reluctance to adopting communality. She notes that some barriers to becoming communal are external, for example, in terms of financial costs. Communal work pays less—or nothing at all, if we are talking about caring for one's own children. Other barriers are internal, invoking threats to masculine identity. Research reveals that "men who take time off from work for family reasons are perceived less positively . . . and earn less money over the course of their career." Act more like a woman, face the consequences borne by women.

Citing the success of the acronym "STEM" in corralling

broad public encouragement for girls in the sciences, Schmader suggests making "HEED" part of our vernacular: *h*ealth care, *e*lementary *e*ducation, and the *d*omestic sphere. Problem is, as Schmader tells me she's found, "People view careers in science and technology as having more worth to society than careers in health care and education. Men, more than women, see HEED careers as having less societal worth. This gender difference is itself partly explained by men's lower endorsement of communal values that focus on care for others. Because HEED careers are not seen as critically valuable to society, and because men are not intrinsically interested in them anyway, there seems to be less of a market for encouraging greater gender balance in care-oriented jobs and roles." Therein lies the problem with our biases: Men see nothing to gain in becoming more like women.

The Trouble with Benign Sexism

Women do more care work for their parents. The adult daughters of aging parents are more likely than adult sons to help with the activities of daily living like bathing, dressing, and feeding. Sons are more likely to perform so-called instrumental tasks like grocery shopping and yard work. The research concluded that while both men and women participate in elder care, women are more likely to take on tasks that are physically draining and that interrupt their daily lives, while men's assistance and involvement is more periodic, circumscribed, and flexible. When it comes to setting their personal priorities aside, be it for their children or their parents, women are the generous sex.

Communality is a good thing. We are flattered at the invocation of our warmth. There will be no movement against it, no #MeToo for pushing back at the assumption of munificence. Unlike hostile sexism, which inspires protest, benevolent sexism wins widespread acceptance, inhibiting collective action for social change. Indeed, while women reject hostile sexism more adamantly than men, they're also at least as likely to endorse the benevolent kind. As Supreme Court justice Ruth Bader Ginsburg has said, "Too few of us are eager to relinquish our place on the pedestal, even one that doubles as a cage." We smile when lauded for our giving, even as we're left little more than a stump.

Benevolent sexism, "an affectionate or chivalrous expression of male dominance," promotes the belief that women have a superior moral compass but also require the care and protection of men, whose needs they exist to fulfill. Behind every successful man there is a woman. Toe that party line and you will reap rewards. Don't call yourself a feminist, at least not within male earshot. As the journalist Rebecca Traister has noted, "Any time women do anything with their lives that is not in service to others, they are readily perceived as acting perversely."

Act perversely and face consequences. Women encounter daily reminders that it is our job to make men feel good. Smile, say male strangers on the street. It starts young. Boarding a plane behind Tess, then five, I watched as an older man seated in first class grinned at her when we made our way down the aisle. She likely scowled at him, as she is wont to do with strangers who look at her. "Why are they looking at me!?!" she often asks me through gritted teeth. Undiscouraged, the man proceeded to poke her firmly in the shoulder while exhorting her to "Smile!" Tess did not comply. Automatically and to my own horror, I found myself all but apologizing to the man for my daughter's failure to obey his instruction. Socialization runs so deep. (I quickly recovered my sanity and told her she never needed to smile for anyone, and I deeply regret not poking that guy back.)

Recently, a listing service I use for my practice—a service that I pay—called to request I take part in a ten-minute interview to help them improve their product. I said no. Undiscouraged, the young male sales associate on the other end of the phone persisted. I said no again, and expressed some irritation with the call, the likes of which in the past had ended in them trying to convince me to sell their service to my friends. Expressing my impatience was unnecessary. I might have just hung up. But his response was biting. "You don't have to get conflictual," he chided me, a paying customer. I hung up feeling guilty. I should've been nicer. Because, clearly, being nice is my job. Would he have responded to George in the same way? I can't know. At least on some level, that young man must have felt entitled to my compliance or my kindness and become angry when it was not forthcoming. Smile!

Women who violate norms of communality, who don't behave as women should, are punished. Research in applied psychology in both the laboratory and the workplace has shown that saying yes to altruistic behavior improves the favorability ratings of men but not women. In contrast, saying no to altruistic behavior increases the negative evaluations of women but not men. "Women neither were given as much credit for their altruism nor treated as tolerantly for their lack of it as were men who behaved identically," write the authors of one 2005 study out of NYU. This is the hostile side of benevolent sexism. "Benevolent" starts to feel like a misnomer.

To avoid negative evaluation, we act in concert with rarely

questioned stereotypes, and sometimes we even embrace them. Conservative activist Phyllis Schlafly opposed the Equal Rights Amendment on the grounds that it would upset the "beautiful way men treat women in this country." Laura in New York says, "I am and other women are conflicted. I love my work. It's my safe haven. It's very important to me. We went to counseling sessions where my husband said, 'You're putting work in front of me.' That was a conscious decision. I feel respected and liked there. But then a part of us wants to be cared for. That may seem like weakness or, I'm not sure what to call it. I have that traditional aspect. I'd like to be treated like a lady. Maybe even order for me sometime."

If embracing one's gentler nature cannot be a 24/7 endeavor, feeling in control of household governance might satisfy other, more prohibited female desires. Psychologists suggest that a woman who believes she is the master of her home is less likely to seek influence outside of it. In 2014, UC Berkeley and Emory social psychologists Serena Chen and Melissa Williams tested this theory in the lab, asking men and women both to imagine how a person might feel when engaged in a variety of household duties, from making a budget to sweeping a floor. Both sexes reported that adults performing tasks involving decision-making were likely to feel more powerful than those engaged in house-keeping. Next, participants were instructed to imagine themselves in a variety of scenarios where they were either the sole manager of their household or a co-manager with their spouse. Women assigned to the solo home management scenario later expressed less interest in workplace power than women in the co-manager one. Men's interest in workplace power was not impacted by their (imagined) domestic role.

"Exercising power over household decisions may bring a semblance of status and control to women's traditional role, to the point where they may have less desire to push against the obstacles to achieving additional power outside the home," explain Williams and Chen. "We propose that power over domestic decision making, in which women are given the ultimate say in household choices that affect others' daily lives, serves to create an illusion of equality in the domain of power. Women's power in the household may appear to compensate for a lack of power in the workplace or public sphere. Ultimately, however, women must at least partially abdicate their role as household decision makers—and men must agree to share such authority—in order to realize true gender equality in both the public and private spheres."

What Chen and Williams highlight is that benevolent sexism is the spoonful of sugar that helps the patriarchy go down. Women are wonderful but childlike, best suited for low-status roles. As Simon Fraser University social psychologist Stephen Wright and University of Osnabrück social psychologist Julia Becker have put it, "despite the clearly patronizing nature of benevolent sexist beliefs, they also can be interpreted as expressing positive affect toward women, can be seen by both women and men as providing personal and group benefits for women, and thus can motivate women to be complicit in the maintenance of the current gender status quo."

Wright and Becker decided to test whether exposure to benevolent and hostile sexism would impact a woman's desire to get involved in social action. Ninety-nine women in a teacher-training program in Germany volunteered for an experiment purportedly about memory. First, they were asked to read six sentences about "common beliefs." Some participants read sentences endorsing benevolent sexism (for example, "Women have a way of caring that men are not capable of"). Others read sentences endorsing hostile sexism (for example, "When women have to work together, they often get into catfights"). A third group read neutral statements about women and men. Next, all ninety-nine subjects completed a handful of measures about fairness in the gender system, the advantages of being a woman, and the likelihood that they would take part in some sort of social protest (for example, "I would participate in a rally demanding equal salaries for women and men"). Finally, they had to select the six sentences they'd initially read from among a group of twenty-four.

In the end, the women who'd read the benevolently sexist statements were the least likely of the three groups to report that they would sign a gender-related petition or distribute flyers designed to raise awareness about gender inequality. Conversely, exposure to hostile sexism increased the likelihood of taking both of these actions. Exposure to just six benevolently sexist statements upped the women's perception that the gender system is fair and that being a woman is advantageous. Then what is there to protest, after all? The benevolently sexist sentences also increased women's positive affect, reducing the number of flyers they were willing to take and the likelihood of signing that petition on behalf of women. Again in contrast, exposure to hostile sexism decreased the perception that the gender system is fair, decreased the perceived advantages of being a woman, and increased negative affect—upping the willingness to engage in gender-related collective action.

This would seem to tell us something about our failure to

rise up en masse—to answer our unfulfilled, rising expectations with revolution, insurgency, and civil unrest—to have acquiesced to our position as the handler of all things. "You're a very good mommy," is all men have to say. Wright and Becker note, "[W]omen adopt belief systems that serve as justifications for existing gender inequality at least in part to make the best of an unfavorable situation rather than challenging it. [Men] flatter women into active cooperation with a patriarchal system by enhancing an illusion of . . . individual and group benefits of being a woman. Thus, benevolent sexism creates a more positive social identity for women and offers a means by which women as individuals can manage within a sexist system." Hostile sexism is squalid and nasty, but at least it inspires a fight. Benign sexism is much more insidious. Lauded for loving kindness, mothers do not feel inspired to resist.

Cautionary Tales

In 2017, *Newsweek* ran the headline "Women over 85 Are Happier Because Their Partner Is Dead by Then, Psychiatrists Say." The article that followed reported on an English study by the National Health Service that asked eight thousand participants to respond to statements like "I've been feeling relaxed" and "I've been feeling good about myself" on a five-point scale ranging from always to never. Based on the responses of those surveyed, the NHS determined that though women report increasing levels of happiness from retirement age on, they are less happy than men over most of their lives. At eighty-five, though, the gender difference flips. In old age, women are happier than men. Asked to explain the finding, Kate Lovett, the dean of the UK's Royal College of Psychiatrists, explained that women "are still more likely to bear the brunt of domestic and caring responsibilities." Over time, those burdens ebb. By eighty-five, women's partners have likely passed away. No longer responsible for the constant care of another, Lovett pointed out, they're happier once their partners have died. Died!

The study is a cautionary tale. I came across gentler versions of that attitude among the non-octogenarians in my interview pool and in articles that I read. Kristin, a mother of two in Ann Arbor, Michigan, said, "I have a friend who's a single mom. She said it would be harder being married. As a single mom, she can't get frustrated with anyone. She just has to do it all. When my husband is on a trip and I'm doing everything, I just do it. There's no point of contention lurking beneath the surface. It's nicer, in a way."

"Why do new mothers hate their husbands?" posed a working woman calling herself Ingrate New Mom to an advice columnist for *The Cut*, a Web offshoot of *New York* magazine. She went on to explain, "I'd love to come downstairs on a Saturday morning and be the one to plop on the couch with my coffee (instead of keeping the 15-month-old from killing himself). I'd love for Jim to worry about milestones or whether the baby needs a hat or not. I guess I'm tired of always asking and feeling like I'm managing an enthusiastic employee who fails to take initiative."

Ask Polly's Heather Havrilesky responded, "Believe me, your current separation of tasks is making you *both* unhappy. Your husband might look relaxed now, but he's not. He knows that you hate his guts. He is wary of this. He feels worried that you will hate him forever. It doesn't feel good for him, either. Your unequal, unbalanced life might feel reasonably okay to him now. He probably thinks he's doing a lot, and sure, he does things! He does lots of stuff really well! But your balance of tasks is not good, and that doesn't benefit him in the long haul. In the big picture, he will wind up with a crabby, silently resentful wife who blames him for breathing oxygen and would rather eat a plate of live maggots than have sex with him."

As bell hooks wrote, "There can be no love when there is domination."

My widowed grandmother had a boyfriend for the last fifteen years of her life. His name was Hans, they'd both fled Nazi Germany, and their South Florida condominiums were not too far apart. Hans wanted to move in with my grandmother, but she adamantly refused, and I remember asking her why. "I'm NOT going to take care of another man," she said pointedly and with rage. I must have been twenty-five. I think I found it funny at the time.

I do not find it funny anymore. I don't want to be happier when my partner is dead. I don't want to wish that I were parenting alone. I don't want to prefer the ingestion of live maggots to sex with my husband. Across cultures, women go into marriage reporting less hope for fulfillment than men. While both sexes demonstrate unrealistic optimism about their relationships—predicting that they are less likely than the average person to be unhappily married or divorced—men are more idealistic than women.

At the outset of their unions, as compared to women, men guess that they are less likely to get divorced; they also estimate a higher likelihood that they will have a happy relationship.

Research has shown that men and women have different expectations for romantic partnerships and that men are ultimately more likely than women to feel satisfied. One explanation is that women have higher expectations around intimacy and emotional support, expectations that men, socialized for distance, can't fulfill. Another is that the role of each spouse differs, with the tasks of married womanhood being more stressful and less gratifying than those left to the married man. Not only does she cook his dinner and care for his children, research has also shown that women make more efforts to generate or maintain good moods in their spouse (smile!). Gretchen, Ingrate New Mom, and I can all attest to that. Acting out male privilege is hardly an exclusively male endeavor.

Together we do this. Men can choose to be blind to the himpathetic lengths women go to, and women can allow them to maintain that blindness. Men have been raised to compete for power, and women to keep their mouths shut. One 1998 study took a close look at twelve newly married couples who all reported enjoying equal partnerships. Despite their own estimations, though, the researchers found that not a single pair ultimately fit the model of equality that they had outlined before the study began.

Sociologist Anne Rankin Mahoney and family therapist Carmen Knudson-Martin defined equality thus (and check yourself out in this mirror): Partners hold equal status, attention to the other in the relationship is mutual, accommodation in the relationship is mutual, and there is shared well-being. Instead, even among this group of couples who volunteered for the study specifically because they truly believed they'd achieved marital parity, Mahoney and Martin found that the women in each of the pairs were more likely than the men to accommodate their partner's desires, to speak of fitting their lives around their partner's schedule, to describe attending to their partner's emotional needs, to worry about upsetting their partner, and to do what their partner wanted. They found: "Most of the couples created an image or myth of equality that was consistent with their expectations and ideals. It seemed to serve as a reassurance, a symbolic representation of their commitment to an equal relationship. For some it was a substitute for practice."

Unentitlement

Entitlement gets a bad rap, but too little of it can leave one wanting. Kyla, thirty-four, the mother of a one-year-old in South Salem, New York, works from home with the help of a part-time babysitter. Her husband's office is a short drive away. She said, "In my mind, there's something about John physically going to work that warrants more of a break. So I feel less entitled to rest and relaxation. I talk about this with my therapist all the time because it's crazy for me to think this way. I'm working on client work in between taking care of Zoey all week and am often just as exhausted. So John is always the one to suggest I need breaks, which is pretty much the only reason I take them. He was the one to suggest I do a spin class every Friday morning, or schedule a haircut, or take a nap. It feels weird to say, but sometimes I think there's something going on with me internally where I think I should never take time to myself. John realized early on that he needs to force me to relax, so he does."

When not explicitly encouraged to give themselves a break,

mothers don't always sign up for one. Studies have shown that women feel a lower sense of claim than men to all sorts of nice things, including payment in exchange for work. In lab settings, women ask for less money than men do and assert that they should work longer, harder, better, and more efficiently for their pay. This seems to carry over to their dealings with their kids: A 2018 data analysis from BusyKid, an app that lets parents pay their children online for chores, found that boys were given twice as much money per week as girls.

In a 2003 study with MBA students involving a simulated job interview, 85 percent of the men reported that they knew their worth, while almost the same percentage of women reported that they did not; in the same study, 70 percent of men expressed the belief that they deserved above-average salaries, while only 30 percent of women did the same.

The gender norm shows up young. A study from 1979 found in children as young as six the same gender gap in self-confidence and entitlement that is found among adults. Family psychologists Philip and Carolyn Cowan believe that women's lack of entitlement is partially responsible for the uneven distribution of family labor. They call it "unentitlement."

Female unentitlement is ubiquitous. In 2009's *Still Failing at Fairness*, educators David Sadker and Karen Zittleman observed that school-age girls take fewer opportunities than boys to raise their hands in class (teachers in their study also called on boys with eight times the frequency). In 2016's *Girls & Sex*, journalist Peggy Orenstein reported that adolescent-to-college-age girls often believe or at least behave as if sex is exclusively about male pleasure (the boys they're involved with don't protest). In *The Silent Sex*, political scientists Christopher

Karpowitz and Tali Mendelberg suggest that women in the public sphere feel less entitled not only to pay but also to authority. And then, too, there is the home.

Stanford sociologist Aliya Rao studies unemployment and how middle-class, dual-earner couples navigate the challenging experience of job loss. Observing families with children in which one of the partners had been laid off, Rao found that even when it came to finding work, women behaved as if they had less right than men to family support. She tells me, "When men lose their jobs, unemployment becomes a really central aspect of family life. It's talked about daily by husbands and wives, especially his job-searching activity. It shapes the home. In families with unemployed men, they'd create offices to facilitate the husbands' job-searching abilities, even in a time when they have fewer resources—building a wall in the living room so he can be at home without being at home, not be disturbed by the kids. With unemployed women, this is not happening. Their unemployment is peripheral. They talk about it but don't emphasize it. There's no creating a space for her. One of the families, the son complained to me, 'The one thing that's changed since my mom has been home is she uses my desk as her work space.'

"The other thing is, with husbands, their wives offer so much encouragement in the job search. It's a really hard process with daily rejection. Wives play an instrumental role in keeping their husbands going. With unemployed women, their husbands weren't doing this emotion work. Women's unemployment is not seen as a problem that needed to be rectified immediately. 'You can be the mom you couldn't be before.' Unemployed dads do a little more child care than when they were working, but not that much more. The reason they give is that they need to job-search, and their wives agree on that. There's no major shift. We might think Dad would pick up the kids all the time. That is not happening. My point is that couples work hard to maintain gender inequalities at a time when it would be easy to dismantle them." Even when their male partners are unemployed and they are working themselves, women do not appear to feel entitled to more help with children, and they don't give themselves a similar break from family work when they are the one searching for a job.

Both male entitlement and female unentitlement are supported by our faith in a just universe. If we imagine that the world is fair—an easier attitude to live with than the opposite—we can stomach sexism, the set of beliefs that legitimate women's subservient role. Men are deserving of their power and influence, and women of their high moral esteem. System justification theory suggests that people have a fundamental psychological need to believe that the system they live under is fair.

The veneer of "complementary but equal" in the gender system casts acceptability on sex roles that mostly benefit men. It serves a palliative function. New York University social psychologist John Jost has spent his career studying system justification, a tendency that is, he writes, "born of an attempt to reduce the cognitive or ideological dissonance that is aroused when citizens profess the value of equality while living in a clearly hierarchical society." When I contact him, he sends me a handful of recent papers he's co-authored. The papers detail experiments that demonstrate how members of low-status groups embrace socially desirable trait ascriptions as a trade-off for their own subordination. You can't tell women that they're too dumb to do anything but stay home and make sandwiches (that would be hostile), but you can point out how their loving nature makes them especially well suited for that task. Social psychology calls this "role justification," and it "contributes to the perceived legitimacy of the status quo by characterizing cultural divisions of labor as not only fair but perhaps even natural and inevitable," Jost notes.

I spent a day immersed in Jost's work before speaking with him, and I told him how glum I felt after reading his findings. "It's a tricky business for a lot of reasons. Nobody wants to be unhappy or depressed," he says. "And it really is depressing if you think about how hard it is to change inequality or injustice. Precisely because people would rather feel good than bad, they respond defensively and engage in more system justification when you point out all the problems. It's not a simple matter. This is what activists do. They put things in your face that you'd rather not think about. Eventually, it gets through. As a society, we are making a bit of progress, but it's not a linear thing. Sometimes it lurches forward. #MeToo came out of nowhere. It says a lot about how much has changed, how behaviors that were tolerated are now the subject of massive moral outrage. And some people feel it's moving too fast and going too far."

It's been half a century since Betty Friedan published *The Feminine Mystique*. Is the glass half empty or half full? Has change come too fast or too slow? Women are so good at child care, we continue to assert, taking that trade-off, complicit in our own subordination. To remain at peace in a system we feel powerless to change, we swallow justifications that support our ongoing servitude.

Lab experiments have shown that research participants randomly assigned to the lower-paid of two groups subsequently come to believe not that their group is being arbitrarily short-changed but, rather, that they are less competent. Better to be a devil in heaven than an angel in hell. Similarly, when research participants are primed to believe in the fairness of a system, there are measurable impacts on their attitudes. In one social psychology experiment at Tulane and University of California, Santa Barbara, men who read statements that supported a belief in meritocracy ("Persistence leads to success" or "Rich people deserve it") went on to demand higher pay for work they'd completed than men who had not been similarly primed.

System-justifying statements had little impact on the amount of pay women asked for. Consistent with other studies, women simply requested less than men across the board. The study's authors concluded, "Elevated feelings of entitlement may . . . blind men to seeing when they are overbenefited, allow them to justify their privileged position, and lead them to regard efforts to 'level the playing field' as unjust. In contrast, a depressed sense of entitlement among women may prevent them from seeing when they are targets of discrimination and reduce the likelihood that they will engage in collective action to challenge the distribution of social goods. In this way, gender differences in feelings of personal entitlement may serve to perpetuate and maintain gender inequality."

As Susan Faludi writes in *Backlash*, "Instead of assailing injustice, many women have learned to adjust to it."

It is time to stop adjusting, to come to terms with the fact that we're better off living uncomfortably with obvious truths than comfortably with well-worn misrepresentations. Disavowing our displeasure has not led to change. Neither has denying it with cries of "At least he helps." Only once we begin to see all sexism as blatantly hostile will there be pushback, an end to justification in each imbalanced home. Jost offers, "One can only speculate (and perhaps hope) that such ideological comforts will be less necessary fifty years from now."

Fifty Years from Now

Carissa in Seattle with the foot surgery told me, "My mom will often say to me, 'We fought for you to have what you have, and yet it's totally crazy and unsustainable, being a full-time working woman.' Societal norms haven't changed that much. We have not created the balance that is needed. It's a daily experience for me and most of my friends."

The cultural-lag hypothesis tells us that group attitudes always drag behind societal change. But exactly how long is that lag supposed to last? At what point is it reasonable to stop calling it a lag? It's been twenty years since men's proportion of caretaking increased in response to greater demands from working mothers. Still, maybe we are too impatient. Maybe a change is gonna come. More likely, as Harry Brighouse and Erik Olin Wright suggest, the norms "are sufficiently robust and deeply entrenched to remain very sticky unless directly undermined."

Remember the research demonstrating that spousal equality promotes marital success and that inequality undermines it? A similar relationship has been found between men and women and society at large. Equality between the sexes is positively related to a citizenry's general happiness. At a national level, as the first rises, so does the second—and for men as much as women. Advancements in the status of women do not seem to come at a cost to men. Men may have a hard time believing this. You'll recall "I'll go along with some of it, equal pay for equal work, that seems fair enough. . . . [But] you can't tell me women's lib means I have to wash dishes, does it?"

Couples vary in their commitment to quashing the lag. In studies, spouses aspiring to equal parenting express awareness about gender politics, share dual commitments to work and family, and feel poorly served by traditional gender roles. They try to reach their goals through actively negotiating family life, questioning gendered entitlements, developing new competencies, and paying mutual attention to family tasks. Equality is not so much an end point as a process.

Responsibility for that process can too easily fall on mothers. Social psychologist Francine Deutsch tells me, "The women who were successful in achieving an equally sharing relationship were pretty relentless, for the most part, in just articulating it. I think most men are not horrible people and have a sense of justice and can hear that, but still, sometimes it has to be more than one time. This dynamic I saw, women doing and doing and doing and then having the blowup and the man just trying to get that under control, 'I'll do a few things.' That's not equality, and it doesn't become equality. I always think of this one woman, when she first got married, it was very traditional. But that stopped working for her, and she told me, 'I just sat him down and said, It's got to be like this, and I'm going to keep pushing until that's what this is.' It's persistence, the belief that this is the right thing, and the willingness to communicate repeatedly about it."

Or, as gender psychologist Sandra Bem has written, women can empower themselves by taking their own preferences, goals, and experiences seriously, and expecting their partners to take them seriously as well. Women must begin to see their own activities "whatever it is that they do and desire—as no less important and no less deserving of special consideration than those of the men in their lives." In the face of what Simone de Beauvoir describes as "constant socialization to consider herself as the object who exists for the pleasure and comfort of the man. . . ."

Of course, all of the above is true. But responsibility for the process must be shared. This is not one more thing for mothers to spearhead alone. Patrick Coleman, the editor at *Fatherly*, said, "I would like to see men really take this on. Like really take it on. Because making little changes and then waiting for society to push us into changing our role will take generations and generations. I think we can change it more quickly if we own those steps. Waiting for or expecting women to hand down a list of demands that we then agree to, I don't think that's going to work. Men need to say, 'We have to do this now.' It's in our power to end it." When parenting is a conscious collaboration, men, like women, track their own responsibilities and think ahead about what their children need. They do not look to their wives for orders or direction. Strong gender egalitarianism means a family life free from assumptions about who does what based on activities deemed more appropriate for fathers or for mothers.

It has been suggested that the political and social moment we now find ourselves in calls on each of us to replace our commitment to individual gain with an ethic of care and collective responsibility. Can parents be at the forefront of that rebellion? Parenthood turns our devotion to narrow self-interest inside out. It requires the kind of generous attention to the good of others that is rarely widely embraced in postmodern life. Or, rather, motherhood does. Fatherhood has yet to get there, but it must if we are ever to achieve our upright goals.

Writing about fifty years ago, the journalist Martha Weinman Lear recalled, "In the early sixties, I knew many women—myself among them—who were doing precisely the same jobs as men, for far less pay. We absorbed it as a natural inequity. Today, even people who call themselves antifeminist insist upon equal pay for equal work. It has passed into the national consciousness as a basic principle, not of feminism—as it clearly was then—but of pure justice."

In the early years of the twenty-first century, I knew many mothers, myself among them, who were working just as hard outside the home as fathers, while also doing far more deep inside it. We absorbed it as a natural inequity. Under some scrutiny, the patina of "natural" dulled. The national consciousness shifted. Mothering and fathering became indiscernible. Social justice triumphed, and parenting was all the rage.

ACKNOWLEDGMENTS

With deep gratitude to my friend Megan Abbott and my agent, Dan Conaway, without whose enthusiasm and encouragement this project would never have been more than just another fleeting idea. To my sister, Cori Carr, my friends Nana Asfour and Mark Swartz, and Andrea Vedder at Writers House for being such kind, generous, and attentive readers whenever I needed them to be (as well as to Kerri Kolen for her early support). Then, too, and not at all least to my editor, Stephanie Hitchcock, and everyone at HarperCollins for never wavering in their passion for and commitment to this book; it has been my pleasure and good fortune to get to have this experience with you.

I am so appreciative of all the parents, academics, and other various experts quoted extensively in these pages. Our conversations were both enlightening and a total hoot. More people than I can name helped me recruit subjects—thank you especially Rona Kobell, Lisa Goren, Marla Garfield, Adrienne Lapidos, Emily Grey Berman, Anjali Naik Polan, Liz Greenberg, and Sarah Granatir Bryan (and Facebook, for allowing me to cast a wider net). Lizzie Fassler, Kate Zolotkovsky, and Ivy and Davin Hatsengate: I could not have asked for better companions as we discussed these (and other) pressing issues against the backdrop of homework and dinner over what is now many years of playdates. I'm so lucky to be sharing this longest shortest time with you.

To my parents, Michael and Helene Lockman, for never trying to hide the fact that marriage is hard, and for sticking it through with fortitude and joy (happy just-belated fiftieth anniversary!). Though you no longer host ACLU mailing parties in your basement, your activism and values taught me to use my mind and to speak it, and I love you very much.

Finally, to my husband, George Kingsley, whose spirit and good humor is best illustrated by the fact that he has taken to calling himself my muse. It is not every man who would offer unflagging support for a book that chronicled the stickiest parts of his marriage, and knowing that you did allowed me to write without hesitation. You are not actually my muse, but something better.

NOTES

Introduction: The Problem That Has No Name

10 "her female undergraduates at Berkeley in the '80s": Arlie Hochschild, *The Second Shift* (New York: Viking Adult, 1989), xiv.

10 "reported on a study of two hundred couples out of Ohio State": Claire Kamp Dush, "Men Share Housework Equally—Until the First Baby," posted 5/10/15, https://www.newsweek.com/men-share-housework -equally-until-first-baby-330347

11 "more theoretically egalitarian times, were no better": Claire Cain Miller, "Millennial Men Aren't the Dads They Thought They'd Be," *New York Times*, July 30, 2015, https://www.nytimes.com/2015 /07/31/upshot/millennial-men-find-work-and-family-hard-to -balance.html

11 "told Pew that their responsibilities were shared equally": "Raising Kids and Running a Household: How Working Parents Share the Load," Pew Research Trends, November 4, 2015, https://www.pewsocialtrends .org/2015/11/04/raising-kids-and-running-a-household-how -working-parents-share-the-load/

11 "survey of parents in eight Western countries": "Sharing Chores at Home: Houses Divided," *The Economist*, October 5, 2017, https://www .economist.com/international/2017/10/05/houses-divided

11 "Why don't men do more?": Scott Coltrane, "Research on Household Labor: Modeling and Measuring the Social Embeddedness of Routine Family Work," *Journal of Marriage and Family* 62, no. 4 (November 2000): 1208–33.

14 "inaugural edition of *Ms.* magazine back in 1971": Jane O'Reilly, "The Housewife's Moment of Truth," *Ms.*, December 20, 1971, http:// nymag.com/news/features/46167/

15 "I have to wash dishes": Ibid.

16 "and their male partners 35 percent": "Time spent in primary activities by married mothers and fathers by employment status of self and spouse . . . 2011–15," Bureau of Labor Statistics, https://www.bls.gov /tus/tables/a7_1115.pdf

16 "held steady since the year 2000": "Time spent in primary activities by married mothers and fathers by employment status of self and spouse . . . 2005–09," Bureau of Labor Statistics, https://www.bls.gov /tus/tables/a7_0509.htm

17 "letters could've been written by the same person": Cheryl Strayed and Steve Almond, "Save Me from This Domestic Drudgery!" *New York Times*, May 8, 2018, https://www.nytimes.com/2018/05/08/style /household-parenting-marriage-share-work.html

17 "more fruitful for understanding and eradicating inequality": Toni Calasanti and Carol Bailey, "Gender Inequality and the Division of Household Labor in the United States and Sweden: A Socialist-Feminist Approach," *Social Problems* 38, no. 1 (February 1991): 34–53.

18 "more threatening than condemning the political": Amy Richards, *Opting In* (New York: Farrar, Straus and Giroux, 2008), 9.

Chapter 1: On How Life Is

19 "tripled the amount of time they spend with their kids since 1965": Kim Parker and Gretchen Livingston, "7 Facts About American Dads," *Pew Research Center*, June 13, 2018, http://www.pewresearch .org/fact-tank/2018/06/13/fathers-day-facts/

19 "up from 26 percent a decade before": "Statistics on Stay-At-Home Dads," National At-Home Dad Network, accessed October 18, 2018, http://athomedad.org/media-resources/statistics/

19 "twice the number there were ten years ago": Ibid.

19 "parenting is extremely important to their identity": "Parenting in America," *Pew Research Center Social & Demographic Trends*, December 17, 2015, http://www.pewsocialtrends.org/2015/12/17/2 -satisfaction-time-and-support/

19 "only twice as many hours in 2010": Suzanne Bianchi, Liana Sayer, Melissa Milkie, and John Robinson, "Housework: Who Did, Does or Will Do It, and How Much Does It Matter?" *Social Forces* 91, no. 1 (September 2012): 55–63.

19 "from under 20 percent to almost 35 percent": Jennifer Hook, "Care in Context: Men's Unpaid Work in 20 Countries, 1965–2003," *American Sociological Review* 71 (August 2006): 639–60.

19 "where of course it has remained ever since": Kim Parker and Wendy

Wang, "Modern Parenthood: Roles of Moms and Dads Converge as They Balance Work and Family," *Pew Research Social & Demographic Trends*, March 14, 2013, http://www.pewsocialtrends.org/2013/03/14/modern-parenthood-roles-of-moms-and-dads-converge-as-they-balance-work-and-family/

20 "spawned the modern, involved father": Sara Raley, Suzanne Bianchi, and Wendy Wang, "When Do Fathers Care? Mothers' Economic Contribution and Fathers' Involvement in Child Care," *American Journal of Sociology* 117, no. 5 (March 2012): 1422–59, https://www.ncbi.nlm.nih.gov/pmc/articles/PMC4568757/

20 "they were their husband's property": Rebecca Traister, *All the Single Ladies* (New York: Simon & Schuster, 2016), 41.

20 "The honorifics 'Miss' and 'Mrs.'": Alexandra Buxton, "Mistress, Miss, Mrs or Ms: untangling the shifting history of women's titles," *New Statesman*, September 12, 2014, https://www.newstatesman.com/cultural-capital/2014/09/mistress-miss-mrs-or-ms-untangling-shifting-history-women-s-titles

20 "legal . . . to fire or refuse to employ a married woman": Susan Thistle, *From Marriage to Market* (California: University of California Press, 2006), 52–53.

20 "every husband 'the head of household'": Susan Faludi, *Backlash* (New York: Crown Publishing, 1991), 81.

21 "her first husband, whom she 'long ago divorced'": Sheila Nevins, "HBO Documentary Head Sheila Nevins On Her Career, Aging and Family," interview by Leonard Lopate, *The Leonard Lopate Show*, WNYC, May 1, 2017. Audio 10:30. https://www.wnyc.org/story/hbo-documentary-filmmaker-sheila-nevins/

21 "When a dad comes, we clap": Jay Miranda, "Why the Hell Do We Clap for the Dads?" *Mom.me*, July 16, 2015, https://mom.me/lifestyle/20953-when-dads-get-praise-stuff-moms-do-all-time/

22 "U.S. states with the highest divorce rates": "Divorce Rate in the United States in 2016," Statista: The Statistics Portal, accessed October 18, 2018, https://www.statista.com/statistics/621703/divorce-rate-in-the-united-states-by-state/

24 "haven't totally caught up to women's expectations": Jill Filipovic, *The H-Spot* (New York: Nation Books, 2017), 141.

24 "new egalitarian couple is way ahead of its time": Carolyn Cowan and Philip Cowan, *When Partners Become Parents* (New York: Routledge, 1999), 97.

25 "since the U.S. began keeping reliable statistics": Paul Raeburn, *Do Fathers Matter?* (New York: Scientific American, 2014), 220.

25 "fewer father-present families": Scott Coltrane, "Fatherhood, Gender and Work-Family Policies," in *The Real Utopias Project: Gender Equality, Transforming Family Divisions of Labor* (Brooklyn: Verso, 2009), 386.

25 "Men are among the 3 to 5 percent of male mammals": Peter Gray and Kermyt Anderson, *Fatherhood* (Massachusetts: Harvard University Press, 2010), 59.

25 "three hours more per week than men without kids": Scott Coltrane, "Fatherhood, Gender and Work-Family Policies," in *The Real Utopias Project: Gender Equality, Transforming Family Divisions of Labor* (Brooklyn: Verso, 2009), 389.

25 "labor is very important to a successful marriage": Abigail Geiger, "Sharing Chores a Key to Good Marriage, Say Majority of Married Adults," *Pew Research Center*, November 30, 2016, http://www .pewresearch.org/fact-tank/2016/11/30/sharing-chores-a-key-to -good-marriage-say-majority-of-married-adults/

25 "more in 'the culture of fatherhood' than in actual behavior": Berna- dette Park, J. Allegra Smith, and Joshua Correll, "The persistence of implicit behavioral associations for moms and dads," *Journal of Experimental Social Psychology* 46 (2010): 809–15.

25 "between two and ten times as much unpaid care": "Why the majority of the world's poor are women," Oxfam International, accessed Octo- ber 18, 2018, https://www.oxfam.org/en/even-it/why-majority-worlds -poor-are-women

26 "paid parental leave exclusively for fathers": Elin Kvande and Berit Brandth, "Fathers on Leave Alone in Norway: Changes and Continuities" in Comparative Perspectives on Work-Life Balance and Gender Equality 6, 29–44 (New York: Springer Publishing, 2017), https://link.springer .com/chapter/10.1007/978-3-319-42970-0_3

26 "compared to men's three": Elizabeth Weingarten, "Unpaid Work Should Be Measured and Valued, but Mostly Isn't," *Financial Times*, January 13, 2017, https://ftalphaville.ft.com/2017/01/13/2182312/guest

-article-unpaid-work-should-be-measured-and-valued-but-mostly
-isnt/?mhq5j=e3

26 "in South Asia, where women carry": Ibid.

26 "men only one": "Employment: Time Spent in Paid and Unpaid Work,
by Sex," OECD.stat, accessed October 20, 2018, https://stats.oecd
.org/index.aspx?queryid=54757

26 "six hours each day collecting water": Anam Parvez Butt, Jane
Remme, Lucia Rost, and Sandrine Koissy-Kpein, "Exploring the Need
for Gender-Equitable Fiscal Policies for Human Economy: Evidence
from Uganda and Zimbabwe," Oxfam, March 2018.

26 "the wealthier the country": Gaelle Ferrant, Luca Maria Pesando,
and Keiko Nowacka, "Unpaid Care Work: The Missing Link in the
Analysis of Gender Gaps in Labour Outcomes," OECD Development
Centre, December 2014, https://www.oecd.org/dev/development-gender
/Unpaid_care_work.pdf

26 "achieve gender equity in their homes": "Men Taking on 50 Percent
of the World's Child Care and Domestic Work Requires Global Goal
and Immediate Action, Reveals State of the World's Fathers Report,"
Men Care: A Global Fatherhood Campaign, June 2017, https://men
-care.org/2017/06/09/men-taking-on-50-percent-of-the-worlds-child
care-and-domestic-work-requires-global-goal-and-immediate-action
-reveals-state-of-the-worlds-fathers-report/

27 "an inequality of crisis proportions": Francine Deutsch, *Halving It All*
(Cambridge, Massachusetts: Harvard University Press, 1999), 5.

29 "they themselves are doing less": Carolyn Cowan and Philip Cowan,
When Partners Become Parents (New York: Routledge, 1999), 97.

30 "to family care as men": Lyn Craig and Killian Mullan, "Parenthood,
Gender and Work-Family Time in the United States, Australia, Italy,
France and Denmark," *Journal of Marriage and Family* 72, no. 5
(October 2010): 1344–61.

30 "caring for their kids": Janet C. Gornick and Marcia K. Meyers, "Institutions That Support Gender Equality in Parenthood and Employment,"
in *The Real Utopias Project: Gender Equality, Transforming Family
Divisions of Labor* (Brooklyn: Verso, 2009), 10.

30 "with the care of their young": Marc H. Bornstein, "Parenting x
Gender x Culture x Time," in *Gender and Parenthood: Biological and*

Social Scientific Perspectives, eds. W. Bradford Wilcox and Kathleen Kovner Kline (New York: Columbia University Press, 2013), 100.

30 "United Nations estimated that women average 2.6 times": UN Women, "Turning Promises Into Action," 2018, http://www.unwomen.org /-/media/headquarters/attachments/sections/library/publications/201 8/sdg-report-summary-gender-equality-in-the-2030-agenda-for -sustainable-development-2018-en.pdf?la=en&vs=949

31 "employed for pay": Janet C. Gornick and Marcia K. Meyers, *The Real Utopias Project: Gender Equality, Transforming Family Divisions of Labor* (Brooklyn: Verso, 2009), 7.

31 "comparativ- time-use studies": Ibid., 10.

31 "relatively large in magnitude": Erika Lawrence, Rebecca J. Cobb, Alexia D. Rothman, Michael T. Rothman, and Thomas N. Bradbury, "Marital Satisfaction Across the Transition to Parenthood," *Journal of Family Psychology* 22, no. 1 (February 2008): 41–50.

31 "at twice the rate for parents": Ibid.

31 "before a child's first birthday": Ibid.

31 "so, too, does the discontent": Jean M. Twenge, W. Keith Campbell, and Craig A. Foster, "Parenthood and Marital Satisfaction: A Meta -Analytic Review," *Journal of Marriage and Family* 65, no. 3 (August 2003): 574–83.

32 "People who are sleep deprived": Amie M. Gordon and Serena Chen, "The Role of Sleep in Interpersonal Conflict: Do Sleepless Nights Mean Worse Fights?" *Social Psychological and Personality Science* 5, no. 2 (2014): 168–75.

32 "time spent on routine household labor": Janeen Baxter, Belinda Hewitt, and Michele Haynes, "Life Course Transitions and Housework: Marriage, Parenthood, and Time on Housework," *Journal of Marriage and Family* 70 (May 2008), 259–72.

32 "average housework hours for men": Ibid.

32 "a man's time in unpaid domestic labor": Ibid.

32 "in the U.S. and elsewhere": Suzanne M. Bianchi and Melissa Milkie, "Work and Family Research in the First Decade of the 21st Century," *Journal of Marriage and Family* 72 (June 2010): 705–25.

32 "confounded scholars for years": Anne-Rigt Poortman and Tanja Van Der Lippe, "Attitudes Toward Housework and Child Care and

the Gendered Division of Labor," *Journal of Marriage and Family* 71 (August 2009): 526–41.

33 "why men do so little": Scott Coltrane, "Research on Household Labor: Modeling and Measuring the Social Embeddedness of Routine Family Work," *Journal of Marriage and Family* 62, no. 4 (November 2000): 1208–33.

33 "the care of others": Suzanne M. Bianchi, Liana C. Sayer, Melissa A. Milkie, and John P. Robinson, "Housework: Who Did, Does or Will Do It, and How Much Does It Matter?" *Social Forces* 91, no. 1 (September 2012): 55–63.

33 "more equitable gender distribution of housework": Liana Sayer, "Gender, Time and Inequality: Trends in Women's and Men's Paid Work, Unpaid Work, and Free Time," *Social Forces* 84, no. 1 (September 2005): 285–303.

33 "change is gradual at best": Sara Raley, Suzanne M. Bianchi, and Wendy Wang, "When Do Fathers Care? Mothers' Economic Contribution and Fathers' Involvement in Childcare," *American Journal of Sociology* 117, no. 5 (May 2005): 1422–59.

33 "father-in-a-room-by-himself": Belinda Campos, Anthony P. Graesch, Rena Repetti, Thomas Bradbury, and Elinor Ochs, "Opportunity for Interaction? A Naturalistic Observation Study of Dual-Earner Families After Work and School," *Journal of Family Psychology* 23, no. 6 (2009): 798–807.

33 "watch lots of television": Suzanne M. Bianchi, John P. Robinson, and Melissa A. Milkie, *Changing Rhythms of American Life* (New York: Russell Sage Foundation, 2006), 121–22.

33 "likelier to get up in the middle of the night": Sarah A. Burgard, "The Needs of Others: Gender and Sleep Interruptions for Caregivers," *Social Forces* 89, no. 4 (June 2011): 1189–1218.

33 "twice as much weekend time engaged in leisure": Claire M. Kamp Dush, Jill E. Yavorsky, and Sarah J. Schoppe-Sullivan, "What Are Men Doing while Women Perform Extra Unpaid Labor? Leisure and Specialization at the Transitions to Parenthood," *Sex Roles* 78, no. 11–12 (June 2018): 715–30.

34 "significantly more unequal than men": Rebecca Erickson, "Why Emotion Work Matters: Sex, Gender, and the Division of Household Labor," *Journal of Marriage and Family* 67 (May 2005): 337–51.

34 "fails to reach parity": Sara Raley, Suzanne M. Bianchi, and Wendy Wang, "When Do Fathers Care? Mothers' Economic Contribution and Fathers' Involvement in Childcare," *American Journal of Sociology* 117, no. 5 (May 2005): 1422–59.

34 "scheduling and keeping track of stuff": "they must use it or lose it": Andrea Doucet, "Can Parenting Be Equal? Rethinking Equality and Gender Differences in Parenting," in *What Is Parenthood?*, eds. Linda C. McClain and Daniel Cere (New York: NYU Press, 2013): 251–75.

34 "personal care, and sleep": Suzanne Bianchi, John Robinson, and Melissa Milkie, *Changing Rhythms of American Family Life* (New York: Russell Sage Foundation, 2007).

34 "levels of co-residential father care": Ross D. Parke, "Gender Differences and Similarities in Parental Behavior," in *Gender and Parenthood: Biological and Social Scientific Perspectives*, eds. W. Bradford Wilcox and Kathleen Kovner Kline (New York: Columbia University Press, 2013), 125.

34 "gender inequality than Hispanics": Emily W. Kane, "Racial and Ethnic Variations in Gender-Related Attitudes," *Annual Review of Sociology* 26 (2000): 419–39.

34 "much more traditional reality:" Carolyn Cowan and Philip Cowan, *When Partners Become Parents* (New York: Routledge, 1999), 93.

34 "All the talk about men and women": Ibid.

34 "daily lives that differ the most": Lyn Craig and Killian Mullan, "Parenthood, Gender and Work-Family Time in the United States, Australia, Italy, France and Denmark," *Journal of Marriage and Family* 72, no. 5 (October 2010): 1344–61.

35 "that figure has not budged": "Time spent in primary activities by married mothers and fathers by employment status of self and spouse . . . 2011–15," Bureau of Labor Statistics, https://www.bls.gov/tus/tables /a7_1115.pdf

35 "in such brief time increments": Mitra Toossi, "A Century of Change: the U.S. Labor Force, 1950–2050," Bureau of Labor Statistics, accessed October 27, 2018, https://www.bls.gov/opub/mlr/2002/05/art2full .pdf

36 "increased their time in child care": Suzanne M. Bianchi, Liana C. Sayer, Melissa A. Milkie, and John P. Robinson, "Housework: Who

Did, Does or Will Do It, and How Much Does It Matter?" *Social Forces* 91, no. 1 (September 2012): 55–63.

36 "predictor of family work performance": Rebecca Erickson, "Why Emotion Work Matters: Sex, Gender, and the Division of Household Labor," *Journal of Marriage and Family* 67 (May 2005): 337–51.

36 "recent gains made in fathers' unpaid work time": Jennifer L. Hook, "Care in Context: Men's Unpaid Work in 20 Countries, 1965–2003," *American Sociological Review* 71 (August 2006): 639–60.

36 "women do less housework and men do more": Suzanne M. Bianchi, Liana C. Sayer, Melissa A. Milkie, and John P. Robinson, "Housework: Who Did, Does or Will Do It, and How Much Does It Matter?" *Social Forces* 91, no. 1 (September 2012): 55–63.

40 "inequality undermines it": Anne Rankin Mahoney and Carmen Knudson-Martin, "Gender Equality in Intimate Relationships," in *Couples, Gender, and Power*, eds. Carmen Knudson-Martin and Anne Rankin Mahoney (New York: Springer Publishing Company, 2009), 6.

40 "responsibilities are shared": W. Bradford Wilcox and Jeffrey Dew, "No One Best Way," in *Gender and Parenthood: Biological and Social Scientific Perspectives*, eds. W. Bradford Wilcox and Kathleen Kovner Kline (New York: Columbia University Press, 2013), 287.

40 "sex within marriage has declined worldwide": Daniel L. Carlson, Amanda J. Miller, Sharon Sassler, and Sarah Hanson, "The Gendered Division of Housework and Couples' Sexual Relationships: A Re-examination," *Journal of Marriage and Family* 78, no. 4 (August 2016): 975–95.

40 "Mothers of kids under four": Paul R. Amato, Alan Booth, David R. Johnson, and Stacy J. Rogers, *Alone Together: How Marriage in America Is Changing* (Cambridge: Harvard University Press paperback edition, 2009), 156.

41 "We are looking for another self": Maria Ray, "This Is the Number One Reason Why Women Cheat," *Marie Claire UK*, December 1, 2017, https://www.marieclaire.co.uk/life/sex-and-relationships/infidelity-why-women-cheat-552935

41 "relationship conflict and mothers' satisfaction": Dana Shawn Matta, "Fathering: Disengaged or Responsive?" in *Couples, Gender, and Power*, eds. Carmen Knudson-Martin and Anne Rankin Mahoney (New York: Springer Publishing Company, 2009), 151.

41 "perceived unfairness predicts both unhappiness and distress for women": Scott Coltrane, "Research on Household Labor: Modeling and Measuring the Social Embeddedness of Routine Family Work," *Journal of Marriage and Family* (November 2000): 1208–33.

41 "free and easy happiness never emerged": Francine M. Deutsch, *Halving It All* (Cambridge: Harvard University Press, 1999), 8.

41 "one full standard deviation": Paul R. Amato, Alan Booth, David R. Johnson, and Stacy J. Rogers, *Alone Together: How Marriage in America Is Changing* (Cambridge: Harvard University Press paperback edition, 2009), 156.

42 "agreed to their respective roles": Claire Cain Miller, "How Same-Sex Couples Divide Chores, and What It Reveals About Modern Parenting," *New York Times*, May 16, 2018, https://www.nytimes.com/2018/05/16/upshot/same-sex-couples-divide-chores-much-more-evenly-until-they-become-parents.html

42 "choices they have made": Carolyn Cowan and Philip Cowan, *When Partners Become Parents* (New York: Routledge, 1999), 97.

43 "new-parent equivalent of a unicorn": Carolyn Cowan and Philip Cowan, *When Partners Become Parents* (New York: Routledge, 1999), 102.

44 "not having enough time to himself": Suzanne M. Bianchi and Melissa Milkie, "Work and Family Research in the First Decade of the 21st Century," *Journal of Marriage and Family* 72 (June 2010): 705–25.

44 "female physicians continue to shoulder": Dhruv Khullar, "Being A Doctor Is Hard. It's Harder For Women," *New York Times*, December 7, 2017, https://www.nytimes.com/2017/12/07/upshot/being-a-doctor-is-hard-its-harder-for-women.html

44 "vast improvements in their health": Jason Schnittker, "Working More and Feeling Better: Women's Health, Employment, and Family Life, 1974–2004," *American Sociological Review* 72 (April 2007): 221–38.

45 "if only for a limited time": Jason Schnittker, "Working More and Feeling Better: Women's Health, Employment, and Family Life, 1974-2004," *American Sociological Review* 72 (April 2007): 221–38.

45 "economists at the Center for American Progress": Michael Madowitz, Alex Rowell, and Katie Hamm, "Calculating the Hidden Cost of Interrupting a Career for Childcare," *Center for American Progress*, June 21, 2016, https://www.americanprogress.org/issues/early-childhood

/reports/2016/06/21/139731/calculating-the-hidden-cost-of-interrupting
-a-career-for-child-care/

45 "report from think tank McKinsey Global Institute": McKinsey Global Institute, "How Advancing Women's Equality Can Add $12 Trillion to Global Growth," mckinsey.com, September 2015, https://www.mckinsey.com/featured-insights/employment-and-growth/how-advancing-womens-equality-can-add-12-trillion-to-global-growth

46 "gender wage gap is really a motherhood gap": Sarah Kliff, "A Stunning Chart Shows the True Cause of the Gender Wage Gap," *Vox*, February 19, 2018, https://www.vox.com/2018/2/19/17018380/gender-wage-gap-child care-penalty

46 "the motherhood wage penalty": Sara Raley, Suzanne M. Bianchi, and Wendy Wang, "When Do Fathers Care? Mothers' Economic Contribution and Fathers' Involvement in Childcare," *American Journal of Sociology* 117, no. 5 (May 2005): 1422–59.

46 "financial rewards for working long hours went up": Sarah Green Carmichael, "Defend Your Research: Working Long Hours Used to Hurt Your Wages—Now It Helps Them," *Harvard Business Review*, November 19, 2013, https://hbr.org/2013/11/defend-your-research-working-long-hours-used-to-hurt-your-wages-now-it-helps-them

46 "gender wage gap would be about 10 percent smaller": Youngjoo Cha and Kim A. Weeden, "Overwork and the Slow Convergence in the Gender Gap in Wages," *American Sociological Review* 79, no. 3 (2014): 457–84.

47 "Pregnancy Discrimination Is Rampant": Natalie Kitroeff and Jessica Silver-Greenberg, "Pregnancy Discrimination Is Rampant Inside America's Biggest Companies," *New York Times*, June 15, 2018, https://www.nytimes.com/interactive/2018/06/15/business/pregnancy-discrimination.html

47 "childless women were 2.1 times more likely": Shelley J. Correll, Stephen Benard, and In Paik, "Getting a Job: Is There a Motherhood Penalty?" *American Journal of Sociology* 112, no. 5 (March 2007): 1297–339.

50 "women should do about two-thirds of household chores": Mary Clare Lennon and Sarah Rosenfield, "Relative Fairness and the Division of Housework: The Importance of Options," *American Journal of Sociology* 100, no. 2 (September 1994): 506–31.

50 "role as wife and mother": Riché J. Daniel Barnes, *Raising the Race: Black Career Women Redefine Marriage, Motherhood, and Community* (New Jersey: Rutgers University Press, 2016), 115.

50 "necessary nor sufficient condition for equally shared parenting": Shannon N. Davis and Theodore N. Greenstein, "Gender Ideology: Components, Predictors, and Consequences," *Annual Review of Sociology* 35 (2009): 87–105.

51 "determining family practices": Scott Coltrane, "Fatherhood, Gender and Work-Family Policies," in *The Real Utopias Project: Gender Equality, Transforming Family Divisions of Labor* (Brooklyn: Verso, 2009), 393.

51 "bulk of tasks at home": Gillian Ranson, *Against the Grain* (Toronto, University of Toronto Press: 2010), 2.

51 "65 percent of millennial men": Claire Cain Miller, "Millennial Men Aren't the Dads They Thought They'd Be," *New York Times*, July 30, 2015, https://www.nytimes.com/2015/07/31/upshot/millennial-men -find-work-and-family-hard-to-balance.html

51 "suits them rather well after all": Rebecca Asher, *Shattered: Modern Motherhood and the Illusion of Equality* (London: Harvill Secker, 2011), 130.

51 "'on top' versus 'underneath' ideologies": Arlie Hochschild with Anne Machung, *The Second Shift* (New York: Penguin Books, 2003).

51 "different interests and skills": Paula England, "The Gender Revolution: Uneven and Stalled," *Gender & Society* 24, no. 2 (March 2010), 149–66.

52 "reduce inconsistency by changing the former": Jennifer L. Hook, "Care in Context: Men's Unpaid Work in 20 Countries, 1965–2003," *American Sociological Review* 71 (August 2006): 639–60.

52 "when the man's ideology is in consideration": Ronald Bulanda, "Paternal Involvement with Children: The Influence of Gender Ideologies," *Journal of Marriage and Family* 66, no. 1 (February 2004): 40–45.

52 "husbands' gender ideology may be": Shannon N. Davis and Theodore N. Greenstein, "Gender Ideology: Components, Predictors, and Consequences," *Annual Review of Sociology* 35 (2009): 87–105.

52 "paternal involvement with child care": Scott Coltrane, "Fatherhood, Gender and Work-Family Policies," in *The Real Utopias Project:*

Gender Equality, Transforming Family Divisions of Labor (Brooklyn: Verso, 2009): 392.

52 "satisfaction than those that don't": Diane N. Lye and Timothy J. Biblarz, "The Effects of Attitudes Toward Family Life and Gender Roles on Marital Satisfaction," *Journal of Family Issues* 14, no. 2 (June 1993): 157–88.

53 "regardless of the gender of those children": Shannon N. Davis and Theodore N. Greenstein, "Gender Ideology: Components, Predictors and Consequences," *Annual Review of Sociology* 35 (2009): 87–105.

54 "stress and burden associated with child care": Randi S. Cowdery, Carmen Knudson-Martin, and Anne Rankin Mahoney, "Mothering: Innate Talent or Conscious Collaboration?," in *Couples, Gender, and Power*, eds. Carmen Knudson-Martin and Anne Rankin Mahoney (New York: Springer Publishing Company, 2009), 137.

54 "a 'marriage between equals discourse'": Anne Rankin Mahoney and Carmen Knudson-Martin, "The Myth of Equality," in *Couples, Gender, and Power*, eds. Carmen Knudson-Martin and Anne Rankin Mahoney (New York: Springer Publishing Company, 2009), 57.

54 "goals of husbands much more than wives": Anne Rankin Mahoney and Carmen Knudson-Martin, "Gender Equality in Intimate Relationships," in *Couples, Gender, and Power*, eds. Carmen Knudson-Martin and Anne Rankin Mahoney (New York: Springer Publishing Company, 2009), 20.

54 "managing fathers seemed to do": Annette Lareau, *Unequal Childhoods: Class, Race and Family Life, Second Edition* (California: University of California Press, 1999), 115.

55 "young women anticipate divorce": Lisa Wade, "The Modern Marriage Trap—and What to Do About It," *Time*, January 11, 2017, http://time.com/money/4630251/the-modern-marriage-trap-and-what-to-do-about-it/

56 "involvement on the part of fathers": Ross D. Parke, "Gender Differences and Similarities in Parental Behavior," in *Gender and Parenthood: Biological and Social Scientific Perspectives*, eds. W. Bradford Wilcox and Kathleen Kovner Kline (New York: Columbia University Press, 2013), 139.

56 "she needs to be more assertive": Anne Rankin Mahoney and Carmen Knudson-Martin, "The Myth of Equality," in *Couples, Gender, and*

Power, eds. Carmen Knudson-Martin and Anne Rankin Mahoney (New York: Springer Publishing Company, 2009), 52.

Chapter 2: The Naturalistic Fallacy

57 "men are more likely than women to credit nature": Kim Parker, Juliana Menasce Horowitz, and Renee Stepler, "On Gender Differences, No Consensus on Nature vs. Nurture," *Pew Research Center Social & Demographic Trends*, December 5, 2017, http://www.pewsocialtrends .org/2017/12/05/on-gender-differences-no-consensus-on-nature -vs-nurture/

60 "actually a cultural habit": Jennifer Hockenberry Dragseth, *Thinking Woman: A Philosophical Approach to the Quandary of Gender* (Eugene, Oregon: Cascade Books, 2015), 32.

60 "hardwired into me": Amy Richards, *Opting In* (New York: Farrar, Straus & Giroux, 2008), 179.

61 "this view is strikingly different": Janet Shibley Hyde, "New Directions in the Study of Gender Similarities and Differences," *Current Directions in Psychological Science* 16, no. 5 (October 2007), 259–63.

61 "rather than old-fashioned and sexist": Cordelia Fine, *Delusions of Gender* (New York: W. W. Norton & Company, 2010), 172.

62 "similar in more ways than not": Janet Shibley Hyde, "New Directions in the Study of Gender Similarities and Differences," *Current Directions in Psychological Science* 16, no. 5 (October 2007), 259–63.

62 "not the other way around": Michael Kimmel, *The Gendered Society* (New York: Oxford University Press, 2000).

62 "efforts to change the existing situation are futile": Anne Fausto-Sterling, *Myths of Gender: Biological Theories About Women and Men* (New York: Basic Books, 1992), 7.

62 "experiment on perceptual style": Deborah A. Prentice and Dale T. Miller, "Essentializing Differences Between Women and Men," *Psychological Science* 17, no. 2 (February 2006): 129–35.

67 "did things begin to change": Lise Eliot, *Pink Brain, Blue Brain: How Small Differences Grow into Troublesome Gaps—and What We Can Do About It* (New York: Mariner Books, 2010), 302.

70 "Scott Coltrane believes": Scott Coltrane, "Research on Household Labor: Modeling and Measuring the Social Embeddedness of Routine

Family Work," *Journal of Marriage and Family* 62, no. 4 (November 2000), 1208–33.

70 "study of young men and women in Iceland": Thoroddur Bjarnason and Andrea Hjalsdottir, "Egalitarian Attitudes Towards the Division of Household Labor Among Adolescents in Iceland," *Sex Roles* 59, no. 1–2 (July 2008): 49–60.

70 "a 2007 study in the U.S.": Francine M. Deutsch, Amy P. Kokot, and Katherine S. Binder, "College Women's Plans for Different Types of Egalitarian Marriages," *Journal of Marriage and Family* 69, no. 4 (November 2007), 919–29.

71 "a mother is better equipped than a father": Kim Parker and Gretchen Livingston, "7 Facts About American Dads," Pew Research Center: FactTank, June 13, 2018, http://www.pewresearch.org/fact-tank/2018/06/13/fathers-day-facts/

72 "survive only a narrow range of circumstances": Lesley Newson and Peter J. Richerson, "The Evolution of Flexible Parenting," in *Evolution's Empress: Darwinian Perspectives on the Nature of Women* (England: Oxford University Press, 2013) 151–62.

72 "*practice* and learning become more important": Sarah Blaffer Hrdy, *Mother Nature* (New York: Ballantine Books, 1999), 155.

73 "places the placenta next to her baby": "!Kung People," Wikipedia, accessed October 29, 2018, https://en.wikipedia.org/wiki/%C7%83Kung_people

73 "Hadza, women give birth in huts": Kristen Herlosky, email to author, November 30, 2017.

73 "first-time parents": Charles T. Snowdon, "Family Life and Infant Care: Lessons from Cooperatively Breeding Primates," in *Gender and Parenthood: Biological and Social Scientific Perspectives*, eds. W. Bradford Wilcox and Kathleen Kovner Kline (New York: Columbia University Press, 2013), 48.

74 "latest products of human evolution.": Katharina Rowold, *The Educated Woman* (New York: Routledge, 2010): 33.

75 "attached to their breast-feeding infants": Sarah Blaffer Hrdy, *Mother Nature* (New York: Ballantine Books, 1999), 310–15.

75 "within the first seventy-two hours.": Ibid., 316.

76 "predispositions to nurture": Ibid., 378.

76 "played out in our recent history": Ibid., 12.

77 "flexible, manipulative opportunists": Ibid., 32.

77 "defended and constrained": Ibid., 496.

77 "you wouldn't want to marry one": Eduardo Fernandez-Duque, Claudia R. Valeggia, and Sally P. Mendoza, "The Biology of Paternal Care in Human and Non-Human Primates," *Annual Review of Anthropology* 38 (2009): 115–30.

78 "remains poorly understood": Ibid.

79 "protection by males for survival": Harriet J. Smith, *Parenting for Primates* (Cambridge: Harvard University Press, 2005), 91–95.

79 "Caretaking behaviors are unisex potentials": Sarah Blaffer Hrdy, *Mother Nature* (New York: Ballantine Books, 1999), 209.

80 "correspondent percentage of necessary calories": Nicholas B. Davies, Ben J. Hatchwell, Timothy Robson, and Terry Burke, "Paternity and Parental Effort in Dunnocks Prunella Modularis: How Good Are Male Chick-feeding Rules," *Animal Behaviour* 43, no. 5, May 1992, 729–45.

80 "children who resembled them spent more time": Marlon R. Tracey and Solomon W. Polachek, "If Looks Could Heal: Child Health and Paternal Investment," *Journal of Health Economics* 57 (January 2018): 179–90.

80 "resulted in involved fatherhood": Eduardo Fernandez-Duque, Claudia R. Valeggia, and Sally P. Mendoza, "The Biology of Paternal Care in Human and Non-Human Primates," *Annual Review of Anthropology* 38 (2009): 115–30.

81 "failures to 'meet sharing obligations'": Michael Gurven and Kim Hill, "Why Do Men Hunt? A Reevaluation of 'Man the Hunter' and the Sexual Division of Labor," *Current Anthropology* 50, no. 1, February 2009, 62–74.

82 "primate species combined": Kelly Lambert and Catherine Franssen, "The Dynamic Nature of the Parental Brain," in *Gender and Parenthood: Biological and Social Scientific Perspectives*, eds. W. Bradford Wilcox and Kathleen Kovner Kline (New York: Columbia University Press, 2013), 32.

82 "'The Birth of a Mother'": Alexandra Sacks, "The Birth of a Mother," *New York Times*, May 8, 2017, https://www.nytimes.com/2017/05/08 /well/family/the-birth-of-a-mother.html

83 "their baby's mother": Ross D. Parke, "Gender Differences and Similarities in Parental Behavior," in *Gender and Parenthood: Biological and Social Scientific Perspectives*, eds. W. Bradford Wilcox and Kathleen Kovner Kline (New York: Columbia University Press, 2013), 136.

83 "testosterone . . . declines": Jennifer Mascaro, Patrick D. Hackett, and James K. Rilling, "Testicular Volume Is Inversely Correlated with Nurturing-related Brain Activity in Human Fathers," *Proceedings of the National Academy of Sciences* 110, no. 39 (September 2013): 15746–51.

83 "to love and care for his infant": Charles T. Snowdon, "Family Life and Infant Care: Lessons from Cooperatively Breeding Primates," in *Gender and Parenthood: Biological and Social Scientific Perspectives*, eds. W. Bradford Wilcox and Kathleen Kovner Kline (New York: Columbia University Press, 2013), 47–48.

83 "electrochemical response to airborne estratetraenol": Warren S. T. Hays, "Human Pheromones: Have They Been Demonstrated?" *Behavioral Ecology and Sociobiology* 54, no. 2 (July 2003): 89–97.

84 "human males have an evolved neuroendocrine architecture": Lee T. Gettler, Thomas W. McDade, Alan B. Feranil, and Christoper W. Kuzawa, "Longitudinal Evidence that Fatherhood Decreases Testosterone in Human Males," *Proceedings of the National Academy of Sciences* 108, no. 39 (2011): 16194–99.

84 "encoded in the DNA of our species": Sarah Blaffer Hrdy, *Mothers and Others* (Cambridge: Harvard University Press, 2011), 161.

84 "fathers had been done": Paul Raeburn, *Do Fathers Matter?* (New York: Scientific American/Farrar, Straus and Giroux, 2014), 10.

85 "President Richard Nixon cited evolution": Jack Rosenthal, "President Vetoes Child Care Plan as Irresponsible," *New York Times*, December 10, 1971, https://www.nytimes.com/1971/12/10/archives/president-vetoes-child-care-plan-as-irresponsible-he-terms-bill.html

85 "just as likely to be calmed by the presence of their fathers as their mothers": "The Critical Importance of Fathers," *Fatherhood Project*, March 31, 2016, http://www.thefatherhoodproject.org/critical-importance-fathers/

85 "mothers and fathers did not differ": Ann M. Frodi, Michael E. Lamb, and Lewis A. Leavitt, "Fathers and Mothers' Responses to the Faces and Cries of Normal and Premature Infants," *Developmental Psychology* 14, no. 5 (September 1978): 490–8.

86 "in the presence of their spouse": Harriet J. Smith, *Parenting for Primates* (Cambridge: Harvard University Press, 2005), 88.

86 "quicker than those of childless adults": Sarah Blaffer Hrdy, *Mother Nature* (New York: Ballantine Books, 1999), 212.

87 "habits of mind and emotion": Ibid., 212.

87 "marked division of labor by sex": Ibid., 213.

87 "equal access to education": Cynthia Russett, *Sexual Science: The Victorian Construction of Womanhood* (Cambridge: Harvard University Press, 1989).

88 "tell them apart at an individual level": Cordelia Fine, *Delusions of Gender* (New York: W. W. Norton & Company, 2010), 165.

89 "accomplishing multiple tasks": Lesley J. Rogers, Paolo Zucca, and Giorgio Vallortigara, "Advantages of Having a Lateralized Brain," *Proceedings of the Royal Society of London: Biological Sciences* 271, no. 6 (December 7, 2004): S420–22.

89 "ambition and original thought": Cordelia Fine, *Delusions of Gender* (New York: W. W. Norton & Company, 2010), 167.

90 "organization and function over time": Janet Shibley Hyde, "New Directions in the Study of Gender Similarities and Differences," *Current Directions in Psychological Science* 16, no. 5 (October 2007), 259–63.

91 "global parental caregiving network": Eyal Abraham, Talma Hendler, Irit Shapira-Lichter, Yaniv Kanat-Maymon, Orna Zagoory-Sharon, and Ruth Feldman, "Father's Brain Is Sensitive to Childcare Experiences," *Proceedings of the National Academy of Sciences* 111, no. 27 (July 2014): 9792–97.

Chapter 3: We Are Raised to Be Two Different Kinds of People

96 "not by biology but by culture": Jennifer Hockenberry Dragseth, *Thinking Woman: A Philosophical Approach to the Quandary of Gender* (Eugene, OR: Cascade Books, 2015), 78.

96 "more women than men are gender existentialists": Kim Parker, Juliana Menasce Horowitz, and Renee Stepler, "On Gender Differences, No Consensus on Nature vs. Nurture," *Pew Research Center Social & Demographic Trends*, December 5, 2017, http://www.pewsocialtrends .org/2017/12/05/on-gender-differences-no-consensus-on-nature -vs-nurture/

98 "another kid enters the picture": Lise Eliot, *Pink Brain, Blue Brain: How Small Differences Grow into Troublesome Gaps—and What We Can Do About It* (New York: Mariner Books, 2010), 121.

98 "girl and boy babies reliably differ": Marilyn Stern and Katherine Hildebrandt Karraker, "Sex Stereotyping of Infants: A Review of Gender Labeling Studies," *Sex Roles* 20, no. 9/10 (1989): 501–22.

98 "baby boys wore nightgowns": Jo B. Paoletti, *Pink and Blue: Telling the Boys from the Girls in America* (Indiana: Indiana University Press, 2012): 100–16.

99 "reliably get them noticed": Virginia Valian, *Why So Slow?: The Advancement of Women* (Cambridge: MIT Press, 1999), 50–1.

99 "traditional homes show less": Judith Blakemore, "The Influence of Gender and Parental Attitudes on Preschool Children's Interest in Babies: Observations in Natural Settings," *Sex Roles* 38, no. 1–2 (January 1998): 73–94.

100 "animals' traits and behaviors": Virginia Valian, *Why So Slow?: The Advancement of Women* (Cambridge: MIT Press, 1999), 69.

100 "per a mid-twentieth-century survey": Sarah Blaffer Hrdy, *Mother Nature* (New York: Ballantine Books, 1999), 252.

101 "longer periods of caretaking touch": Anne Fausto-Sterling, Jihyun Sung, David Crews, and Cynthia Garcia-Coll, "Multimodal Sex-Related Differences in Infant and in Infant-Directed Maternal Behaviors During Months Three Through Twelve of Development," *Developmental Psychology* 51, no. 10 (2005), 1351–66.

101 "women's behavior accommodated": Alice H. Eagly and Wendy Wood, "The Origins of Sex Differences in Human Behavior: Evolved Dispositions Versus Social Roles," *American Psychologist* 54, no. 6 (1999): 408–23.

102 "gender polarization, and biological essentialism": Alice Eagly, "Bridging the Gap Between Gender Politics and the Science of Gender," review of *The Lenses of Gender*, by Sandra Lipsitz Bem, *Psychological Inquiry* 5, no. 1 (1994), 83–85.

102 "Nobel Prize for making people feel included": Neil Levy, "Understanding Blindness," review of *The Essential Difference*, by Simon Baron-Cohen, *Phenomenology and the Cognitive Sciences* 3, no. 3, September 2004, 323.

103 "systematically curtailed and repressed": Nancy J. Chodorow, *Feminism and Psychoanalytic Theory* (New Haven: Yale University Press, 1989), 6–7.

104 "having power over others": Michael Ian Black, "The Boys Are Not All Right," *New York Times*, February 21, 2018, https://www.nytimes.com/2018/02/21/opinion/boys-violence-shootings-guns.html

104 "stigma of being girl-like": Virginia Valian, *Why So Slow?: The Advancement of Women* (Cambridge: MIT Press, 1999), 53–55.

105 "influence only other girls": Lise Eliot, *Pink Brain, Blue Brain: How Small Differences Grow into Troublesome Gaps—and What We Can Do About It* (New York: Mariner Books, 2010), 266–67.

105 "members of the second sex": Eleanor E. Maccoby, *The Two Sexes: Growing Up Apart, Coming Together* (Cambridge: Harvard University Press, 1999), 64–65.

105 "Stonewalling behavior makes it difficult for wives": Anne Rankin Mahoney and Carmen Knudson-Martin, "The Social Context of Gendered Power," in *Couples, Gender, and Power*, eds. Carmen Knudson-Martin and Anne Rankin Mahoney (New York: Springer Publishing Company, 2009), 8.

106 "co-parent most harmoniously": Timothy J. Biblarz and Judith Stacey, "How Does the Gender of Parents Matter?," *Journal of Marriage and Family* 72, no. 1 (February 2010): 3–22.

107 "initiated into the codes and scripts of patriarchal manhood": Carol Gilligan, *Joining the Resistance* (Cambridge: Polity, 2011): 26.

107 "the most gender-enforcing experience in a woman's life": Bonnie Fox, "The Formative Years: How Parenthood Creates Gender," *Canadian Review of Sociology & Anthropology* 38, no. 4 (2001): 373–90.

107 "gender factory": Sarah Fenstermaker Berk, *The Gender Factory: The Apportionment of Work in American Households* (New York: Plenum Press, 1985).

107 "13 percent of women who give birth each year": "Maternal Mental Health," World Health Organization, accessed October 27, 2018, http://www.who.int/mental_health/maternal-child/maternal_mental_health/en/

107 "equally prevalent in men": "Even Men Get the Blues After Childbirth,"

American Psychological Association, August 19, 2018, https://www
.apa.org/news/press/releases/2018/08/men-after-childbirth.aspx

108 "by the gender of others": Eleanor E. Maccoby, *The Two Sexes: Growing Up Apart, Coming Together* (Cambridge: Harvard University Press, 1999), 9.

108 "[T]he good woman cared for others": Carol Gilligan, *Joining the Resistance* (Cambridge: Polity, 2011), 17.

110 "the experience of being fully human.": Jonah Gokova, "Challenging Men to Reject Gender Stereotypes," in *The Essential Feminist Reader*, ed. Estelle B. Freedman (New York: Modern Library, 2007), 422.

110 "people who care are doing women's work": Carol Gilligan, *Joining the Resistance* (Cambridge: Polity, 2011): 19.

111 "maximize your paycheck": Marc and Amy Vachon, *Equally Shared Parenting* (New York: Penguin Group, 2010), 125.

111 "hire that labor out": Scott Coltrane, "Fatherhood, Gender and Work-Family Policies," in *The Real Utopias Project: Gender Equality, Transforming Family Divisions of Labor* (Brooklyn: Verso, 2009), 391.

111 "every additional dollar earned by her husband": Saniv Gupta, "Autonomy, Dependence, or Display? The Relationship Between Married Women's Earnings and Housework," *Journal of Marriage and Family* 69, no. 2, May 2007, 399–417.

112 "living below one's means": Marc and Amy Vachon, *Equally Shared Parenting* (New York: Penguin Group, 2010), 55.

113 "happy place to be": Ibid., 30.

113 "wanted to be equals": Ibid., 9.

117 "half of their girlfriends' birth control": Rebecca Traister, *All the Single Ladies* (New York: Simon & Schuster, 2016), 239.

121 "increasingly traditional attitudes about the home": Jenny Anderson, "Are Millennials More Likely Than Their Parents to Think Women's place Is in the Home?" Quartz, March 31, 2017, https://qz.com/946816 /millennials-are-more-likely-than-their-parents-to-think-womens -place-is-in-the-home/

122 "Pepin and Cotter reach a conclusion": David Cotter and Joanna Pepin, "Trending Toward Traditionalism? Changes in Youths' Gender Ideology," *Council on Contemporary Families*, March 30, 2017, https:// contemporaryfamilies.org/2-pepin-cotter-traditionalism/

122 "28.8 percent of employed wives earned more": U.S. Census Bureau, "Historical Income Tables: Families, Table F-22, Married Couple Families with Wives' Earning Greater than Husbands' Earnings: 1981-2017," https://www.census.gov/data/tables/time-series/demo/income -poverty/historical-income-families.html

122 "households with an unemployed male partner": "Husband and Wife Employed in 48 Percent of Married Couple Families in 2015," Bureau of Labor Statistics, May 2, 2016, https://www.bls.gov/opub/ted/2016 /husband-and-wife-employed-in-48-percent-of-married-couple-families -in-2015.htm

122 "exaggerate the husband's income": Claire Cain Miller, "When Wives Earn More Than Husbands, Neither Partner Likes to Admit It," *New York Times*, July 17, 2018, https://www.nytimes.com/2018/07/17 /upshot/when-wives-earn-more-than-husbands-neither-like-to-admit -it.html

123 "YouGov survey of British adults": "YouGov Survey Results," YouGov: What the World Thinks, September 12, 2016, https://d25d2506sfb94s .cloudfront.net/cumulus_uploads/document/8jcokpgzqg/Internal Results_160912_NameswithRela_AgeGenderBreak_W.pdf

123 "family ahead of themselves": Emily Fitzgibbons Shafer, "Hillary Rodham Versus Hillary Clinton: Consequences of Surname Choice in Marriage," *Gender Issues* 34, no. 4 (December 2017): 316–32.

123 "men expressed harsher attitudes": Ibid.

124 "passing down the maternal surname": "YouGov Survey Results," YouGov: What the World Thinks, September 12, 2016, https://d25d2506sfb94s .cloudfront.net/cumulus_uploads/document/8jcokpgzqg/Internal Results_160912_NameswithRela_AgeGenderBreak_W.pdf

124 "under 3 percent had taken their wives' names": Emily Fitzgibbons Shafer and MacKenzie A. Christensen, "Flipping the (Surname) Script: Men's Nontraditional Surname Choice at Marriage," *Journal of Family Issues* (2018): 1–20.

125 "I would have presented my marriage license": James Kosur, "When I Decided to Take My Wife's Last Name, I Was Shocked by How Different the Process Is for Men," *Business Insider*, December 19, 2015, https://www.businessinsider.com/i-took-my-wifes-last-name-and-was -shocked-by-how-different-the-process-is-for-men-2015-12

125 "largely non-economic": Paula England, "The Gender Revolution: Uneven and Stalled," *Gender & Society* 24, no. 2 (March 2010), 149–66.

126 "those that are female typed": Janeen Baxter, Belinda Hewitt, and Michele Haynes, "Life Course Transitions and Housework: Marriage, Parenthood, and Time on Housework," *Journal of Marriage and Family* 70 (May 2008), 259–72.

128 "maintain an uneven exchange": Chimamanda Ngozi Adichie, *Dear Ijeawele, or A Feminist Manifesto in Fifteen Suggestions* (New York: Knopf, 2017), Location 258, Kindle.

128 "resilient sex in widowhood": Kei M. Nomaguchi, "Are There Race and Gender Differences in the Effect of Marital Dissolution on Depression?" *Race, Gender & Class* 12, no. 1 (2005), 11–30.

130 "but it is not an achievement": Chimamanda Ngozi Adichie, *Dear Ijeawele, or A Feminist Manifesto in Fifteen Suggestions* (New York: Knopf, 2017), Location 258, Kindle.

130 "single women (but not others) reported wanting lower salaries": Leonardo Bursztyn, Thomas Fujiwara, and Amanda Pallais, "'Acting Wife:' Marriage Market Incentives and Labor Market Incentives," *American Economic Review* 107, no. 11 (2017): 3288–3319.

130 "support their own individual well-being": Anne Rankin Mahoney and Carmen Knudson-Martin, "The Social Context of Gendered Power," in *Couples, Gender, and Power*, eds. Carmen Knudson-Martin and Anne Rankin Mahoney (New York: Springer Publishing Company, 2009), 17.

131 "females can be just as sexist as men": bell hooks, *Feminism Is for Everybody* (New York: Routledge, 2015), xii.

131 "feel more responsible than men for this work": Rebecca Erickson, "Why Emotion Work Matters: Sex, Gender, and the Division of Household Labor," *Journal of Marriage and Family* 67 (May 2005): 337–51.

132 "better (and deserved) away from them": Jacqueline Rose, "Mothers: An Essay on Love and Cruelty," interview by Tracy Morgan, *New Books in Psychoanalysis*, New Books Network, audio, 9:50, https://newbooksnetwork.com/jacqueline-rose-mothers-an-essay-on-love-and-cruelty-farrar-straus-and-giroux-2018/

133 "and individual resistance": Cecilia L. Ridgeway and Shelley J. Correll,

"Unpacking the Gender System: A Theoretical Perspective on Gender Beliefs and Social Relations," *Gender & Society* 18, no. 4 (August 2004), 510–31.

Chapter 4: The Default Parent

134 "women 'adapt' their work arrangements": David J. Maume, "Gender Differences in Providing Urgent Childcare Among Dual-earner Parents," *Social Forces* 87, no. 1 (September 2008): 273–97.

135 "Mothers feel a greater sense of responsibility.": Anne Roeters, Tania Van Der Lippe, and Esther S. Kluwer, "Parental Work Demands and the Frequency of Child-Related Activities," *Journal of Marriage and Family* 71 (December 2009): 1193–204.

136 "material interdependencies": Stephanie Coontz, *The Way We Never Were* (New York: Basic Books; Revised, Updated edition, 2016), 50.

136 "dependence and obligation": Ibid., 63.

137 "out the window": Francine M. Deutsch, *Halving It All* (Cambridge: Harvard University Press, 1999), 228.

137 "although he's really helpful": Ibid., 45.

138 "supposed to be infringed upon": Ibid., 89.

139 "fathers less harshly than mothers": Ashley J. Thomas, P. Kyle Stanford, and Barbara W. Sarnecka, "No Child Left Alone: Moral Judgments about Parents Effect Risk Estimates to Children," *Collabra* 2, no. 1 (2016): 10.

140 "stimulate marital tension between mothers and fathers": Susan Walzer, "Thinking About the Baby: Gender and Divisions of Infant Care," *Social Problems* 43, no. 2 (May 1996), 219–34.

140 "was all hers": Francine M. Deutsch, *Halving It All* (Cambridge: Harvard University Press, 1999), 159.

142 "not held accountable for that kind of thing": Janet N. Ahn, Elizabeth L. Haines, and Malia F. Mason, "Gender Stereotypes and the Coordination of Mnemonic Work within Heterosexual Couples: Romantic Partners Manage their Daily To-Dos," *Sex Roles* 77, no. 7 (March 2017): 1–18.

142 "less mnemonic work than women do": Ibid.

144 "reflects on them as parents": Susan Walzer, *Thinking About the Baby: Gender and Transitions into Parenthood* (Philadelphia: Temple University Press, 1998), 33.

144 "of course so often go together": Jacqueline Rose, "Mothers: An Essay on Love and Cruelty," interview by Tracy Morgan, *New Books in Psychoanalysis*, New Books Network, audio, 4:20, https://new booksnetwork.com/jacqueline-rose-mothers-an-essay-on-love-and -cruelty-farrar-straus-and-giroux-2018/

144 "connected it to their babies' well-being": Susan Walzer, *Thinking About the Baby: Gender and Transitions into Parenthood* (Philadelphia: Temple University Press, 1998), 43.

145 "failing in both roles at all times": Shira Offer, "The Costs of Thinking About Work and Family: Mental Labor, Work-Family Spillover, and Gender Inequality Among Parents in Dual-Earner Families," *Sociological Forum* 29, no. 4 (December 2014): 91–36.

146 "Am I being a good mother?": Susan Walzer, *Thinking About the Baby: Gender and Transitions into Parenthood* (Philadelphia: Temple University Press, 1998), 35.

148 "open to what she is telling me": Alice Miller, *For Your Own Good: Hidden Cruelty in Childrearing and the Roots of Violence* (New York: Farrar, Straus & Giroux, 1983), 258.

148 "expected their marriages to be partnerships": Susan Walzer, *Thinking About the Baby: Gender and Transitions into Parenthood* (Philadelphia: Temple University Press, 1998), 41.

150 "compensate for lowered partner investment": Michael Gurven and Kim Hill, "Why Do Men Hunt? A Reevaluation of 'Man the Hunter' and the Sexual Division of Labor," *Current Anthropology* 50, no. 1, February 2009, 62–74.

151 "men's willingness to contribute is": Lynn Prince Cooke, "'Doing' Gender in Context: Household Bargaining and Risk of Divorce in Germany and the United States," *American Journal of Sociology* 112, no. 2 (September 2006): 442–72.

152 "the influences of under- and overbenefiting": Kathryn J. Lively, Lala Carr Steelman, and Brian Powell, "Equity, Emotion, and Household Division of Labor Response," *Social Psychology Quarterly* 73, no. 4 (2010): 358–79.

152 "men are more emotionally sensitive to underbenefiting": Ibid.

154 "flat-out denial": Francine M. Deutsch, *Halving It All* (Cambridge: Harvard University Press, 1999), 74.

156 "offer ideas to their colleagues": Heather Murphy, "Picture a Leader: Is She a Woman?" *New York Times*, March 16, 2018, https://www.nytimes .com/2018/03/16/health/women-leadership-workplace.html

156 "cult of female sacrifice": Jill Filipovic, *The H-Spot: The Feminist Pursuit of Happiness* (New York: Nation Books, 2017), 29.

157 "ratio in father's to mother's child care time": Lyn Craig and Killian Mullan, "Parenthood, Gender and Work-Family Time in the United States, Australia, Italy, France and Denmark," *Journal of Marriage and Family* 72, no. 5 (October 2010): 1344–61.

157 "Frenchwomen can have both a career and kids.": Pamela Druckerman, *Bringing Up Bébé: One American Mother Discovers the Wisdom of French Parenting* (New York: Penguin Books, 2012), 194.

158 "warm-blooded American citizens": Jessica Weiss, "'Fraud of Femininity:' Domesticity, Selflessness, and Individualism in Responses to Betty Friedan," in *Liberty and Justice for All? Rethinking Politics in Cold War America*, ed. Kathleen G. Donohue (Amherst: University of Massachusetts Press, 2012), 124–41.

158 "even our college audiences branded it as 'communist'": Sandra Lipsitz Bem, *An Unconventional Family* (New Haven: Yale University Press, 1998), 80.

158 "the housewife-mother": Betty Friedan, *The Feminine Mystique* (New York: W. W. Norton & Company, 2013), 36.

159 "tanks women's happiness": Jill Filipovic, *The H-Spot* (New York: Nation Books, 2017), 29.

160 "not willing to pay": Riché J. Daniel Barnes, *Raising the Race: Black Career Women Redefine Marriage, Motherhood, and Community* (New Brunswick, NJ: Rutgers University Press, 2016), 9.

160 "costly performance": Ibid., 42.

160 "more from their husbands": Ibid., 104–5.

160 "comfort and pleasure": bell hooks, *Feminism Is For Everybody* (New York: Routledge, 2015), 50.

165 "a generally sour attitude": Barack H. Obama, *The Audacity of Hope* (New York: Vintage reprint edition, 2008), 531–32.

165 "Michelle decided to make peace with the situation": Rebecca Johnson, "Michelle Obama: The Natural," *Vogue*, September 2007, https:// www.vogue.com/article/michelle-obama-the-natural

169 "the flight from intimacy": Drake Baer, "Japan's Huge Sex Problem Is Setting Up a 'Demographic Time Bomb' for the Country," *Business Insider*, July 1, 2015, https://www.businessinsider.com/half-of-japanese-people-arent-having-sex-2015-7

169 "a demographic time bomb": Chris Weller, "7 Countries at Risk of Becoming 'Demographic Time Bombs,'" *Business Insider*, August 14, 2017, https://www.businessinsider.com/countries-becoming-demographic-time-bombs-2017-8

170 "committed to increasing men's time in child care": Julia Glum, "Japan Population Problem: Government Adopts Paternity Leave, Nursery School Measures to Increase Birth Rate," *International Business Times*, March 20, 2015, https://www.ibtimes.com/japan-population-problem-government-adopts-paternity-leave-nursery-school-measures-1854084

170 "incoherence in the levels of gender equity": Peter McDonald, "Societal Foundations for Explaining Low Fertility: Gender Equity," *Demographic Research* 28, no. 34 (May 2013): 981–94, https://www.demographic-research.org/volumes/vol28/34/28-34.pdf

170 "We could end humanity this way": Suzanne Moore, "The Womb Is a Battlefield," review of *Mothers: An Essay on Love and Cruelty*, by Jacqueline Rose, *New Statesman*, April 8, 2018, https://www.newstatesman.com/culture/books/2018/04/jacqueline-rose-s-book-offers-clear-sighted-analysis-what-it-means-be-mother

171 "fertility falls to low levels": Thomas Anderson and Hans-Peter Kohler, "Low Fertility, Socioeconomic Development and Gender Equity," *Population and Development Review* 41, no. 3 (September 2015): 381–407.

Chapter 5: 24-Hour Lifelong Shifts of Unconditional Love

175 "journalist Heather Wilhelm notes": Heather Wilhelm, "The Supposed 'Horror Show' of Motherhood," *National Review*, May 4, 2018, https://www.nationalreview.com/2018/05/motherhood-portrayal-in-media-wrong-benefits-outweigh-cost/

177 "intensive mothering over a thirty-year period": Susan J. Douglas and Meredith W. Michaels, *The Mommy Myth: The Idealization of Motherhood and How It Has Undermined All Women* (New York: Free Press, 2004), 6.

177 "a noxious delusion, one that isn't suitable for real women": Manohla Dargis, "In the Comedy 'Tully,' Mom's Struggle Is Real," *New York Times*, May 3, 2018, https://www.nytimes.com/2018/05/03/movies /tully-review-charlize-theron.html

178 "a socially constructed reality": Sharon Hays, *The Cultural Contradictions of Motherhood* (New Haven: Yale University Press, 1996), 13.

178 "the ever-present mother": Cameron Macdonald, "What's Culture Got to Do with It? Mothering Ideologies as Barriers to Gender Equity," in *The Real Utopias Project: Gender Equality, Transforming Family Divisions of Labor* (Brooklyn: Verso, 2009), 415.

178 "depending on whom you ask": Elisabeth Badinter, *The Conflict: How Overzealous Motherhood Undermines the Status of Women* (New York: Picador, 2010), 153–66.

179 "more important than her own convenience": Sharon Hays, *The Cultural Contradictions of Motherhood* (New Haven: Yale University Press, 1996), 85.

179 "the ideal of motherhood they hold": Cameron Macdonald, "What's Culture Got to Do with It? Mothering Ideologies as Barriers to Gender Equity," in *The Real Utopias Project: Gender Equality, Transforming Family Divisions of Labor* (Brooklyn: Verso, 2009), 419.

180 "mother-appropriate activities": Anita Garey, *Weaving Work and Motherhood* (Philadelphia: Temple University Press, 1999), 26–27.

180 "innocent infants": Elisabeth Badinter, *The Conflict: How Overzealous Motherhood Undermines the Status of Women* (New York: Picador, 2010), 97.

181 "Intensive Parenting Attitudes Questionnaire": Miriam Liss, Holly H. Schiffrin, Virginia H. Mackintosh, Haley Miles-McLean, and Mindy J. Erchull, "Development and Validation of a Quantitative Measure of Intensive Parenting Attitudes," *Journal of Family Studies* 22, no. 5 (July 2012): 621–36.

182 "predicted lower life satisfaction": Miriam Liss, Holly H. Schiffrin, and Kathryn M. Rizzo, "Maternal Guilt and Shame: The Role of Self-discrepancy and Fear of Negative Evaluation," *Journal of Child and Family Studies* 22, no. 8 (2013): 1112–19.

183 "the former is bad for kids": Holly H. Schiffrin, Miriam Liss, Haley Miles-McLean, Katherine A. Geary, Mindy J. Erchull, and Taryn Tashner, "Helping or Hovering? The Effects of Helicopter Parenting

on College Students' Well-Being," *Journal of Child and Family Studies* 23, no. 3 (April 2014): 548–57.

183 "mostly bad for mothers": Kathryn M. Rizzo, Holly H. Schiffrin, and Miriam Liss, "Insight into the Parenthood Paradox: Mental Health Outcomes of Intensive Mothering," *Journal of Child and Family Studies* 22, no. 5 (July 2013): 614–20.

184 "Luca plays Legos in the next room": "Hilary Duff Doesn't Feel Guilty About 'Me Time' (And You Shouldn't Either!)," *Parents*, https://www.parents.com/parents-magazine/parents-perspective/hilary-duff-doesnt-feel-guilty-about-me-time-and-you-shouldn't/

185 "buffering women through the myriad challenges": Suniya S. Luthar and Lucia Ciciolla, "Who Mothers Mommy? Factors that Contribute to Mothers' Well-Being," *Developmental Psychology* 51, no. 12 (December 2015): 1812–23.

188 "men and women in family work": Sarah M. Allen and Alan J. Hawkins, "Maternal Gatekeeping: Mothers' Beliefs and Behaviors That Inhibit Greater Father Involvement in Family Work," *Journal of Marriage and Family* 61, no. 1 (February 1999): 199–212.

189 "mothers reported more traditional beliefs": Brent A. McBride, Geoffrey L. Brown, Kelly K. Bost, Nana Shin, Brian Vaughn, and Bryan Korth, "Paternal Identity, Maternal Gatekeeping, and Father Involvement," *Family Relations* 54, no. 3 (July 2005): 360–72.

189 "A 2008 study out of Ohio State": Sarah J. Schoppe Sullivan, Geoffrey L. Brown, Elizabeth A. Cannon, and Sarah C. Mangelsdorf, "Maternal Gatekeeping, Co-parenting Quality, and Fathering Behavior in Families with Infants," *Journal of Family Psychology* 22, no. 3 (208) 389–98.

189 "salient maternal identity": Ruth Gaunt, "Maternal Gatekeeping: Antecedents and Consequences," *Journal of Family Issues* 29, no. 3 (2008), 373–95.

189 "better predictors of gatekeeping": Sarah J. Schoppe-Sullivan, Lauren E. Altenburger, Meghan A. Lee, Daniel J. Bower, and Claire M. Kamp Dush, "Who Are the Gatekeepers? Predictors of Maternal Gatekeeping," *Parenting: Science and Practice* 15, no. 3 (2015), 166–86.

190 "less powerful than themselves": Sharon Hays, *The Cultural Contradictions of Motherhood* (New Haven: Yale University Press, 1996), 153.

190 "situation that already exists": Rebecca Asher, *Shattered: Modern Motherhood and the Illusion of Equality* (London: Harvill Secker, 2011), 142.

193 "hold on tight to that responsibility": Amy Richards, *Opting In* (New York: Farrar, Straus & Giroux, 2008), 173–74.

194 "If it were just a question of survival": Mary Blair Loy, *Competing Devotions: Career and Family Among Women Executives* (Cambridge: Harvard University Press, 2003), 19.

195 "to offset atypical ones": Saniv Gupta, "Autonomy, Dependence, or Display? The Relationship Between Married Women's Earnings and Housework," *Journal of Marriage and Family* 69, no. 2 (May 2007): 399–417.

195 "hewed closer to gendered norms": Jennifer L. Hook, "Women's Housework: New Tests of Time and Money," *Journal of Marriage and Family* 79, no. 1 (February 2017), 179–98.

196 "his sense of failure": John Gordon Simister, "Is Men's Share of Housework Reduced by 'Gender Deviance Neutralization'? Evidence from Seven Countries," *Journal of Comparative Family Studies* 43, no. 3 (May 2013), 311–26.

196 "It's not hard to feel good about your spouse making money": Jason Zinoman, "The Strategic Mind of Ali Wong," *New York Times*, May 3, 2018, https://www.nytimes.com/2018/05/03/arts/television/ali-wong -netflix-hard-knock-wife.html

196 "to be appreciated for them": Francine M. Deutsch, *Halving It All* (Cambridge: Harvard University Press, 1999), 96.

198 "invisible violence of the institution of motherhood": Adrienne Rich, *Of Woman Born: Motherhood as Experience and Institution* (New York: Norton, 1986).

199 "unrelated to the children's well-being": Douglas B. Downey, James W. Ainsworth-Darnell, and Mikaela J. Dufur, "Sex of Parent and Children's Well-Being in Single Parent Households," *Journal of Marriage and Family* 60, no. 4 (1998), 878–93.

199 "an easily acquired taste": Sarah Blaffer Hrdy, *Mother Nature* (New York: Ballantine Books, 1999), 501.

200 "parenting support from their networks": Maeve Duggan, Amanda Lenhart, Cliff Lampe, and Nicole B. Ellison, "Parents and Social

Media," Pew Research Center, July 16, 2015, http://www.pewinternet
.org/2015/07/16/parents-and-social-media/

200 "looked upon as a bad parent": Deni Kirkova, "Millennial Mothers
Take Parental Rivalry to New Levels as They 'Obsess over Brands
and Success' Thanks to Social Media," *Daily Mail*, May 4, 2014,
https://www.dailymail.co.uk/femail/article-2619957/Social-media
-obsessed-millennial-mothers-parental-rivalry-new-levels.html

201 "moms report that it is their job alone to share photos online":
"Sharenting: Why Mothers Post About Their Children on Social
Media," *The Conversation*, March 9, 2018, http://theconversation
.com/sharenting-why-mothers-post-about-their-children-on-social
-media-91954

201 "new mothers . . . may use Facebook": Sarah J. Schoppe-Sullivan, Jill
E. Yavorsky, Mitchell K. Bartholomew, Jason M. Sullivan, Meghan A.
Lee, Claire M. Kamp Dush, and Michael Glassman, "Doing Gender
Online: New Mothers' Psychological Characteristics, Facebook Use,
and Depressive Symptoms," *Sex Roles* 76, no. 5 (March 2017), 276–89.

202 "has shown inimitable resolve": Cameron Macdonald, "What's Cul-
ture Got to Do with It? Mothering Ideologies as Barriers to Gender
Equity," in *The Real Utopias Project: Gender Equality, Transforming
Family Divisions of Labor* (Brooklyn: Verso, 2009), 424.

202 "their extramaternal identities": Elisabeth Badinter, *The Conflict:
How Overzealous Motherhood Undermines the Status of Women*
(New York: Picador, 2010), 153–66.

202 "What's wrong with me that I don't think to ask him?": Jacqueline
Rose, "Mothers: An Essay on Love and Cruelty," interview by Tracy
Morgan, *New Books in Psychoanalysis*, New Books Network, audio
7:20, https://newbooksnetwork.com/jacqueline-rose-mothers-an-essay
-on-love-and-cruelty-farrar-straus-and-giroux-2018/

Chapter 6: Successful Male Resistance

205 "gender order privileging men over women": Scott Coltrane, "Father-
hood, Gender and Work-Family Policies," in *The Real Utopias Project:
Gender Equality, Transforming Family Divisions of Labor* (Brooklyn:
Verso, 2009), 401.

210 "author Roxane Gay has called it": Roxane Gay, "The Facts and the
Furious," interview by Ophira Eisenberg, *Ask Me Another*, NPR, De-

cember 15, 2017, https://www.npr.org/templates/transcript/transcript
.php?storyId=571107993

211 "take responsibility for misogyny and patriarchy": George Yancy,
"#IAmSexist," *New York Times*, October 24, 2018, https://www.nytimes
.com/2018/10/24/opinion/men-sexism-me-too.html

212 "to say yes when asked": Linda Babcock, Maria P. Recalde, Lise
Vesterlund, and Laurie Weingart, "Gender Differences in Accepting
and Receiving Requests for Tasks with Low Promotability," *American
Economic Review* 107, no. 3 (March 2017): 714–47.

213 "the ones who will raise their hands": Lise Vesterlund, "Why Women
'Volunteer' at Work," interview by Jonathan Capehart, *Midday on
WNYC*, New York Public Radio, July 23, 2018.

214 "seem eager to do so": Sarah Blaffer Hrdy, *Mother Nature* (New York:
Ballantine Books, 1999), 497.

215 "Men do not pause to consider": David L. Dickinson and Jill Tiefen-
thaler, "What Is Fair? Experimental Evidence," *Southern Economic
Journal* 69, no. 2 (2002): 414–28.

215 "monetary prize to stellar performance": Kristi J. K. Klein and Sara D.
Hodges, "Gender Differences, Motivation, and Empathic Accuracy:
When It Pays to Understand," *Personality and Social Psychology
Bulletin* 27, no. 6 (June 1, 2001): 720–30.

215 "born to consider others all the time": Nancy Eisenberg and Randy
Lennon, "Sex Differences in Empathy and Related Capacities," *Psychological Bulletin* 94, no. 1 (July 1983): 100–31.

216 "social ties of the participants are frayed": Christopher Karpowitz and
Tali Mendelberg, *The Silent Sex: Gender, Deliberation, and Institutions* (Princeton, NJ: Princeton University Press, 2014), 63.

216 "to work hard at child care": bell hooks, *Feminism Is for Everybody*
(New York: Routledge, 2015), 82.

219 "countries not offering that time": Jennifer Hook, "Care in Context:
Men's Unpaid Work in 20 Countries, 1965–2003," *American Sociological Review* 71 (August 2006): 639–60.

219 "high-earning wife meant higher risk of divorce": Christine R.
Schwartz and Pilar Gonalons-Pons, "Trends in Relative Earnings and
Marital Dissolution: Are Wives Who Outearn Their Husbands Still
More Likely to Divorce?" RSF: *Russell Sage Foundation Journal of
the Social Sciences* 24, no. 4 (2016): 218–36.

220 "Violating this norm can cause discomfort": H. Colleen Stuart, Sue Moon, and Tiziana Casciaro, "The Oscar Curse: Status Dynamics and Gender Differences in Marital Survival," *SSRN Electronic Journal* (January 2011), https://papers.ssrn.com/sol3/papers.cfm?abstract _id=1749612

220 "CEOs are twice as likely to divorce": Valentina Zarya, "Being Promoted May Double Women's Odds of Getting Divorced," *Fortune*, March 5, 2018, http://fortune.com/2018/03/05/promotion-women-divorce/

220 "deferentially and unassumingly": Christopher Karpowitz and Tali Mendelberg, *The Silent Sex: Gender, Deliberation, and Institutions* (Princeton, NJ: Princeton University Press, 2014), 60.

221 "more ambitious than he is": Raymond Fisman, Sheena S. Iyengar, Emir Kamenica, and Itamar Simonson, "Gender Differences in Mate Selection: Evidence from a Speed Dating Experiment," *Quarterly Journal of Economics* 121, no. 2 (May 2006): 673–97.

221 "in society as a whole": Sharon Hays, *The Cultural Contradictions of Motherhood* (New Haven: Yale University Press, 1996), 163.

222 "what became known as the Pygmalion effect": Katherine Ellison, "Being Honest About the Pygmalion Effect," *Discover*, December 2015, http://discovermagazine.com/2015/dec/14-great-expectations

223 "Teacher Expectation Project": Christine M. Rubie-Davies, "Teacher Expectations and Student Self-Perceptions: Exploring Relationships" (PhD diss., University of Auckland, 2004).

223 "improved performance on standardized tests": Katherine Ellison, "Being Honest About the Pygmalion Effect," *Discover*, December 2015, http://discovermagazine.com/2015/dec/14-great-expectations

224 "negative stereotype about one's group applies": Cordelia Fine, *Delusions of Gender* (New York: W.W. Norton & Company, 2010), 30.

224 "uncertainty for women about their own ability": Ibid.

224 "Caucasian men perform worse": Toni Schmader, "Stereotype Threat Deconstructed," *Current Directions in Psychological Science* 19, no. 1 (March 2010): 14–18.

224 "they are trying to avoid": Ibid.

225 "ratio of men to women in the room is high": Cordelia Fine, *Delusions of Gender* (New York: W.W. Norton & Company, 2010), 35.

225 "Even the gender of an experimenter can cue the stereotype threat":

Sabrina Solanki and Di Xu, "Looking Beyond Academic Performance: The Influence of Instructor Gender on Student Engagement and Attitudes in STEM Fields," *American Educational Research Journal 55*, no. 4 (2018): 801–35.

226 "The so-called demand characteristics of the prison experiment": Jared M. Bartels, "The Stanford Prison Experiment in Introductory Psychology Textbooks: A Content Analysis," *Psychology Learning & Teaching* 14, no. 1 (2015): 36–50.

226 "diffuse the damage it can do": Toni Schmader, "Stereotype Threat Deconstructed," *Current Directions in Psychological Science* 19, no. 1 (March 2010), 14–18.

228 "a dysfunctional but familiar system": Robert Kegan and Lisa Laskow Lahey, *Immunity to Change: How to Overcome It and Unlock the Potential in Yourself and Your Organization* (Boston: Harvard Business School Publishing, 2009).

230 "hard to identify and address": Anne Rankin-Mahoney and Carmen Knudson-Martin, "Beyond Gender: The Process of Relationship Equality," in *Couples, Gender and Power*, eds. Carmen Knudson-Martin and Anne Rankin-Mahoney (New York: Springer Publishing Company, 2009), 73.

231 "decreasing rigid demarcations between the genders": Bernadette Park and Sarah Banchefsky, "Leveraging the Social Role of Dad to Change Gender Stereotypes of Men," *Personality and Social Psychology Bulletin* 44, no. 9 (September 2018): 1380–94.

231 "who must use it or lose it": Andrea Doucet, "Can Parenting Be Equal? Rethinking Equality and Gender Differences in Parenting," in *What Is Parenthood?*, eds. Linda C. McClain and Daniel Cere (New York: New York University Press, 2013): 251–75.

231 "divorce and separation rates have also been falling": Katrin Benhold, "In Sweden, Men Can Have It All," *New York Times*, June 9, 2010, https://www.nytimes.com/2010/06/10/world/europe/10iht-sweden .html?action=click&contentCollection=Europe&module=Related Coverage&region=EndOfArticle&pgtype=article

232 "one year at their single-sex school": Nilanjana Dasgupta and Shaki Asgari, "Seeing Is Believing: Exposure to Counterstereotypic Women Leaders and Its Effect on the Malleability of Automatic Gender Stereo-

typing," *Journal of Experimental Social Psychology* 40, no. 5 (2004): 642–58.

233 "be competitive, get rich, get laid.": Michael Kimmel and Lisa Wade, "Ask a Feminist: Michael Kimmel and Lisa Wade Discuss Toxic Masculinity," *Signs*, http://signsjournal.org/kimmel-wade -toxic-masculinity/

236 "shoots up to two thirds": Sarah Blaffer Hrdy, *Mothers and Others* (Cambridge: Harvard University Press, 2011), 150.

236 "ways to maintain collaboration": Randi S. Cowdery, Carmen Knudson-Martin, and Anne Rankin Mahoney, "Mothering: Innate Talent or Conscious Collaboration?," in *Couples, Gender, and Power*, eds. Carmen Knudson-Martin and Anne Rankin Mahoney (New York: Springer Publishing Company, 2009), 137.

236 "Supporting Father Involvement Project": "Supporting Father Involvement: An Evidence Based Program," Supporting Father Involvement Program, accessed October 30, 2018, http://supportingfatherinvolv ementsfi.com /supporting-father-involvement-an-evidence-based-program/

237 "to teach Bringing Baby Home": Hannah Eaton, email to author, July 27, 2018.

237 "mothers in the study as well": Alyson F. Shapiro and John M. Gottman, "Effects on Marriage of a Psycho-Communicative-Educational Intervention with Couples Undergoing the Transition to Parenthood, Evaluation at 1-Year Post Intervention," *The Journal of Family Communication* 5, no. 1 (2005): 1–24.

238 "men talking to women interrupt": Adrienne Hancock and Benjamin Rubin, "Influence of Communication Partner's Gender on Language," *Journal of Language and Social Psychology* 34, no. 1 (December 2014): 46–64.

238 "when another woman was speaking": Kieran Snyder, "How to Get Ahead as a Woman in Tech: Interrupt Men," *Slate*, July 23, 2014, https:// slate.com/human-interest/2014/07/study-men-interrupt-women -more-in-tech-workplaces-but-high-ranking-women-learn-to -interrupt.html

238 "Barack Obama said": Irin Carmon, "What Women Really Think of Men," *New York Times*, December 9, 2016, https://www.nytimes.com /2016/12/09/opinion/sunday/what-women-really-think-of-men.html/

241 "Yalom instructs Marvin": Irvin D. Yalom, *Love's Executioner & Other Tales of Psychotherapy* (New York: Basic Books, 1989): 267–68.

Chapter 7: What Are We Trying to Achieve

243 "typical gender schemas have obscured": Patricia Adair Gowaty, "Biological Essentialism, Gender, True Belief, Confirmation Biases, and Skepticism," in *APA Handbook of the Psychology of Women: History, Theory, and Battlegrounds* (Washington, DC: American Psychological Association, 2018): 145–64.

246 "reorganized for the better": Jacqueline Rose, "Mothers: An Essay on Love and Cruelty," interview by Tracy Morgan, *New Books in Psychoanalysis*, New Books Network, audio, 10:50, https://new booksnetwork.com/jacqueline-rose-mothers-an-essay-on-love-and -cruelty-farrar-straus-and-giroux-2018/

247 "decision-making power was often assigned": Mignon R. Moore, "Gendered Power Relations Among Women: A Study of Household Decision Making in Black, Lesbian Stepfamilies," *American Sociological Review* 73, no. 2 (2008): 335–56

248 "women are more likely": Harry Brighouse and Erik Olin Wright, "Strong Gender Egalitarianism," in *The Real Utopias Project: Gender Equality, Transforming Family Divisions of Labor* (Brooklyn: Verso, 2009), 86.

249 "Manne told *Jezebel*,": Stassa Edwards, "Philosopher Kate Manne on 'Himpathy,' Donald Trump, and Rethinking the Logic of Misogyny," Jezebel, August 2, 2018, https://jezebel.com/philosopher-kate-manne -on-himpathy-donald-trump-and-r-1822639677

252 "the exact opposite is true for dad": Bernadette Park, J. Allegra Smith, and Joshua Correll, "The Persistence of Implicit Behavioral Associations for Moms and Dads," *Journal of Experimental Social Psychology* 46 (2010): 809–15.

253 "*Other* than the man": Jennifer Hockenberry Dragseth, *Thinking Woman: A Philosophical Approach to the Quandary of Gender* (Eugene, OR: Cascade Books, 2015), 88.

253 "women participate, too": Ibid., 86.

253 "less than 8 percent, are of women": Elana Lyn Gross, "The Five Female Historical Statues in New York City Are Decorated for International Woman's Day," *Forbes*, March 8, 2018, https://www.forbes.com/sites

/elanagross/2018/03/08/the-five-female-historical-statues-in-new-york-city-are-decorated-for-international-womens-day/#116866077c26

253 "Alice in Wonderland, and Mother Goose": Andy Battaglia, "New York City Launches 'She Built NYC' Commission for Public Art on Women's History," *Art News*, June 20, 2018, http://www.artnews.com /2018/06/20/new-york-city-launches-built-nyc-commission-public-art -womens-history/

253 "'symbolically annihilated' in the media": Gaye Tuchman, "The Symbolic Annihilation of Women by the Mass Media," in *Culture and Politics*, eds. Lane Crothers and Charles Lockhart (New York: Palgrave Macmillan, 2000), 150–74.

254 "the journalist doing the reporting": Ed Yong, "I Spent Two Years Trying to Fix the Gender Imbalance in My Stories," *The Atlantic*, February 6, 2018, https://www.theatlantic.com/science/archive/2018/02/i-spent -two-years-trying-to-fix-the-gender-imbalance-in-my-stories/552404/

254 "women have not become less like women": Elizabeth L. Haines, Kay Deaux, and Nicole Lofaro, "The Times They Are a-Changing . . . or Are They Not? A Comparison of Gender Stereotypes, 1983–2014," *Psychology of Women Quarterly* 40, no. 3 (2016), 353–63.

255 "men's underrepresentation in communal roles": Alyssa Croft, Toni Schmader, and Katharina Block, "An Underexamined Inequality: Cultural and Psychological Barriers to Men's Engagement with Communal Roles," *Personality and Social Psychology Review* 19, no. 4 (2015): 343–70.

255 "never completely disappears": Lise Eliot, *Pink Brain, Blue Brain: How Small Differences Grow into Troublesome Gaps—and What We Can Do About It* (New York: Mariner Books, 2010), 258.

255 "than the young women do theirs": Christopher Karpowitz and Tali Mendelberg, *The Silent Sex: Gender, Deliberation, and Institutions* (Princeton, NJ: Princeton University Press, 2014), 54.

256 "work as community organizers": Stephanie Coontz, *The Way We Never Were* (New York: Basic Books; Revised, Updated edition, 2016), 200.

256 "men are rightly more powerful": Cecilia L. Ridgeway and Shelley J. Correll, "Unpacking the Gender System: A Theoretical Perspective on Gender Beliefs and Social Relations," *Gender & Society* 18, no. 4 (August 2004): 510 –31.

257 "involved with academic citizenship work": Bruce MacFarlane, "Women Professors, Pay, Promotion, and Academic Housekeeping," wonkhe .com, June 4, 2018, https://wonkhe.com/blogs/women-professors -pay-promotion-and-academic-housekeeping/

258 "circumscribed, and flexible": Margaret B. Neal and Leslie B. Hammer, "Working Couples Caring for Children and Aging Parents," *Journal of Marriage and Family* 70, no. 2 (May 2008): 565–66.

259 "readily perceived as acting perversely": Rebecca Traister, *All the Single Ladies: Unmarried Women and the Rise of an Independent Nation* (New York: Simon & Schuster, 2016), 132.

260 "study out of NYU": Madeline E. Heilman and Julia J. Chen, "Same Behavior, Different Consequences: Reactions to Men's and Women's Altruistic Citizenship Behavior," *Journal of Applied Psychology* 90, no. 3 (May 2005): 431–41.

262 "abdicate their role as household decision makers": Melissa J. Williams and Serena Chen, "When 'Mom's the Boss': Control over Domestic Decision Making Reduces Women's Interest in Workplace Power," *Group Processes & Intergroup Relations* 17, no. 4 (2014): 436–52.

262 "current gender status quo": Julia C. Becker and Stephen Wright, "Yet Another Dark Side of Chivalry: Benevolent Sexism Undermines and Hostile Sexism Motivates Collective Action for Social Change," *Journal of Personality and Social Psychology* 101, no. 1 (February 2011): 62–77.

263 "willingness to engage in gender-related collective action": Ibid.

265 "of domestic and caring responsibilities": Sydney Pereira, "Women over 85 Are Happier Because Their Partner Is Dead by Then, Psychiatrists Say," *Newsweek*, December 14, 2017, https://www.newsweek .com/women-over-85-are-happier-because-their-partner-dead-then -psychiatrists-say-748067

266 "than have sex with him": Heather Havrilesky, "Ask Polly: Why Do New Mothers Hate Their Husbands," *The Cut*, June 6, 2018, https:// www.thecut.com/2018/06/ask-polly-why-do-new-mothers-hate-their -husbands.html

266 "when there is domination": bell hooks, *Feminism Is for Everybody* (New York: Routledge, 2015), 103.

266 "they will have a happy relationship": Ying-Ching Lin and Priya

Raghubir, "Gender Differences in Unrealistic Optimism About Marriage and Divorce: Are Men More Optimistic and Women More Realistic?" *Personality and Social Psychology Bulletin* 31, no. 2 (2005), 198–207.

267 "maintain good moods in their spouses": Eleanor E. Maccoby, *The Two Sexes: Growing Up Apart, Coming Together* (Cambridge: Harvard University Press, 1999), 218.

267 "there is shared well-being": Anne Rankin Mahoney and Carmen Knudson-Martin, "Gender Equality in Intimate Relationships," in *Couples, Gender, and Power*, eds. Carmen Knudson-Martin and Anne Rankin Mahoney (New York: Springer Publishing Company, 2009), 11.

268 "it was a substitute for practice": Anne Rankin Mahoney and Carmen Knudson-Martin, "The Myth of Equality," in *Couples, Gender, and Power*, eds. Carmen Knudson-Martin and Anne Rankin Mahoney (New York: Springer Publishing Company, 2009), 50.

269 "more efficiently for their pay": Christopher Karpowitz and Tali Mendelberg, *The Silent Sex: Gender, Deliberation, and Institutions* (Princeton, NJ: Princeton University Press, 2014), 55.

269 "twice as much per week as girls": "Gender Pay Gap Starts with Kids in America," in Blog, *Making News by BusyKid*, June 29, 2018, https://busykid.com/2018/06/29/gender-pay-gap-starts-with-kids-in-america/

269 "30 percent of women did the same": Christopher Karpowitz and Tali Mendelberg, *The Silent Sex: Gender, Deliberation, and Institutions* (Princeton, NJ: Princeton University Press, 2014), 61.

269 "children as young as six": Ibid., 55–56.

269 "They call it 'unentitlement.'": Carolyn Pape Cowan and Philip A. Cowan, *When Partners Become Parents* (New York: Routledge, 1999), 196.

269 "called on boys with eight times the frequency": David Sadker and Karen R. Zittleman, *Still Failing at Fairness: How Gender Bias Cheats Girls and Boys in School and What We Can Do About It* (New York: Scribner, 2009), 7–11.

269 "the boys they're involved with don't protest": Peggy Orenstein, *Girls & Sex: Navigating the Complicated New Landscape* (New York: HarperCollins, 2016), 7–11.

270 "but also to authority": Christopher Karpowitz and Tali Mendelberg, *The Silent Sex: Gender, Deliberation, and Institutions* (Princeton, NJ: Princeton University Press, 2014), 51.

270 "less right than men to family support": Aliya Rao, "Unemployed: What Men's and Women's Divergent Experiences Tell Us About Gender Inequality," (PhD diss., University of Pennsylvania, 2016).

271 "living in a clearly hierarchical society": Jaime L. Napier, Hulda Thorisdottir, and John T. Jost, "The Joy of Sexism: A Multinational Investigation of Hostile and Benevolent Justifications for Gender Inequality and Their Relations to Subjective Well-Being," *Sex Roles* 62, no. 7–8 (April 2010): 405–19.

272 "perhaps even natural and inevitable": John T. Jost and Aaron C. Kay, "Exposure to Benevolent Sexism and Complementary Gender Stereotypes: Consequences for Specific and Diffuse Forms of System Justification," *Journal of Personality and Social Psychology* 88, no. 3 (April 2005): 498–509.

273 "perpetuate and maintain gender inequality": Laurie T. O'Brien, Brenda Major, and Patricia Gilbert, "Gender Differences in Entitlement: The Role of System Justifying Beliefs," *Basic and Applied Social Psychology* 34, no. 2 (2012), 136–45.

273 "have learned to adjust to it": Susan Faludi, *Backlash: The Undeclared War Against American Women* (New York: Broadway Books; Anniversary Edition, 2006), 72.

274 "very sticky unless directly undermined": Harry Brighouse and Erik Olin Wright, "Strong Gender Egalitarianism," in *The Real Utopias Project: Gender Equality, Transforming Family Divisions of Labor* (Brooklyn: Verso, 2009), 87.

274 "positively related to a citizenry's general happiness": Ozlem Yorulmaz, "Relationship Between Happiness and Gender Inequality Index," *Research in World Economy* 7, no. 1 (2016): 11–20.

275 "not so much an end point as a process": Anne Rankin Mahoney and Carmen Knudson-Martin, "Beyond Gender," in *Couples, Gender, and Power*, eds. Carmen Knudson-Martin and Anne Rankin Mahoney (New York: Springer Publishing Company, 2009), 70.

277 "but of pure justice": Martha Weinman Lear, "'You'll Probably Think I'm Stupid'," *New York Times*, April 11, 1976, https://www.nytimes.com/1976/04/11/archives/youll-probably-think-im-stupid-era.html

INDEX

ABOUT THE AUTHOR

DARCY LOCKMAN is a former journalist turned psychologist. Her first book, *Brooklyn Zoo,* chronicled the year she spent working in a city hospital's psychiatric ward. Her writing has also appeared in *The New York Times* and *The Washington Post*, among others. She lives with her husband and daughters in Queens.